4

Ebury Press
London

Contents

Introduction

Our interest is in enriching the experience of living by simplifying it, by paring it down to what is essential. Get rid of everything which is unnecessary and distracting and you are left with what actually matters. We share a passion for the details of living and eating. This book is intended as a record of those details and of the choices we have found support perfectly the way we want to live.

Most of us are familiar with the effect paring down has on architecture. The process is as relevant to cooking and eating, simply less thoroughly explored. Our desire to examine this subject and to provide a source of recipes which would be used every day led us to a collaboration which has drawn widely on the experiences of both our professional and private lives.

The first chapter takes a look at that most personal of rooms, the kitchen. The resourceful cook can assemble a dinner with a trestle table, a bucket of water and a primus gas stove, but it is unlikely to be a serene experience. The process of cooking—in a well-conceived kitchen with sound equipment—should be smooth and pleasurable. Fashionably it is alleged that all you need are a few items of basic equipment, but we don't accept this. Having 'the kit' will make your life that much more enjoyable. At the end of the book we define that kit—paring down, not to a skeletal minimum, but seeking the best.

From the kitchen, we move on to consider texture, taste, fragrance and temperature—the cornerstones of quality relevant to every ingredient and dish. Texture is

perhaps the most neglected of these, yet it accounts for the sensuality of food—the milky succulence of a grilled scallop, the jammy inside of a ripe fig, the silken elasticity of a skein of melted mozzarella, or exquisite softness of melting butter. Food can have all the flavour in the world but fail to excite without the careful coaxing of an ingredient's better nature. Food can only be truly great if a cook is prepared to be pedantic and the less there is going on, the more pedantic he or she needs to be. Hot food on cold plates can ruin an otherwise great experience. Equally there are very few dishes that will 'hold' in a low oven. Better to choose food designed to be cooked in advance and dispense with the worry.

From there we embark on a collection of recipes designed to cater for all seasons and occasions. We have taken our approach to feeding our own families as a starting point. Far from being eclectic, we are creatures of habit and return to a handful of foods and dishes time and time again. In keeping with our upbringing, these derive from Europe and the Mediterranean. The approach goes something like roast chicken one night, pasta the next, a salad another and so on—basically the things we feel comfortable cooking and eating. Using these as a framework, we have tried simply to broaden things out, hence the seven different recipes for roasting a chicken and almost as many for cooking spaghetti and noodles.

When we cook or entertain, our interest lies in perfection, rather than having a stab at something different or overly ambitious every time. Our aim is the ultimate

tomato salad, the perfect roast potatoes and so on, moving on to ways of varying these basics. Food is invariably presented simply, to give individual ingredients the chance to shine, so we can fully appreciate their particular flavours and textures.

And then we come to that perennial dilemma, how to entertain. It seems as though the gap between what we want to provide and what we are able to is ever widening. A 30-minute, after-work three course menu is wishful thinking. There are ways around it mind you—often the mere suggestion of a first course and something sweet to finish is enough. A few grissini and some goat's cheese crushed with olive oil to dip into before dinner, and a plate of mascarpone-filled Medjool dates doused in maple syrup with after-dinner coffee will suffice.

To an extent, we are all bound by social convention. There is the notion that to honour your guests, food must display a certain intricacy, to show that you have gone to an effort. This suggests a bizarre measure between the sort of food you offer and how much you value your guests, which brings us full circle back to the dinner party charade. We're not alone as a culture, or in history for that matter, the point is whether there is any place for this approach within our hectic modern lives.

Surely the ideal is to narrow the gap between how we eat on a daily basis and how we entertain, given that the spirit of entertaining at its most gracious is about inviting people to join you at your table? There is no need for the style of food to change from one occasion to another. You will simply want to linger longer and the menu needs to take that into account.

Towards the end of the book, we get down to the serious business of defining our kit, cataloguing a library of everything essential to the kitchen, from equipment to tableware, down to linen and flowers. We've tried to go beyond the kitchen handbook that lists everything by its function and instead recommended our preferred manufacturers, having tested products and explored the production process.

If you are considering investing in a set of saucepans, for example, you may want to know about the different properties of stainless steel, aluminium, copper and cast iron, in order to make an informed choice that suits your needs. We've all had enough of the beautiful saucepan that burns everything and the ugly one that cooks like a dream. Everything we have listed has had to satisfy cook and architect alike.

How many people end up with three sets of glasses—albeit incomplete and never used for the colour of wine intended—several sets of cutlery and as many sizes of plate? We have pared glasses, china and cutlery down to a restrained minimum, intended as a starting point. The tendency when you have too much equipment is that it ceases to function as a whole.

As it is, nearly everything we have chosen finds its roots in the past. Contrary to the belief that modern equates with futuristic, our choice of china is the traditional Wedgwood Queensware, first produced in the eighteenth century.

The range appears undesigned compared to most contemporary tableware. The nature of newly designed plates is the same as a newly conceived dish—the designer or cook is under pressure to do something slightly different. The irony about Wedgwood is that it really is different because nobody else is producing anything as unselfconscious.

The result of all this—we hope —is one of harmony, where there is nothing to distract from the food and the wine, and the vital process of enjoying yourself.

John Pawson and Annie Bell

Kitchen Design

The design of the kitchen is often the most difficult task for the architect. However sophisticated, the result all too often fails to perform. There are so many considerations and elements that need to be included and the balance of aesthetics and practicality needs to be finely tuned. Added to this, the kitchen is an area about which we all have strong feelings—it is one of the most personal rooms in the home. As well as being the place where we cook and eat, at any one time it may function as office, laundry and living room.

Everyone has some idea of what they want from their kitchen. While aesthetic preferences differ, it is helpful to distil the kitchen down to its essential elements, as there are certain considerations that are applicable to any cook.

Various specialist designers create bespoke kitchens and, while they produce well conceived spaces, there is a tendency to complicate the overall result by creating a different design for every function. We shy away from this approach, instead veering towards spaces that are more uniform and flexible in their use. To respond to a cook's varied needs, areas and storage should have multiple uses. When design is very specific, however suited to the intended task, it does tend to limit use. The drawer fitted with wooden pegs to hold plates in place cannot be used for pots and pans, just as glass shelves intended for glasses will not be strong enough to hold heavier ware.

Aesthetically, focusing a design on quality and simplicity also affords the kitchen a timelessness.

The elements we have taken as being essential are the same ones that have been included in kitchens throughout history. It doesn't matter whether the kitchen is in a mud-hut in Bali or a penthouse in New York, there are certain requirements without which you cannot begin cooking.

Worktop and floor

The work surface is the single most important feature of a kitchen, not only in terms of its function, but also its conspicuousness. Being an essential feature, it seems logical to accentuate it even further by giving it substance and using a material that feels good to touch. Our hands are repeatedly in contact with the worktop, whether we are preparing vegetables, unwrapping a piece of cheese, or wiping down after cutting a loaf of bread.

The choice of material at John's house is stone, from Lecce in Italy, possessed of a warm honey-coloured beauty that takes its cue from the solid stone counters of the traditional salting larder and marble surfaces of the dairy. Chosen to be the same material as the floor thereby minimising the number of different materials, its sheer length in the kitchen creates the feeling of a path. Stone has the advantage over any other material that it can be used outside as well as in, creating a seamless floor that connects the two areas. The downside of this material is its tendency to stain— a spillage of coffee, red wine or beetroot will all tell a tale—so it must be sealed before use. It should also be said that stone is relatively unforgiving and likely to shatter any glass or crockery dropped on to it.

Other possibilities are steel and wood. Visually stainless steel is at its best presented as a thick slab, which somehow avoids laboratory associations. This surface takes on the colour that surrounds it, glowing pink in the reflection of a vase of flowers—at times it is even delicate. Since so many pans and handles are made from the same material, there is less visual disruption than with other surfaces.

Stainless steel has the advantage of being durable, with a slight give that is kinder on china than stone, but it's hard to keep clean and not suitable for every situation. The inevitable scratches that appear are unavoidable, but with time will even out and even add to its appeal. Special cleaners are available. To avoid traces of water marks, a surface should be wiped over with a teatowel or other soft linen cloth after it has been washed.

Wood possesses a particular softness and can also be used to work on directly. It does, however, need to be sealed on a regular basis, and care must be taken with hot pans. Dark woods are better than light, and those with a tight grain are preferable—walnut is especially appealing.

The custom of building units and work surfaces at a height of 900mm is a strange one. You don't have to be unusually tall to find a unit some 50mm higher that much kinder on the back and a more natural height to work with.

Somewhere to put things

In John's kitchen all those quirky spice jars and packets of sugar and coffee are stored behind cool white screens. This isn't solely for

aesthetic purposes. Kitchens, if they are being used properly, breathe grease in the steam emitted by any pan on the hob in the throes of frying, grilling or braising. Those decorative pots and casseroles on the top shelf that rarely get an airing, invariably have to be scrubbed of a sticky layer before they can be used. Open kitchens do have their charms, especially in the country, but they are hard work to maintain.

The bank of low white doors at John's house opens to reveal drawers of varying depths. It is a system that allows for every pot or pan to be pulled out with ease, without the need to unpack an entire cupboard to get to the back. It is equally accommodating of small jars and packets that at eye level in a cupboard become invisible beyond the front row.

Sink

A sink is a workstation with running water as well as a trough for dirty dishes. When we did away with the butler we did away with the generous nature of his sink as well. The shrinking of sinks in the twentieth century to a size that scarcely accommodates a saucepan turns the process of washing up into a circus of elbows and splashed water. Limited space certainly makes it difficult to clean large pots and pans properly. There's no absolute in size, but your sink should ideally accommodate your largest pan or griddle and the racks from your hob and oven. Beyond the drudge of washing up, a big sink is that much more accommodating towards ingredients, whether the task is peeling potatoes, scrubbing mussels or washing spinach.

Failing one large sink, two smaller ones can be a good option, provided they are of sufficient depth, and allow you to soak dishes and prepare food at the same time. If you are reliant on a single sink, then it will be well served by a tall bar waste that peeks over the top of the water, allowing for disposal of slops, even when the sink is full.

A tap is often failing in design. The ideal is a single source of water from a tap that swivels and is high enough to fit any large pans underneath it. The tap at John's house stands out as a graceful curve—in fact, the only one in the kitchen—and it performs its task extremely well. The knobs have been relocated below the sink and redesigned as levers that turn anti-clockwise. It is the same design of lever that services the gas on the hob, so to the eye there is just one row of tools.

Hobs and your heat source

Preference of heat source is a cultural consideration, swayed in this country by the availability of North Sea Gas.

Gas hobs

Our personal fondness for gas has partly to do with the control it offers the cook, but also the pleasure of cooking over a naked flame. We have an in-built understanding of the naked flame —if it's burning low, it is obvious that the heat will be gentle, while if it blazes we know instantly that the heat is fierce. We can direct the cooking with minute precision. Combine gas with state of the art pans and you have the ultimate in performance.

Ceramic hobs

The cooking zones on a ceramic hob heat up by means of a coiled wire, the heat being a combination of conducted heat from the surface and radiated heat from the element. While faster in response than a traditional electric coil, the surface still takes time to respond to a change in temperature. If a pan of milk is about to boil over, a quick turn of the appropriate knob won't help —you will need to remove the pan.

Induction hobs

Within this space-age technology the pan only heats up when it comes into contact with the hob. The salesman's trick is to place a £10 note between the pan and the surface of the hob to illustrate the efficacy of the magnetic field in only heating the saucepan. In theory, the area surrounding the hob stays cool, although the pan itself will transfer some heat.

Induction hobs are popular on the Continent but they have been comparatively slow to catch on here, perhaps because they lack the atavistic charm of gas. Their sleek lines and efficiency may well make them the hob of the future. If induction hobs were adopted in professional kitchens, chefs would benefit from a lower ambient temperature in summer.

Halogen hobs

In this type of hob heat is radiated from special tubes. Despite their initial popularity, objections from consumers about the brightness of the light and the expense of replacing the tubes have led to their decline.

Standard electric hobs

These are the least responsive of all hob types.

Hob size

It is extraordinary how badly designed many hobs are. It's not uncommon for a shiny stainless steel 4-ring hob to accommodate no more than two large pans, when clearly it should have room for four good-sized frying pans or saucepans. We favour hobs that are even larger than this. The average household will be able to make good use of a 5-ring hob, upwards of 900mm in width. Not that you often have five pans on the go at once, but because food in various stages of preparation and cooling finds a natural space on top of the stove. It may be a roast chicken that is resting, a clafoutis which is cooling, or a pan of soup that you are planning on reheating later. A stove-top kettle is more easily accommodated too.

We particularly favour a large central ring, either a solid iron simmer plate or a fish burner, that takes on the task of finishing off the gravy in the roasting pan while the meat is resting. It also takes care of those maslin pan days when you are simmering a large quantity of stock, chutney or marmalade.

Lighting

In a kitchen that is used as an eating area as well as a workstation, the lighting needs to be flexible. It must allow the cook to see their ingredients and what is going on at the bottom of a pan, at the same time providing an ambience conducive to relaxing over dinner— ideally without having to hop up and down turning lights up and down, or on and off to achieve it. The conventional solution is a light over the worktop and a candle on the table, but indirect or hidden light sources controlled by a dimmer

provide a more subtle and kinder light that swathes the whole room in the same atmosphere.

Machines

Our intention here is to determine a balance, ridding the kitchen of those items it doesn't need while retaining anything that makes a genuine contribution. Each valued appliance must outweigh the space it takes up and the hassle of cleaning.

All machines intrude into the peace of the home. While an oven and a fridge are necessities and a dishwasher an extremely desirable accessory, it is worth assessing just how necessary most other domestic appliances are. This is not to say that you shouldn't own a bread-maker, a state-of-the-art juicer or a computerised espresso maker, but these are personal choices. Of those that are necessities, the additional features advertised in the name of advance should be treated with circumspection—many are more likely to cause frustration for the user than solve any problems.

Oven

A standard 600mm oven is often too small, even for an average dinner to serve six. If you are roasting a good-sized joint, it can be difficult to fit in a tray of roast potatoes, let alone anything else. It is worth considering scaling up to one large oven, at least 900mm in width. This allows you to roast meat, potatoes and vegetables simultaneously and at the same level—essential if you have designs on crispy, golden potatoes and a sticky, caramelised roast.

Fan ovens have their critics, but are to be commended for achieving consistently good results. There are no pockets of heat, so food cooks evenly. They are more effective at browning potatoes and cook more quickly than a standard oven too. The downside has to be the aggressive nag of the fan which continues as long as the oven takes to cool down. An oven that sports both fan and conventional options allows for the greatest flexibility. Not only can you choose how you cook food, but when you are in pursuit of peace or quiet conversation, you can opt to use the conventional oven.

Dishwasher

Is there anything to be said for washing up by hand? There may be some individuals who find washing up therapeutic, but probably only on an occasional basis. Aside from a handful of items, such as handmade earthenware, silver, bone-handled knives, crystal and anodised aluminium which should always be washed by hand, it can beat its human counterpart hands down in achieving really clean plates and utensils. And it performs another useful function in sterilising everything without special chemicals, reducing the risk of infection. The main requisites are that the machine should function quietly and offer environmentally-friendly washing programmes, including modest water usage.

Fridges and freezers

The fridge makes a curious status symbol, but status symbol it has become. It is no longer enough for our means of chilling food to be discreet and efficient. The huge double-fronted fridges that come complete with ice-maker are large enough to service a small restaurant. In households that have succumbed, they are rarely more

than a quarter full. Even filled
to capacity they are wholly
impractical, especially when the
butter works its way to the back
and you have to unpack the entire
shelf to get at it.

The most practical solution
has to be two smaller fridges, one
that can be reserved for drinks and
jars of things, the other for fresh
ingredients. A salad drawer is
essential, and frost-free fridges
are that much easier to maintain.
Beyond this there are few features,
saving quietness, that are worth
paying huge amounts for.

Waste disposal

An insinkerator is effective at
masticating biodegradable waste
from the kitchen, but it does so
with an extraordinary lack of grace.
To be sitting within earshot of a
waste-disposal unit doing its stuff
is to shatter the peace of after-
dinner conversation. There is
something unnatural about these
conveniences—perhaps it is the
nature of the waste they ingest.
A conscientious country dweller
would simply trail out to the
compost heap.

And yet the build up of waste
in the average household on a
typical day is frightening and
England, in particular, is a rubbish
heavy nation. In France the bottle
bank is a legal obligation—if glass is
found in with the rubbish you can
be fined. And nor is it simply
bottles that can be taken to a
collection point—the small village
square may sport three different
bins for various types of carton and
other recyclable kitchen waste.
We have some way to go.

Extractors

There is no ideal solution. It helps to
place an extractor motor as far
away from the source as you can,
but in a city this usually means
dumping your noise on a neighbour.
In a well-ventilated kitchen there is
no real need for an extractor—just
keep the room well-aired and throw
open the windows if you need to.

Cornerstones of Quality

'It is an implicit obedience of the rules of the Creator, who, having ordered us to eat in order to live, invites us to do so with appetite, encourages us with flavour, and rewards us with pleasure'.
Jean Anthelme Brillat-Savarin

Texture

It is easy to see why flavour features so predominantly in our lives. We are totally familiar with the charms of strawberries, basil and lemon. Their flavours are tangible, marketable and can even be synthesized. In broader terms, sets of flavours collectively define the food of different countries in a way that speaks to people worldwide.

Texture is elusive. It is the secret weapon of top chefs around the world who aren't simply creating dishes that are technically brilliant and tasty. It is the allure of how food feels in the mouth that separates the mundane or competent from the extraordinary. But texture is not easily attainable or even describable. It's also totally unmarketable. Unlike flavour, texture can rarely be captured beyond the instant of its perfection —one reason why there will never be a truly great convenience food. Roasted meat, sliced, cooled and sent back to the oven, cannot be more than satisfactory, any more than the deep-fried samosa that sees a second life.

In our eyes, texture is the single most important aspect of quality—so much so that the book has been largely built around it. There are certain ingredients and dishes that sell themselves on the basis of this alone—oysters and scallops, the lightly poached egg, molten Livarot, Parma ham,

risottos, soufflés, mashed and roast potatoes, homemade ice-cream and pastry, to name a few.

If the texture of a food is perfect, the experience may be diminished by a lack of flavour, but it won't be totally ruined. However, the reverse doesn't apply. Mashed potato made with the finest potatoes and untreated yellow cream will prove a task to eat if it's dry and lumpy. While mash that is perfectly silky, so liberally enriched with butter, milk or cream it almost drops from the fork, will still be exquisite to eat, even if the flavour isn't as good as it might be.

If food has the wrong texture, be it raw or cooked, there may be a number of reasons. It could be down to the conditions in which the fruit or vegetable was grown. It may be due to handling—scallops that are soaked prior to being sold, for example, often fail to caramelise in the pan on account of the water they exude. It may be due to the age of an ingredient—a radish that was crisp when harvested, its tops healthy and green, will lose its bite turning sadly flaccid. In the case of a manufactured ingredient, it could be down to the processing. Spaghetti, that is forced through a modern plastic die will be so slippery that any sauce will drip off, while a traditional bronze die creates a roughened surface which the sauce will cling to. It may, of course, be to do with the way a particular food is cooked, or the recipe itself.

Taste

We perceive flavour through our sense of taste, together with our sense of smell. Taste is a response to the sensations of sweet, sour, bitter and salty. When one of these is predominant within a food, it is generally better appreciated if it is subtle. When the sensations are combined, there is more leeway to accentuate them. An over-sweet strawberry mousse can be countered by a squeeze of lemon. An acidic salad dressing can be tempered by a pinch of sugar. The secret of really good fudge and toffee is the addition of a measure of salt, even though it cannot be detected within the finished confection.

Regions of India, known for the complexity and intensity of their food, add to the art of balancing the four sensations a fifth dimension—heat provided by chillies.

When food is served very simply, the art lies in bringing out its flavour, highlighting what is already there. In the West this is fulfilled at the table by the provision of salt and pepper, but the principle applies to every ingredient—first determine its qualities and then seek to balance and accentuate them. As the great French maitre de chocolat Christian Constant once remarked, 'sugar is to cocoa what salt is to food'. Intensity has to do with enhancing other taste sensations by way of contrast.

Temperature

A fine, hot dinner is easily ruined if it is served on cold plates. China at room temperature absorbs the warmth from whatever food it comes into contact with. One can almost forgive those electric plate-warmers that look like a concertinaed oven glove. The pragmatic approach is to place the plates over a saucepan of boiling vegetables or in the oven, or to run them under a hot tap—a last

resort. The ideal is a well-designed oven that has a built-in warming drawer, or a small warming oven.

Temperature is more critical to some foods than others. A soufflé, risotto or pasta are all at their best eaten piping hot. Whereas a roast chicken, a joint of beef or lamb, and roasted vegetables are all equally delicious when they have cooled a little—in fact, actually benefit from resting. Chill them, however, and all that changes, not least the texture. Chill a roast chicken and—even if you bring it back up to room temperature again—it will never regain the succulence it had when it was hot or newly cooled.

Refrigeration, while a great convenience, performs few favours for cooked dishes. In addition to altering and hardening textures, it dampens flavour and diminishes it over time. The latter cannot be blamed solely on refrigeration, as many flavours are volatile and waver over time. The fragrance of spices, for instance, is never so pungent as at the moment they are freshly ground. There are a few exceptions to this rule. Stews improve if refrigerated overnight, or for up to a couple of days, because their flavours have time to mingle.

The real luxury is a larder that stores foods just below room temperature, without subjecting them to the dry ferocity of the fridge. This preserves various foods, including cheeses, cakes, chutneys, jams and butter.

As to freezing, the only foods we recommend you freeze are fresh stocks, tomato sauces, creamed soups, ices and sorbets. In addition, if you are reliant on a mail-order supplier for quality meat and fish, then it is better to buy in quantity and freeze, than to eat fresh produce of an inferior provenance. Though any number of cooked dishes can be frozen, it is always somewhat to their detriment. It's one thing to deep-freeze a Shepherd's Pie because you have some left over, quite another to make it with the intention of stocking up the freezer.

Fragrance

The fragrance of a food, as it wafts in the air we breathe, is implicit to our enjoyment and recognition of what we are eating. We only have to consider the loss of appetite that occurs when a common cold impairs our sense of smell to understand its role. Our memories are encapsulated and defined by aromas we have experienced throughout our lives, from the smell of squid sizzling on a grill that evokes a Greek holiday, to the aroma of freshly ground coffee that transports you to the alley where you were first acquainted with it as a child.

Our sense of smell is extraordinarily complex, far more sophisticated than our sense of taste. It is the vehicle of appetite. Like texture it is elusive, and bound up with the complex volatile aromas that define flavour. As well as evoking memories, it has a powerful effect on our emotions or reactions. Some of this is cultural conditioning. You can acquire an appreciation of durian fruit and fermented fish products, but it's unlikely you're born with it. The appreciation of sweet-smelling foods is broader. The scent of an orange and almond cake emerging from the oven, or nectarines poaching with spices in a syrup speaks a universal language.

To Begin

Radishes with Butter and Sea Salt

This is not so much a recipe as a reminder of the best way to honour a tufted bunch of radishes. First nip off their whiskery root, liberally smear them with creamy fresh butter, and then dip them into sea salt. It's an age-old pleasure that relies on all three ingredients being of exemplary good character. With some bread on the side it makes for vintage grazing, simple enough to serve at a moment's notice, good enough for any occasion.

Breakfast radish is as unlikely a title as you could conceive for a salad vegetable you would never dream of eating at that hour of the morning. Freshness is of the essence. Their foliage helps to determine this—it should be lively, not limp—and radishes should bite with audible clarity. To encourage this, store them in the fridge, wallowing in icy water.

Unsalted butter should be lightly chilled and taste unmistakably of fresh cream. The more Norman it is the better.

Maldon sea salt is by far and away the most subtle of its genre and the appropriate choice here.

Bread with an open weave, faint sourness and tawny crumb is the ideal complement.

King Prawns with Garlic

One of the best bits of a prawn is its shell; it is this that infuses a bisque with its classy scent. As bisques are murderous soups to make we haven't included any, but the same joys are to be had here as the prawn shells perfume the pan juices. Mop them up with a hunk of crusty white bread. King prawn usually means tiger prawn, but if you feel like pushing the boat out then langoustines or Dublin Bay prawns will be even more delectable.

Serves 4
6 tablespoons extra virgin olive oil
28 raw tiger prawns in shell, heads removed (about 275g)
2 garlic cloves, peeled and minced
½ teaspoon minced red chilli
Sea salt, black pepper
3 tablespoons white wine
Squeeze of lemon juice
1 heaped tablespoon chopped flat-leaf parsley
Crusty white bread, to serve

Heat the oil in a frying pan over a high heat. Add the prawns, garlic and chilli and cook, turning the prawns, for 2–3 minutes until they are pink, seasoning them as you go. Add the wine and just a little lemon juice and cook until the wine reduces and the sauce amalgamates, about 1 minute more. Serve scattered with the chopped parsley, and accompanied by a big plate of bread.

Oysters with Shallot Vinegar

To enter into the debate over whether native or Pacific oysters are preferable is to assume you are spoilt for choice in the first place. And natives, if you find them, are pricey even outside a restaurant. In their defence they take some seven years to reach maturity, compared to Pacific oysters that take half that time. Natives are a small button of a bivalve compared to the fleshy Pacific oyster, but in the eyes of those who know they are more complex, offering up a metallic bitterness in their wake, and complexity is something connoisseurs love. But if you have only ever known the saline naivety of Pacific oysters then you will likely have learned to love them, and they are not to be sniffed at, scooped out of their shell with a crusty morsel of buttered bread and washed down with a glass of chilled Chablis.

Gaining entry
With an oyster cracker
For Pacific oysters, the easiest way by far to access the morsel of your heart's desire is to take an oyster cracker to it. Hold the oyster cup-side down in your hand. Punch a hole at the very edge of the oyster at the frilly end where the muscle is weakest. Slip the knife into the hole and work it round to cut through the muscle, then lift off and discard the upper shell, pick out any stray shell splinters and place the oyster with its juices on a plate.

With an oyster knife
If you are fortunate enough to be opening natives, or you are an old hand with an oyster knife, then first wrap your non-knifeholding hand tightly in a teatowel to protect it.

Hold the oyster cup-side down in your wrapped hand, and carefully insert the top of the oyster knife in the hinge, then work it backwards and forwards to cut through it. Use the knife to lever the shell up, and cut through the ligament that joins the oyster to the upper shell. Lift off and discard the upper shell, pick out any stray shell splinters and place the oyster and its juices on a plate.

Serves 4
1 tablespoon finely chopped shallots
2 tablespoons cider vinegar
6 to 12 oysters per person, depending on your appetite
White bread and unsalted butter, to serve

Combine the shallots and vinegar in a small bowl. Open all the oysters and arrange them on a large platter. Serve them as soon as possible, with the shallot vinegar. Accompany with a plate of bread and some butter.

Taramasalata and Melba Toast

There must be generations who have never tasted real taramasalata. Anyone who has will remember. It relies on smoked cod's roe, a tawny sac not unlike a pair of trousers in shape, streaked with dark red veins, which slits open to reveal a granular sticky paste. At first taste it's sweet and iodine-rich, and this subsides to a curious bitterness, a taste easily acquired. Just a little spread on to Melba toast or French bread with some oily black olives in tow makes for a thirst-inducing appetiser.

Serves 6
3 slices of slightly stale white bread, crusts removed
400 g smoked cod's roe (225g prepared weight)
Juice of 1 lemon
1 large organic egg yolk
425 ml groundnut oil
Extra virgin olive oil and cayenne pepper, to serve

Break up the bread, place it in a bowl and cover with water. Slit the cod's roe open, scrape out the pulp and put in a food processor. Whizz together with half the lemon juice, then add the egg yolk. Squeeze out the water from the bread using your hands. With the motor running, add the bread through the funnel to make a thick, creamy paste. Slowly drizzle in half the groundnut oil as if you were making mayonnaise. Add half of the remaining lemon juice, then drizzle in the rest of the oil.

Taste the taramasalata to see whether it needs any more lemon. It should be the palest salmon-pink in colour, about as thick as whipped cream and just as light. If it seems too thick, then add a drop or two of warm water.

Scoop the taramasalata into a bowl, drizzle over a little olive oil and dust with cayenne pepper.

Melba toast
Melba toast harks back to a world when divas and prima donnas held the world captive. Thin brittle wafers, warped and curled at the edges like a forty-five left out in the sun, were the hallmark of a good restaurant. It is a toast of character, that cannot be prevailed upon to slot neatly into a rack, nor can it be buttered without first being broken.

Making melba toast
Providing you make this toast on the day, you can do it hours in advance of eating. It might seem adventurous to use interesting types of bread, but there is nought that works so well as thinly sliced white, processed to kingdom come.

Preheat the grill and remove the crusts from day-old thinly sliced white bread. Toast on both sides to a pale gold, then slit each piece in two using a sharp bread knife. Scrape away the crumb from the uncooked sides with a blunt table knife. Now toast it again, uncooked side uppermost, watching it continuously. During this second toasting it curls impressively. Melba toast should be completely dry and brittle. Serve at room temperature, stacked into a precarious pile, with lots of unsalted butter or whatever you are dipping it into.

Crushed Goat's Cheese and Anchoiade

This feisty pair of Provencal pastes derives from the kind of warm weather clime we spend our winters dreaming of; the type that encourages a leisurely aperitif and amuse-gueule outdoors. Anchoiade is summer food; goat's cheeses too are in their prime at this time of year. You can serve any mixture of crudités with the goat's cheese dip and anchoiade—slivers of fennel, radishes with tops attached, cherry tomatoes and slender grissini.

Serves 6
Crushed goat's cheese
225 g medium-mature goat's cheese, such as Crottin de Chavignol
3 tablespoons extra virgin olive oil
Black pepper
Few slivers of spring onion

Anchoiade
4 garlic cloves, peeled
16 salted anchovies in oil
15 green olives, pitted
150 ml extra virgin olive oil
1 teaspoon sherry vinegar

To serve
Crudités (fennel slices, radishes, cherry tomatoes etc, grissini)

Remove the rind from the cheese and crumble into a bowl. Mash to a coarse paste with the olive oil and a little black pepper. Spoon into a bowl and scatter over a few slivers of spring onion.

For the anchoiade, put the garlic, anchovies and olives in a food processor and work to a coarse purée. Add the olive oil and vinegar and process to a smooth paste.

Serve the goat's cheese dip and anchoiade with the crudités.

Bagna Cauda and Crudités

This orgy of anchovies and garlic fused into a warm, buttery emulsion is saved from depravity by the vegetables dipped into it. To follow, you can scramble eggs with whatever bagna cauda is left in the pot, then pile them on to crisp buttered brown toast.

Serves 4
Vegetables
750 g assorted vegetables (carrots, fennel, radishes, celery hearts, red or orange peppers, pattypan squashes or courgettes, button mushrooms etc)

Bagna cauda
75 g unsalted butter
4 garlic cloves, peeled and crushed
75 g salted anchovies in oil
8 tablespoons extra virgin olive oil
100 ml white wine
3 tablespoons double cream

Trim and cut up the vegetables, and arrange them attractively in piles on a large plate. Melt the butter with the garlic in a pan over a very gentle heat. Add the anchovies and mash them up as much as possible. Add the oil and continue heating; the sauce at this point will be separated. Heat the wine in a small saucepan and bubble until it is well reduced and syrupy.

Add the cream to the bagna cauda and whisk until it amalgamates. Then gradually whisk this into the reduced wine, to make a smooth creamy beige sauce. Ideally serve the sauce straightaway, although it can be gently reheated and whisked until it is smooth; it shouldn't boil however. Serve the bagna cauda in a central bowl for everyone to dip into.

Roasted Garlic, Toasted Goat's Cheese and Parma Ham

Roast garlic is about diving in with your fingers and squeezing the creamy insides from their papery casing before licking your fingers clean of the garlicky oil. It is a dextrous pleasure to indulge in with a drink before dinner in the company of friends. It makes a welcome aside to a plate of salami, some olives, gherkins and bread for dipping into the oil. But best of all try it with toasted goat's cheese and Parma ham.

Ideally you want semi-matured or demi-sec goat's cheeses; Crottins de Chavignol are made for the job. Mature goat's cheeses too can be used, but will be that much more pungent. The cheese should bake to an almost mousse-like consistency within, while being crusty and golden on the outside.

Serves 6
Roasted garlic
6 large heads of garlic
5 thyme sprigs
Sea salt, black pepper
4 tablespoons extra virgin olive oil
25 g unsalted butter

Toasted goat's cheese
3 semi-mature goat's cheeses
1 tablespoon marjoram leaves (optional)
3 tablespoons extra virgin olive oil

To serve
18 slices of Parma ham
Pain de Campagne, or other coarse-textured white or sourdough bread

Preheat the oven to 150°C, fan oven 140°C, gas 2. Cut the top off each head of garlic to reveal the cloves and place in a shallow baking dish. Tuck the sprigs of thyme in here and there, season well. Drizzle with the olive oil and dot with the butter. Cover with foil and cook in the oven for 2 hours, basting every so often. Leave until cool enough to handle, or cool to room temperature if you prefer.

For the toasted cheese, preheat the oven to 220°C, fan oven 200°C, gas 7. Place the goat's cheeses in a shallow ovenproof dish, scatter over the marjoram leaves if using and trickle over the oil. Bake for 10–12 minutes until golden and crusty at the edges. The cheese should retain its shape while being soft and melted inside.

Place the roasted garlic and its oil, the hot toasted goat's cheese, Parma ham and some bread centrally on the table for everyone to help themselves.

Parma Ham with Parsnip Salad

For such an unlikely combination, parsnips and Parma ham go together like a dream. There is a sense of deja vu in the way the flavour of one brings out the flavour of the other; could it be because pigs are fond of parsnips? Whatever the reason, this is something to graze on while standing around.

Serves 6
700 g parsnips, peeled
1 tablespoon red wine vinegar
1 teaspoon Dijon mustard
Sea salt, black pepper
7 tablespoons olive oil
4 tablespoons raisins
4 tablespoons coarsely chopped
flat-leaf parsley
250 g Parma ham

Bring a pan of salted water to the boil. Cut the parsnips in half, then halve the thicker ends lengthways. Add the parsnips to the pan and boil for 7–10 minutes until tender. Drain and leave in a sieve to allow surface water to evaporate.

While the parsnips are cooking, make the dressing. Whisk the vinegar with the mustard and seasoning, then add the oil. Slice the parsnips diagonally and place in a bowl. Toss with the dressing, and mix in the raisins and parsley.

To serve, lay the Parma ham out on plates and spoon the salad to one side.

Chicken Liver Parfait

Formality only ever detracts from the pleasure of eating, whether it's the setting or the way food is presented. Terrines are like little boys squeezed into woollen coats with velvet collars. The temptation is to ruffle up their hair, undo their top button and point them in the direction of the nearest puddle. When did a single prim and proper slice of terrine ever entice you to eat it? Parfait, dolloped by the spoonful from a bowl, has infinitely more allure.

Serves 4
225 g unsalted butter
225 g chicken livers, trimmed of
fatty membranes
1 bay leaf
2 thyme sprigs
Sea salt, black pepper
1 shallot, peeled and
finely chopped
1 garlic clove, peeled and
finely chopped
2 tablespoons Calvados or brandy
1 tablespoon crème fraîche
Freshly grated nutmeg

To serve
Chutney, cocktail gherkins, silverskin pickled onions, radishes, toasted walnut bread

Melt 25g of the butter in a large frying pan over a medium heat. When the foam starts to subside, add the chicken livers, herbs and seasoning. Sauté for about 3 minutes until the livers are golden on the outside but still pink in the centre, turning them halfway through cooking.

Discard the herbs and tip the chicken livers with any pan juices into a blender.

Melt another knob of butter in the pan, add the shallot and garlic and sweat for a couple of minutes until glossy and translucent. Add the Calvados and simmer until it has all but disappeared. Tip the contents of the frying pan into the blender and purée with the crème fraîche. Leave this to cool for about 20 minutes.

Dice the remaining butter and add to the blender. Process until the parfait is really smooth and creamy. Add a grinding of nutmeg and adjust the seasoning. We like to pass the parfait through a fine sieve to ensure it's as silky as possible, but you don't have to.

Spoon the parfait into a bowl, smooth the surface, cover and refrigerate for up to 2 days until required. Leave it out of the fridge for 20 minutes before serving to allow to soften. Serve the parfait by the spoonful, accompanied by chutney, gherkins, pickled onions, radishes and toasted walnut bread.

Pain d'Epices with Chicken Liver Parfait

The same joys of marrying pâté de foie gras with something sweet apply to a chicken liver parfait. In particular with toasted pain d'épices and a splodge of redcurrant sauce. Assembled in miniature these can be passed round as an appetiser before dinner with a glass of kir or other sweet aperitif. Any leftover pain d'épices can be eaten as a cake for tea, or toasted and spread with butter. If you do not have time to make pain d'épices, you can use brioche instead.

125 g plain flour
125 g icing sugar
1½ teaspoons ground cinnamon
2 teaspoons baking powder
175 g unsalted butter, softened
4 medium organic eggs, separated
40 g caster sugar

To serve
2 tablespoons redcurrant jelly
1 tablespoon freshly squeezed orange juice
120 g chicken liver parfait

Preheat the oven to 180°C, fan oven 170°C, gas 4. Butter a 1.8 litre loaf tin. Sift the flour, icing sugar, cinnamon and baking powder together. Cream the butter and egg yolks in a food processor or mixer, then gradually incorporate the dry ingredients. If using a processor, transfer the mixture to a bowl.

Whisk the egg whites in a bowl until softly peaking, then gradually add the sugar, whisking well with each addition until you have a glossy meringue. Lightly fold into the cake mixture, a third at a time.

Pour into the prepared tin and tap on the surface to eliminate large air bubbles. Bake for 55–60 minutes until the surface is deep beige in colour. To test whether it is cooked, gently press the top; if it feels at all wet or spongy then bake for a little longer. Run a knife around the sides and turn out on to a rack to cool.

To serve, heat the redcurrant jelly with the orange juice until melted, then cool. Toast thin slices of pain d'épices under a grill and cut into squares. Spread with the parfait and top with a little dollop of redcurrant sauce.

Guacamole and Corn Chips

This is the smooth dipping variety of the classic avocado salad that can range so widely in texture. Coloured corn chips are, surprisingly enough, wholly natural. Corn comes in every colour of the rainbow, and so far blue, yellow and red chips have made it into packets. They're one of the healthier crisps on the market that you can dish up with impunity and pride, as the flavour of sea salt and toasted corn shine through, but try to buy organic ones.

Serves 6
Guacamole
4 avocados
1 tomato, about 90g
⅛ red onion, chopped
1 teaspoon chopped red chilli
2 tablespoons lime juice
2 tablespoons coriander leaves
Sea salt, black pepper

To serve
Cayenne pepper
Extra virgin olive oil
Corn chips

Halve the avocados and scoop the flesh into a food processor. Immerse the tomato in boiling water for 20 seconds, and then into cold water. Peel off the skin, remove the core and coarsely chop the flesh. Add the tomato to the food processor with the remaining ingredients and process to a coarse purée. Turn into a bowl. Just before serving, dust with cayenne pepper and drizzle with olive oil. Accompany with corn chips.

Quail's Eggs, Savoury Salt and Grissini

There was a time when it was deemed good manners to peel your guests' quail's eggs, and then society got real. These days it's quite acceptable to leave everyone to peel their own. After all, there is pleasure to be had from the task of gently rolling a cooked egg on the surface of the table to crackle its shell before breaking the membrane and peeling it off.

Serves 6
1 heaped tablespoon Maldon sea salt
1 heaped teaspoon celery salt
36 quail's eggs
Grissini, to serve

Combine the sea and celery salts and divide between two bowls so everyone can reach them at the table. It is easier to cook the eggs in two batches. Bring a pan of water to the boil, gently lower the eggs into the water and boil for precisely 2½ minutes. Remove them with a spoon and immerse in a large bowl of cold water. This is important to stop the yolk cooking; it should be set on the outside, but still slightly runny within. Serve the quails' eggs with the grissini and salt to dip into, letting everyone peel their own.

Naked Mozzarella

Providing your mozzarella is fresh and oozing buttermilk there is little you can do to improve on it. Enjoy its milky sourness, at the very most with a bowl of olives and a sliced tomato, seasoned with salt and pepper.

Dressed Mozzarella

One step beyond this is to anoint mozzarella modestly with a light film of olive oil and a squeeze of lemon.

Serves 4–6
4 buffalo mozzarella, drained
Sea salt, black pepper
2 tablespoons coarsely chopped flat-leaf parsley
Extra virgin olive oil, for drizzling
Squeeze of lemon juice

Cut the mozzarella into 5mm thick slices. Layer the slices in rows in a container, about 20 by 15cm. As you do so, season them lightly with salt and pepper, scatter over the parsley and drizzle with olive oil. Cover and leave in a cool place until ready to eat. Just before serving, squeeze over a little lemon juice.

Mozzarella with Warm Tomato Dressing

That little bit more thrilling than mozzarella with raw tomato.

Serves 4
8 plum tomatoes
¾ teaspoon caster sugar
Sea salt, black pepper
1 tablespoon finely shredded basil
2 tablespoons extra virgin olive oil
4 buffalo mozzarella cheeses

Cut a cone from the top of each tomato and remove the core. Plunge the tomatoes into a small pan of boiling water for 20–30 seconds, then refresh in cold water and slip off the skins. Dice the tomatoes and mix with the sugar, seasoning, basil and olive oil in a small saucepan. Heat very gently until warm, but not so hot that the dressing cooks.

Slice the buffalo mozzarellas and lay in a circle on a plate so the slices overlap. Pile the warm tomato dressing in the centre, and serve straightaway.

Box-baked Livarot

The invention of a brilliant new idea or design creates in the best of us a confused reaction, delighted that the brilliant new thing now exists, kicking ourselves that we didn't come up with it first. Whoever came up with the enlightened notion of baking a whole cheese in its box is a genius, but we're not quite sure who it was, there are several claimants. Camembert baked in its box has been doing the rounds for a couple of years now. We prefer Livarot for the task, providing it is AOC which means buying it from a reputable cheese shop. It's one of the three classic cheeses of Normandy, originally produced by monks in the area. It's unpasteurised and has a supple creamy texture that belies its pungency. You may like to serve some Parma ham with this too.

Serves 2
1 petit Livarot, about 270g, in its box
Belgian chicory leaves, to serve

Preheat the oven to 150°C, fan oven 140°C, gas 2. Remove any waxed paper surrounding the cheese, and place it back in its box. Now tie a piece of string around the sides of the box to secure it, and bake for 25 minutes.

Transfer the cheese to the table, take off the wooden lid and then using a spoon carefully peel back the surface rind. Now dip in with leaves of Belgian chicory, much as you would a fondue.

Pissaladière—sautéed onions, anchovies and Niçoise olives smeared over a doughy pizza base —is best enjoyed in the environs of Nice, the appetite whetted by the scent of dough baking as you pass the entrance to the shop. This particular rendition, tempered to suit our weather and lack of local colour, is more delicate and built precariously on a foundation of puff pastry. Serve it on a plate with a fork, with or without a salad. It's especially good around elevenses if you missed out on breakfast.

Serves 4–6
Base
250 g puff pastry

Top
900 g beefsteak tomatoes
  4 tablespoons extra virgin olive oil
  2 Spanish onions, peeled, halved and sliced
  1 teaspoon sea salt
  1 garlic clove, peeled and finely chopped
  2 heaped tablespoons tomato purée
  1 bay leaf
  2 thyme sprigs
  ½ teaspoon caster sugar
    Black pepper
  15 saffron threads, ground and blended with 1 tablespoon of boiling water
  75 g black olives, pitted and halved
  10 salted anchovies in oil, drained
  1 tablespoon marjoram leaves

Cut a cone from the top of each tomato and remove the core. Plunge the tomatoes into a pan of boiling water for 20–30 seconds, refresh in cold water and slip off the skins. Coarsely chop the flesh.

Heat 2 tablespoons olive oil in a large saucepan over a medium-low heat. Add the onions with the sea salt and sweat for 8–10 minutes until soft and translucent, adding the garlic towards the end of this time. Add the tomatoes and tomato purée and cook for about 5 minutes, stirring occasionally, until the tomatoes collapse.

Add the herbs, sugar and pepper to taste. Simmer, uncovered, over a low heat until reduced down to a thick purée, about 35–40 minutes. Add the saffron liquid towards the end. Remove the herbs and cool to room temperature.

While the purée is cooking, prepare the pastry base. Preheat the oven to 210°C, fan oven 200°C, gas 7. Roll out the pastry thinly on a lightly floured surface to a rectangle, about 25 by 35cm. Place on a baking sheet, line with foil and weight down with a heavy roasting tray; this needn't fit exactly, but should be as close as possible to the dimensions of the pastry. Bake for 17–20 minutes until lightly golden, then remove the roasting tray and foil.

Trim the edges of the pastry and spread the purée in a thin layer over the surface. Scatter over the olives, anchovies and marjoram, and drizzle with the remaining 2 tablespoons olive oil. Bake for 10 minutes, then leave to stand for 15–20 minutes, or cool to room temperature before serving. Cut into squares and lift on to plates, using a palette knife.

A well-crafted quiche is sufficiently soignée to pass as an appetiser in miniature, as well as making a great lunch.

The secret of a luxurious filling is to achieve a loose set. The worst possible scenario is a predominance of beaten eggs with just a drop of milk, which is guaranteed to be as tough as rubber. Of a good quiche the reverse is true, unashamedly indulgent the custard consists predominantly of cream with just enough egg to set it.

Quiches and tarts benefit from 10 minutes standing around after they come out of the oven, time for the pastry to crisp and the filling to set. They are also delicious just cooled. If you chill them, however, the filling firms up and you lose that wonderful creaminess. They do reheat, though the pastry is never quite as crisp.

The pastry
Homemade shortcrust pastry is short and buttery, crumbly and good enough to eat on its own. That said, shop-bought pastry is adequate if you're not in the mood to make it. One of the secrets of making pastry is lightness of touch. It helps to work as fast as you can, which explains why food processors do the job so well.

For a good quiche, it is important to use a sufficiently deep tin. To avoid uncooked or stodgy pastry, you will need to bake the pastry case blind (without its filling) until it starts to colour. This will ensure that the pastry emerges from its second baking perfectly golden and short.

Shortcrust pastry
225 g plain flour
  Pinch of sea salt
150 g unsalted butter, chilled and diced
  1 medium organic egg, separated

Place the flour and salt in a food processor, add the butter and process until the mixture resembles fine crumbs. Incorporate the egg yolk, then with the motor running trickle in just enough cold water to bring the dough together in lumps. Transfer to a large bowl and gather into a ball using your hands.

Resting the pastry
Wrap the pastry in clingfilm and chill for at least 1 hour. It can be chilled for up to 2 days, or frozen.

Lining the tin and baking blind
Preheat the oven to 190°C, fan oven 180°C, gas 5. Knead the pastry until it is pliable, then roll out thinly on a lightly floured surface and carefully lift into a 23cm tart tin, 4cm deep, with a removable base. Press into the edge of the tin and trim the top using a knife, reserving the trimmings. Prick the base with a fork and line with foil, tucking it over the top edge. Now weight it with baking beans—a dried pulse will do nicely and can be reused.

Bake the case for 15 minutes, then remove the foil and baking beans. If any part of the side has shrunk more than it should, patch with a little of the reserved pastry. Brush the inside of the case with egg white, then bake for another 10 minutes until it is lightly coloured. This glaze helps to seal the pastry and prevent the custard from soaking into it.

A good quiche Lorraine is a fine assembly of warm crumbly pastry and salty snippets of bacon in a custard that is puffed and light enough to wobble precariously as it emerges from the oven.

Serves 6
23 cm tart case, 4cm deep, baked blind (see left)

Filling
250 g smoked streaky bacon, rind removed and cut into 1cm dice
300 ml whipping cream
150 ml milk
  3 medium organic eggs
  1 medium organic egg yolk
  1 teaspoon Dijon mustard
  1 teaspoon grainy mustard
  Black pepper
175 g Gruyère cheese, grated

Preheat the oven to 190°C, fan oven 180°C, gas 5. Separate out the pieces of bacon, place them in a large frying pan and cook over a very low heat until the fat begins to render. Increase the heat to medium and cook, stirring frequently, until the bacon begins to colour and crisp, then scatter it over the base of the tart case.

Whisk together the remaining ingredients, except the cheese, until smooth. (You shouldn't need salt, the bacon and cheese provide this). Whisk in half of the cheese, then pour the custard into the tart case. Scatter the remaining cheese over the top and bake for 35 minutes until golden and puffy.

Remove the collar, leaving the tart to stand on the metal base for 10 minutes. Although best eaten hot, this quiche can be reheated.

Salmon, Red Onion and Anchovy Tart

Serves 6
23 cm tart case, 4cm deep, baked blind (see page 51)

Filling
450 g salmon fillet, skinned
150 ml milk
Sea salt, black pepper
150 ml white wine
150 ml whipping cream
2 medium eggs
1 medium egg yolk
6 tablespoons chopped mixed parsley, basil, chives and dill
3 salted anchovies in oil, halved lengthways
¼ red onion, finely sliced
Vegetable oil

Place the salmon in a small pan with the milk and seasoning. Bring to a simmer then cover, leaving a small gap for the steam to escape. Cook over a low heat for 3 minutes. Take off the heat, cover tightly and leave for 30 minutes, by which time the fish should be just cooked. Pour the wine into another small pan and reduce by half.

Preheat the oven to 190°C, fan oven 180°C, gas 5. Whisk together the cream, eggs and egg yolk in a bowl. Add the fish liquor and wine, then the herbs and seasoning.

Using a fork, coarsely flake the salmon in the saucepan, then scatter over the base of the pastry case. Pour on the custard and lay the anchovies on top. Toss the onion in a bowl with enough oil to coat, and scatter on top of the quiche. Bake for 35–40 minutes until golden, puffy and set. Remove the collar and leave the tart to stand on the base for 10 minutes. This tart is equally good served hot or cold.

Spinach, Feta and Tomato Tart

Feta and tomato make for lively sunny flavours, for when you're in that kind of mood.

Serves 6
23 cm tart case, 4cm deep, baked blind (see page 51)

Filling
450 g baby spinach, picked over and washed
400 ml whipping cream
2 medium organic eggs
1 medium organic egg yolk
1 tablespoon freshly grated Parmesan
1 garlic clove, peeled
Sea salt, black pepper
200 g feta cheese, cut into 1cm dice
125 g cherry tomatoes, halved
Vegetable oil

Put the spinach in a large saucepan with just the water clinging to the leaves after washing, pressing it down to get it all in. Cover with a tight-fitting lid and cook over a low heat for 10 minutes until wilted and tender, stirring halfway through. Drain the spinach into a sieve, pressing out as much water as possible (otherwise the moisture will seep down into the pastry). Tip the spinach on to a board and coarsely chop it with a large sharp knife.

Preheat the oven to 190°C, fan oven 180°C, gas 5. Whisk together the cream, eggs, egg yolk and Parmesan. Either purée the garlic in a press or chop it, sprinkle over a little salt and crush to a paste using the flat of a knife. Whisk this into the custard and season with salt and pepper. Mix in the spinach, then gently fold in half the feta. Transfer this filling to the tart case.

Toss the halved cherry tomatoes and remaining feta with just enough oil to coat them and scatter over the top of the tart. Grind over some pepper and bake for 35–45 minutes until golden, puffy and set in the centre. Remove the collar, leaving the tart to stand on the metal base for 10 minutes. This tart is equally delicious served warm or at room temperature.

Aubergine, Goat's Cheese and Pesto Tarts

These tarts are as enjoyable eaten in the hand as with a knife and fork. The recipe makes a little more pesto than you will need but, given the universal appeal of pasta and pesto, this is no bad thing.

Makes 6
1 large aubergine, thinly sliced
Extra virgin olive oil, for brushing
Sea salt, black pepper
2 red peppers
350 g puff pastry
1 organic egg, beaten
150 g medium mature goat's
    cheese, sliced
Cayenne pepper, for dusting

Pesto
15 g pine nuts
1 small garlic clove, peeled
40 g basil leaves
6 tablespoons extra virgin olive oil
25 g Parmesan cheese,
    freshly grated

Preheat the oven to 200°C, fan oven 190°C, gas 6. Brush the aubergine slices on both sides with olive oil, lay on a baking sheet and season with salt and pepper. Roast for 20–25 minutes until they are lightly coloured; at the same time roast the peppers, then wrap them in two plastic bags, one inside another. Once they are cool enough to handle, slip off the skins, halve and remove the core and seeds.

While the vegetables are roasting, make the pesto. Place all the ingredients, except the Parmesan, in a food processor and work to a purée. Add the cheese and season to taste.

Roll out the puff pastry thinly and cut 6 rectangles, each about 15 by 10cm. Lay the aubergine slices on the pastry rectangles so they overlap, leaving a border to allow for shrinkage. Put a slice of red pepper on top, brush this with olive oil and season. Brush the pastry rim with beaten egg. Bake the tarts for 17 minutes.

Spoon a heaped teaspoon of pesto down the length of each tart and lay the sliced goat's cheese on top. Bake for a further 3 minutes. Dust the goat's cheese with a little cayenne pepper and serve hot, or at room temperature.

Bruschetta

Bruschetta in its basic incarnation, surely the best of all, is a soggy affair of over-ripe tomato and lots of very green olive oil—both in colour and flavour—absorbed by a sturdy slice of toasted white bread. A French campagne loaf is probably the most widely available crumb that suits—anything will do but please, no ciabatta.

Makes 1
1 thick slice coarse-textured
    white bread
1 garlic clove, peeled (optional)
Extra virgin olive oil, for drizzling
1 over-ripe tomato
Sea salt

Toast the bread and if you feel so inclined, give it a few half-hearted swipes with a garlic clove —a hint of garlic is fine but nothing too boisterous. Place the toast on a plate and drizzle generously with olive oil.

Your tomato should be ripe to the point of bursting. If it hasn't already done so, use a knife to make an incision and break it open using your fingers, working over the toast. Squeeze out the seeds— one of the best bits that fashion would have us discard—then mash the flesh on to the surface. Throw away the tomato skin and core. Crumble over a few flakes of sea salt and splash over a little more olive oil.

Bloody Mary

Knowing how to fix a mean Bloody Mary is an essential social skill. Even if you never turn your hand to shaking a Martini or stirring a Whisky Sour, there are certain occasions when this is the only drink that fits the bill. It is a task that normally falls on whichever man in the house is feeling most delicate, he who is best placed to gauge a balance between its peppery bite and the warmth of the vodka in a way that hits the spot with sheer precision. The author of this particular version is Chris Bell; it would be unkind to suggest its success lay with an experience of hangovers, he just happens to make a great Bloody Mary.

Makes a jug to serve 4
300 ml vodka
    Ice cubes
850 ml tomato juice
    Juice of 2 lemons
  2 tablespoons Worcestershire
    sauce
  4 dashes of Tabasco
    Sea salt
    Celery salt
    Black pepper

Measure the vodka into a jug, add a generous number of ice cubes and stir for about 1 minute. Pour in the tomato juice. Add the lemon juice, the Worcestershire sauce, Tabasco, some sea salt and a conservative pinch of celery salt. Stir well, tasting to make sure it leaves a warming sense of well being. Pour into glasses and grind over some black pepper to serve.

Salted Almonds

To bring out the best in almonds they need a slow roasting, a little sea salt and the finest dusting of cayenne pepper.

Serves 4–6
  1 teaspoon unsalted butter
225 g whole blanched
    almonds, skinned
  3 tablespoons sea salt
    Cayenne pepper, for dusting

Preheat the oven to 150°C, fan oven 140°C, gas 2. Grease a baking tray with the butter and lay the almonds in a thin layer on top. Bake for 45 minutes until the nuts have toasted to a pale creamy gold. Scatter the sea salt over a sheet of baking parchment, tip the almonds on top and rub the salt through them. Wrap the paper up into a package and set aside for at least 1 hour, preferably several. On unwrapping the nuts, shake off the excess salt and dust with a suspicion of cayenne pepper.

White Onion Soup

This is in the vichyssoise league of creamed soups. Garnish at your whim, a few croûtons (see page 060) scattered on top won't go amiss.

Serves 4–6
70 g unsalted butter
1 kg white onions, peeled, halved and sliced
3 thyme sprigs
Sea salt, black pepper
150 ml white wine
700 ml chicken stock
200 ml crème fraîche

Melt the butter in a large saucepan over a low heat. Add the onions and thyme, sprinkle with a heaped teaspoon of sea salt and sweat for 30 minutes, stirring frequently to prevent them colouring. By the end they should be lusciously silky and soft. Pour in the wine, increase the heat slightly and simmer until it is well reduced. Add the chicken stock, bring to a simmer and cook gently for about 15 minutes.

Discard the thyme sprigs and purée the soup in batches in a blender, adding the crème fraîche and a grinding or two of black pepper. Check the seasoning. Return the soup to a clean saucepan and reheat gently. Serve in warmed bowls.

Stock

Within professional circles the art of making stock is worthy of a PhD; you enter the trade as an apprentice and graduate as a sorcerer. Lesson one—good stock, good soup. To which end you need bones, not any old bones but ones with a bit of breeding. And lots of different vegetables, spices and wine, that will afford your brew its complex magnificence. At which point most of us lose interest. All is not lost however; a simple stock is better than no stock at all.

The starting point for our stock is the leftover Sunday roast chicken carcass. Not wishing to waste it we pop it into a pot, cover with water and leave it to gently simmer for an hour or so. The stock can then be boiled down to enrich it further until it tastes singularly of chicken. If you add vegetables to the pot you will end up with a more complex flavour, but by the time the stock has been included in a recipe that complexity will probably be lost.

Stock cubes are a no-no; rather water than the artifice of all those hydrogenated nasties. Shop-bought fresh stocks vary alarmingly in quality; some are little better than reconstituted stock cubes. We recommend Sainsbury's own label stocks. Amass those you use on a regular basis in the freezer.

Chicken Stock
1 chicken carcass, post-roast
Water
Sea salt

Put the chicken carcass in a saucepan that will hold it snugly, and add water to cover by 2cm. Bring to the boil and skim off any foam on the surface. Add a good teaspoon of salt and simmer for 1 hour. Strain the stock. Taste and, if it seems at all insipid, return to the pan and reduce by up to half to concentrate the flavour. Leave to cool, then cover and chill. Skim off any fat from the surface before use.

Croûtons
The impostors that come with pre-packed Caesar salad only bring shame to the name. Crisp homemade croûtons are a small touch that will make the most humble soup happy. All you need is some day-old white bread, sliced 1cm thick, and groundnut oil for shallow-frying.

Cut the crusts off the bread and dice, using a sharp chopping knife rather than a bread knife, which will tear the crumb. Heat a 3–4mm depth of groundnut oil in a frying pan until it is hot enough to immerse a cube of bread in bubbles. Add a single layer of bread cubes to the pan and fry them, tossing occasionally, until evenly gold and crisp. Remove with a slotted spoon and drain on kitchen paper, then leave to cool.

Croûtons are at their best the day they are made.

White Bean Soup

This pale and interesting soup is titivated with a drizzle of basil oil. Celery salt, with its old-fashioned musty scent, plays a subtle but crucial role in enhancing the flavour of the haricot beans and celery.

Serves 6
2 tablespoons extra virgin olive oil
1 onion, peeled and chopped
2 shallots, peeled and chopped
1 garlic clove, peeled and finely chopped
1 celery heart, sliced
300 g dried haricot beans, soaked overnight
2 litres vegetable stock
Sea salt, white pepper
Celery salt

Basil oil
25 g basil leaves
6 tablespoons extra virgin olive oil

Heat the olive oil in a large saucepan. Add the onion, shallots, garlic and celery and sweat for 5–10 minutes until soft, but not coloured. Drain the soaked haricot beans and add to the pan with the stock. Bring to the boil and simmer for 1¼ hours.

Meanwhile, make the basil oil. Bring a small pan of water to the boil. Add the basil leaves, then immediately tip them into a sieve to drain. Purée in a blender with the olive oil, then pass through a sieve into a small bowl.

Allow the soup to cool slightly, then purée in a blender, seasoning with pepper and a little salt. Pass through a sieve into a clean pan. Add a generous sprinkling of celery salt. Reheat the soup as required and ladle into warmed bowls. Add a swirl of basil oil to serve.

Gingered Carrot Soup

The most delicious-ever carrot soup courtesy of Bryan Leech and Martin Marley who run Kilgraney, a decadent country house hotel just outside Dublin. The orange juice imparts an all-important kick and brings out the flavour of the carrots. Try to use big fat organic ones with lots of flavour, and a good fresh chicken stock.

Serves 4–6
40 g unsalted butter
1 large onion, peeled, halved and sliced
2 tablespoons fresh root ginger, peeled and finely chopped
700 g carrots, peeled and roughly chopped
1.2 litres chicken stock
150 ml freshly squeezed orange juice
Sea salt, white pepper
Crème fraîche and snipped chives, to serve

Melt the butter in a large saucepan. Add the onion and ginger and sauté until the onion is soft but not brown. Add the carrots and sauté for a further minute or two, then stir in the stock and bring to the boil. Cover, turn the heat down and simmer for 30 minutes or until the carrots are very tender.

Allow the soup to cool a little, then purée in batches in a blender and return to a clean pan. Add the orange juice and season to taste. To serve, reheat the soup over a low heat. Adjust the seasoning and ladle into warmed bowls. Spoon a little crème fraîche into each bowl and scatter over a few chives.

Leek and Potato Soup

Surprisingly different from vichyssoise, this is more earth mother, and wholesome.

Serves 6
50 g unsalted butter
700 g trimmed leeks, sliced
1 Spanish onion, peeled and chopped
200 ml white wine
1.3 litres chicken or vegetable stock
170 g maincrop potato, peeled and thinly sliced
Sea salt, black pepper
200 g unsmoked streaky bacon, diced
Snipped chives, to serve

Melt the butter in a large saucepan over a medium-low heat. Add the leeks and onion and sweat for 8–10 minutes, stirring occasionally, until they are silky and soft, but not coloured. Add the wine and reduce until syrupy. Meanwhile, bring the stock to the boil in a separate pan.

Add the sliced potato to the leeks and stir for 1 minute, then pour on the boiling stock. Season and simmer for 10 minutes. In the meantime, heat a dry frying pan over a medium-low heat, add the bacon and fry for 7–8 minutes until browned and crisp, stirring occasionally. Remove with a slotted spoon to a bowl.

Using a food processor, briefly whizz the soup in batches to a textured slurry. Return to a clean saucepan, taste to check the seasoning and gently reheat. Ladle the soup into warm bowls and scatter with the bacon and chives to serve.

Butternut Squash Soup

Sister to pumpkin soup with the same smooth, creamy orange good looks, but that little bit sweeter.

Serves 6
1 litre chicken stock
900 g butternut squash flesh (about 1.5kg unprepared weight), cut into large chunks
300 g crème fraîche, plus 2 tablespoons
Sea salt, black pepper
½ teaspoon caster sugar
75 g unsalted butter, diced
Freshly ground nutmeg

Bring the stock to the boil in a large saucepan. Add the squash, bring back to the boil, cover and simmer over a low heat for about 15 minutes.

Cool slightly, then purée the soup in batches in a blender with the 300g crème fraîche, a generous sprinkling of sea salt and the sugar. Transfer to a large bowl. Add the butter and season with black pepper and nutmeg. Stir until the butter melts, then taste and add a little more salt if necessary. Pass through a fine sieve into a clean pan. Reheat gently and serve in warmed bowls, with a teaspoon of crème fraîche melting in the centre.

Courgette and Lemon Soup

This textured soup is fast and furious to prepare. And yes, if you can't get fresh peas or can't be bothered to pod them, you can use frozen, but don't cheat on the chicken stock. The vegetables should still have some bite so heed the cooking times; courgettes collapse capriciously if allowed too long in the pan.

Serves 4
700 ml strong, well-seasoned fresh
   chicken stock
  3 tablespoons olive oil
  1 red onion, peeled and chopped
225 g maincrop potatoes, peeled and
   cut into 1cm dice
700 g courgettes, trimmed, halved
   and thinly sliced
   Finely grated zest of 1 lemon
150 g shelled peas (preferably fresh)
 40 g coarsely chopped
   flat-leaf parsley
   Juice of ½ lemon
   Sea salt, black pepper
   Freshly grated Parmesan,
   to serve

Bring the chicken stock to the boil in a medium pan. Heat the olive oil in a large saucepan over a medium heat, add the onion and sweat for several minutes until soft and translucent. Add the potato, courgettes and lemon zest, and cook for 2–3 minutes. Pour on the boiling stock and simmer for 3 minutes. Add the peas and parsley and simmer for a further 3 minutes.

Transfer a third of the soup to a food processor and whizz briefly to break the vegetables up. Return to the saucepan, add the lemon juice and taste for seasoning; this soup needs plenty. Serve in warm bowls accompanied by the Parmesan.

Cream of Cauliflower Soup

An understated soup Alice Waters' style where not even stock interferes with the taste of the cauliflower. Try serving it with a poached egg (see page 068) in the middle.

Serves 4–6
  2 cauliflowers
 25 g unsalted butter
  1 onion, peeled and sliced
  4 tablespoons crème fraîche
   Sea salt
   Freshly grated nutmeg
   Chervil sprigs, to serve

Break the cauliflower up into florets and set aside a handful as a garnish. Melt the butter in a large saucepan. Add the onion and cauliflower with a little water and sweat for about 15 minutes, without letting them colour. Add water to cover, bring to a simmer, cover and cook over a medium heat for 25 minutes. Meanwhile, add the reserved florets to a pan of boiling salted water and parboil for 6–8 minutes, so they retain some bite.

Purée the soup in batches in a blender, return it to the saucepan and gently reheat. Add the crème fraîche and season with salt and nutmeg to taste. Serve very hot, garnished with the cauliflower florets and chervil sprigs.

Wild Mushroom Soup

The wider the variety of mushrooms, the merrier this soup will be. Every wild mushroom is possessed of its own unique scent distinctive enough to shine through the others, so creating a soup that is rich and complex.

Serves 4
  5 tablespoons extra virgin olive oil
500 g mixed wild and cultivated
   mushrooms, trimmed and
   thinly sliced
  2 red onions, peeled and chopped
  3 garlic cloves, peeled and
   finely chopped
300 ml white wine
850 ml strong, well-seasoned
   chicken stock
  1 bay leaf
   Croûtons, to serve (see page 060)

Heat 2 tablespoons oil in a large saucepan over a medium-high heat. Add half the mushrooms and sauté, stirring frequently, until soft; transfer to a bowl. Repeat with the rest of the mushrooms, adding them to the bowl.

Heat the remaining 1 tablespoon oil in the pan, add the onions and garlic and sweat for several minutes until softened. Add the wine and cook this right down to a syrupy consistency. Return the mushrooms to the pan, add the chicken stock and the bay leaf, bring to a simmer and cook for 10 minutes.

Using a slotted spoon, transfer a third of the mushrooms to a food processor and pulse to chop finely, then return them to the saucepan. To serve, ladle the soup into warm bowls and place a spoonful of croûtons in the centre.

Mussel Soup with Tomato and Chilli

The bite of chilli midwinter is always a welcome warmer.

Serves 4
1.5 kg mussels in shell
150 ml white wine
3 garlic cloves, peeled
5 tablespoons extra virgin olive oil (approximately)
4 tablespoons chopped flat-leaf parsley
400 g can chopped tomatoes
1 dried red chilli, finely chopped
4 slices of baguette, 1cm thick

Clean the mussels (see page 102) and place in a large saucepan with the wine. Cover and cook over a high heat for 5 minutes by which time they should have opened. Lift them out into a bowl, and decant the cooking liquor, discarding the gritty bit at the bottom. At this stage you may like to shell half the mussels, though it's not essential.

Finely chop 2 garlic cloves. Heat 3 tablespoons oil in a large saucepan over a medium heat. Add the chopped garlic and half the parsley and sizzle for 30 seconds until the garlic starts to colour. Add the tomatoes and chilli, lower the heat and cook gently for about 15 minutes, stirring occasionally, until the oil rises to the surface. You can prepare to this point in advance.

To serve, add the mussel liquor to the tomato base and heat. Add the mussels, cover and reheat for 2–3 minutes, stirring once. Toast the bread; rub with the reserved garlic clove and place in 4 warmed soup bowls. Splash with olive oil, then ladle the soup on top. Scatter over the remaining parsley and splash with a little more olive oil.

Garlic Soup with a Poached Egg

Those who believe in garlic as a universal panacea are bound to feel better after a bowl of this—no shrinking violet with its whole two heads. Combined with raw egg yolk and melted cheese it is deliciously earthy. Your thyme should be soft-leafed rather than hard and woody.

Serves 4
2 heads of garlic, broken into cloves and peeled
3 thyme sprigs, plus 1 heaped teaspoon thyme leaves
1 bay leaf
850 ml light chicken stock
150 ml dry vermouth
4 tablespoons extra virgin olive oil (approximately)
Sea salt, black pepper
8 slices French bread, 1cm thick
Splash of white wine vinegar
4 large organic eggs
150 g Gruyère cheese, finely grated

Place the garlic, thyme sprigs and bay leaf in a medium saucepan with the stock, vermouth, 3 tablespoons olive oil, a heaped teaspoon of sea salt and a grinding of black pepper. Bring to the boil, then lower the heat and simmer gently for 30 minutes. Strain the soup through a sieve into a clean pan, pressing the garlic through. Add the thyme leaves and taste to check the seasoning.

While the soup is cooking, preheat the oven to 190°C, fan oven 180°C, gas 5. Lay the slices of French bread in a single layer in a baking dish and toast in the oven for 5 minutes until dried out. Brush both sides of the toast with olive oil and return to the oven for a further 10–12 minutes until the bread croûtes are lightly golden.

Bring a large pan of water to the boil and acidulate it with a dash of vinegar. Turn the heat down low until the water is barely at a trembling simmer. Stir to create a whirlpool and break in the eggs, one at a time. Once they rise to the surface, trim off any ragged tails of white and cook for about 4 minutes in total.

While the eggs are cooking, reheat the soup. Place two croûtes in each of 4 warmed shallow soup bowls. Using a slotted spoon lift the eggs, one at a time, and place on top of the croûtes. Ladle the soup over the top. Serve accompanied by the cheese.

Risotto Soup with Herbs and Poached Egg

Sloppier than a risotto but just as hearty, this will serve as the focal point of lunch or supper with a salad to follow. Like a risotto however, it demands to be eaten as soon as it's ready.

Serves 6
Splash of white wine vinegar
6 large organic eggs
2 litres vegetable stock
Sea salt, black pepper
70 g unsalted butter
1 red onion, peeled and finely chopped
1 garlic clove, peeled and finely chopped
300 g risotto rice
200 ml white wine
300 g watercress leaves and tender stems
50 g flat-leaf parsley leaves and tender stems
25 g mint leaves (1 large bunch)
Several tarragon sprigs (leaves only)
50 g Parmesan cheese, freshly grated, plus extra to serve

To poach the eggs, bring a large pan of water to the boil and acidulate it with a dash of vinegar. Turn the heat down low until the water is barely at a trembling simmer. Stir to create a whirlpool and break in three of the eggs, one at a time. Once they rise to the surface trim off any ragged tails of white and cook for about 4 minutes in total. Using a slotted spoon lift out the eggs, one at a time, and place in a bowl of cold water. Poach the remaining eggs in the same way and add to the bowl.

Bring the vegetable stock to the boil, season and keep it at a steady simmer.

Melt 40g butter in a large saucepan. Add the onion and sweat without colouring for 4–5 minutes, then add the garlic. A few moments later add the rice and cook, stirring, until it is translucent.

Pour in the wine and cook until it has been absorbed. Then add the stock a couple of ladlefuls at a time, ensuring each addition is absorbed before adding any more. Continue in this way, cooking the risotto for 20–25 minutes; the rice should still be firm to the bite. Towards the end of cooking, bring a medium pan of water to the boil to reheat the eggs.

Melt the remaining butter in another large saucepan, add the watercress and herbs and sweat until they wilt. Pour in the remaining stock and cook for 1 minute. Transfer to a food processor and process until the watercress and herbs are finely chopped. Add to the risotto; it should be nice and soupy.

Gently reheat the soup, stir in the Parmesan and adjust the seasoning. Drop the poached eggs into the boiling water for 1–1½ minutes to reheat. Ladle the soup into warmed bowls and place a poached egg in the centre of each. Serve accompanied by more Parmesan at the table.

Gazpacho

This chilled Spanish soup is as rich and flavourful as the tomatoes that go into it, so try to use really sweet ones—if not cherry, then another small variety. There are a million and one garnishes that can be served with gazpacho and often are, but a splash of olive oil and a few croûtons (see page 060) would seem most respectful of the soup.

Serves 4
1.1 kg cherry tomatoes
1 cucumber, peeled and roughly chopped
1 garlic clove, peeled and chopped
1 heaped teaspoon minced fresh red chilli
2 heaped teaspoons chopped onion
275 ml extra virgin olive oil
1 teaspoon red wine or sherry vinegar
2 heaped teaspoons caster sugar
2 rounded teaspoons sea salt
Grinding of black pepper
Extra virgin olive oil, to serve

Place all the ingredients for the soup in a blender and work to a purée, then pass through a sieve into a large bowl. You will need to do this in batches. Cover and chill for at least 1 hour, but not for longer than necessary.

To serve, ladle the chilled soup into bowls and splash some olive oil over each one.

Vichyssoise with Smoked Salmon

The reputation of this soup precedes it. It is bettered only by a spoonful of caviar.

Serves 6
450 g potatoes, peeled and cut up
50 g unsalted butter
280 g white of leek, sliced
2 sticks of celery heart, sliced
150 ml white wine
850 ml chicken stock
Sea salt, white pepper
300 ml single cream
180 g smoked salmon, cut into thin strips
Finely chopped chives, to serve

Add the potatoes to a pan of salted water and cook until tender. Drain and press them through a sieve. Melt the butter in a large saucepan, add the leek and celery and sweat over a very low heat for 12–15 minutes, stirring frequently to avoid colouring. Add the wine and cook until well reduced. Then add the chicken stock and some seasoning. Bring to the boil, cover and simmer over a low heat for 20 minutes. Purée the soup in a blender, then transfer to a bowl and whisk in the puréed potato. Pass through a fine sieve, stir in the cream and taste for seasoning.

To serve hot, gently reheat the soup without boiling. Place a few strips of smoked salmon in each warmed soup bowl and ladle the soup on top; the heat of the soup will cook the salmon. Scatter over some chives and serve.

Alternatively, serve the vichyssoise lightly chilled. Ladle into bowls, drape with a few strips of smoked salmon and scatter over some chopped chives.

Beetroot and Apple Soup

Beetroot soup promises a vermilion hue of enviable intensity. A garnish of sautéed spring onion and melting crème fraîche is the ideal contrast.

Serves 6
80 g unsalted butter
2 onions, peeled and chopped
2 garlic cloves, peeled and finely chopped
700 g uncooked beetroot, trimmed, peeled and sliced
2 apples, peeled, cored and sliced
200 ml dry cider
1.2 litres chicken stock
Sea salt, black pepper
3 bunches of spring onions, trimmed and sliced
3 tablespoons crème fraîche

Melt 50g of the butter in a large saucepan over a low heat, add the onions and garlic and sweat for 5–8 minutes until soft and glossy, stirring occasionally. Add the beetroot and apples and sweat for a further 5 minutes, again stirring from time to time. Add the cider and reduce until syrupy, then add the stock. Season and bring to the boil. Lower the heat, cover and simmer for 30 minutes. Purée the soup in batches in a food processor, or a blender if you prefer a very smooth soup. Return to the pan and check the seasoning.

About 10 minutes before the soup will be ready, heat the remaining butter in a frying pan and sweat the spring onions over a low heat for about 8 minutes until soft, seasoning them and stirring often. If necessary reheat the soup gently. Ladle it into warm bowls; pile the spring onions in the centre with a heaped teaspoon of crème fraîche on top. Serve straightaway.

The born-again poached egg that has so readily draped itself around the neck of every smoked haddock fillet and muffin that has allowed, seems a wholly British infatuation. And without wanting to embrace the culture in the extreme, nothing else can dress up an otherwise understated lunch with such nonchalant glamour especially when the egg is poached to perfection—an opaque casing of white enclosing a liquid yolk with just the thinnest curdy lining around the outside. By design the warm sticky yolk cascades over whatever happens to be underneath it.

Makes 4
Splash of white wine vinegar
4 large organic eggs

Bring a large saucepan of water to the boil. Add a good splash of wine vinegar, turn the heat down and keep the water at a trembling simmer. The water must not boil while the eggs are poaching.

Break the eggs one at a time into a tea cup (or use 4 teacups). Gently stir the water into a whirlpool using a large spoon and drop the eggs into it. They will sink to the bottom of the pan, leaving strands of white floating. After about 2 minutes the eggs will rise to the surface. Cook them for 2 minutes longer, then remove the eggs using a slotted spoon, trimming off the tendrils of white against the side of the pan.

Either serve straightaway or cool the eggs in a sink of cold water. To reheat, simply plunge them into simmering water or hot soup for 1½ minutes then serve.

This is duly rich, so all you need is a green salad with, or after it.

Serves 4

125 g unsalted butter
225 g trimmed leeks, thinly sliced
1 bay leaf
1 teaspoon plain flour
1 to 2 teaspoons milk
150 ml double cream
Sea salt, black pepper
2 large slices day-old white bread, crusts removed and diced
5 large organic eggs
2 teaspoons vegetable oil
50 g Gruyère cheese, grated

Heat 25g butter in a small non-stick saucepan and sweat the leeks with the bay leaf until soft. Blend the flour with the milk, then mix with the cream. Add to the leeks and season. Bring to a simmer and cook very gently, stirring frequently, for 8 minutes. Remove the bay leaf.

For the croûtons, melt the 100g butter in a frying pan, skim off the surface foam, decant the clear liquid and discard the milky residue. Heat the clarified butter in the frying pan until hot enough to surround a cube of bread with bubbles. Add the bread and cook, tossing, until crisp and golden. Drain on kitchen paper.

Preheat the grill. Lightly whisk the eggs with seasoning in a bowl. Heat the oil in a 23cm frying pan until very hot; tip out the excess. Add the eggs and scramble rapidly for 30 seconds until almost set. Leave undisturbed for another 30 seconds, then spoon the hot leeks on top and scatter over the cheese. Place under the grill until the cheese is melted and bubbling. Serve at once, scattered with croûtons.

A lot of twaddle is written about scrambled eggs, how you need to take the best part of half an hour to cook them and so forth. Nothing is to be gained by cooking them this slowly, you only serve to tire out your arm and waste 25 minutes. Certainly the eggs do have to be gently coaxed into thickening without forming overly large curds, but a non-stick saucepan, a wooden spoon and a gentle heat should see you through.

As ever texture is everything—all too often eggs are over-scrambled until they are dry and rubbery. To arrive at the table with the correct consistency, you have to stop cooking the eggs while they are still too runny. Not only does the heat of the pan continue to cook them, but also the residual heat of the eggs means they will continue to set in the minutes that pass before you lift fork to mouth. We prefer to hold back on the cream and butter, and to rely for creaminess on extra egg yolks. Serve scrambled eggs with toasted brioche, or with smoked salmon, or Buttered Spinach with Garlic (see page 204).

Serves 2

3 large organic eggs, plus
2 extra yolks
Splash of milk
Sea salt, black pepper
Knob of unsalted butter

Whisk the eggs and egg yolks in a bowl with the milk and some seasoning. Pour them into a non-stick saucepan and add a knob of butter. Place the pan over a low heat and after a couple minutes once they've begun to warm up, stir constantly with a wooden spoon, making sure you cover the base of the saucepan. The eggs will begin to thicken; once they reach the consistency of custard remove the pan from the heat, continuing to stir. The eggs should be thick and creamy without being set; if necessary pop them back on the heat momentarily to thicken them a little bit more, and so on until you achieve the right consistency. With no time to waste, divide between two plates and serve straightaway.

Goat's Cheese Frittata

If you are partial to ham and eggs, serve this with a thin slice of honey-roast ham to the side and some tomato chutney.

Serves 4
8 medium organic eggs, whisked
Sea salt, black pepper
150 g medium-mature goat's cheese, cut into 1cm dice
2 tablespoons finely chopped chives
2 tablespoons extra virgin olive oil
15 g unsalted butter

Preheat the oven to 240°C, fan oven 230°C, gas 9. Whisk the eggs in a bowl with some seasoning, then fold in the goat's cheese and chives. Don't worry about the herbs floating to the surface, as they'll be scrambled into the mixture at the next stage.

Heat the olive oil in a 23cm frying pan with a heatproof handle. Once it is hot, tip in the eggs and scramble rapidly for about 30 seconds using a fork until they are half set. Remove the pan from the heat and dot the butter over the surface of the frittata. Place in the oven for 5–6 minutes by which time it should be firm, puffed up and lightly golden. Serve the frittata cut into wedges.

Tomato Frittata

This emerges from the grill puffed and golden at the edges, and gooey in the centre. Rush it to the table and serve straight from the pan.

Serves 3–4
2 plum tomatoes
Vegetable oil, for cooking
4 large organic eggs, plus 2 extra yolks
2 tablespoons double cream
Sea salt, black pepper
50 g Gruyère cheese, grated
50 g Emmental cheese, grated

Bring a small pan of water to the boil and immerse the tomatoes for 20 seconds, then transfer them to a bowl of cold water to cool. Drain, slip off the skins and slice thinly, discarding the ends. Brush the upper sides with oil. Whisk the eggs and egg yolks in a bowl with the cream and some seasoning. Combine the cheeses in another bowl.

Preheat the grill. Heat a little oil in a 23cm frying pan with a heatproof handle and, once it is smoking, tip out the excess. Pour in the eggs and scramble rapidly with a fork for about 30 seconds until about a third is set. Cook for a further 45–60 seconds, sprinkling over the cheese and laying the tomatoes in an overlapping circle with a slice in the centre; season the tomatoes. Now place under the grill for about 2 minutes until the edges of the omelette are puffy and lightly coloured. Serve at once, in wedges.

Souffléed Omelette

Having long been of the opinion that omelettes are one of the hardest feats to pull off, a visit to La Mère Poulard in Mont St Michel, famed for its omelettes, offered more proof. Their formula for making souffléed omelettes appeared to be a cinch, but having tried it at home, how they achieve their golden crust with eggs and butter alone remains a mystery. They certainly don't add Parmesan, but you do achieve the same results, and it really is a cinch.

Serves 2
4 medium organic eggs, separated
   Sea salt, black pepper
40 g Parmesan cheese,
   freshly grated
40 g semi-salted butter

Heat a 25cm cast-iron frying pan over a medium-low heat for 4–5 minutes. Meanwhile whisk the egg whites in a bowl until stiff. In another bowl, whisk the yolks with a pinch of salt and some pepper, then fold in the egg whites in two goes. Finally fold in the Parmesan.

Take the pan off the heat, add the butter and swill until it is melted, then return to the heat. Tip in the omelette mixture and smooth the surface to even it out. Cook for 4–6 minutes until the underside is a deep crusty gold and the uncooked surface feels warm to the touch. Lift the edges of the omelette with a palette knife to see how it's doing.

Loosen the omelette around the sides and carefully fold one half over, then slip it on to a large plate. Cut it in two and serve with the mousse that spills out from the inside spooned beside it.

Souffléed Omelette with Gruyère

Another souffléed omelette for all those cooks whose nerves are set jangling at the thought of having to roll an omelette out of the pan. Genuinely easy—assuming you can whisk an egg white—and every bit as luxurious as a soufflé baked in the oven.

Serves 2
3 large organic eggs, separated, plus 2 extra yolks
   Sea salt, black pepper
25 g Parmesan cheese, freshly grated, plus extra to serve
10 g unsalted butter
50 g Gruyère cheese, grated

Preheat the grill. Whisk the egg yolks in a large bowl with some seasoning, using a fork. Stiffly whisk the egg whites in another bowl. Carefully fold half into the yolks, and then fold in the rest, together with the Parmesan. Warm a 25cm frying pan with a heatproof handle over a low heat. Add the butter to the pan and turn the heat up. Once it melts, add the omelette mixture, spreading it over the base of the pan with the back of a spoon. Cook for 1 minute.

Scatter the cheese over the omelette and put under the grill for 30–60 seconds until it is melted. Loosen the edges and fold the omelette in half. Cut in two and serve on warmed plates, scattered with a little more Parmesan.

Cheddar Cheese Soufflé

The combination of a mature farmhouse Cheddar and Parmesan ensures this soufflé is rich and aromatic. Do not be alarmed by the amount of butter used to line the dish, it ensures the soufflé glides upwards with no resistance.

Serves 4

For the dish

115 g unsalted butter
50 g Parmesan cheese, freshly grated

Soufflé

50 g unsalted butter
50 g plain flour
300 ml milk
175 g mature Cheddar cheese, grated
Sea salt, black pepper
Freshly grated nutmeg
4 large organic eggs, separated, plus 3 extra egg whites
2 tablespoons freshly grated Parmesan cheese

To prepare the dish, clarify the butter by melting it in a small saucepan. Skim off the white foam on the surface and pour off the clear yellow liquid, leaving behind the milky residue in the base. Swill the inside of a 20cm soufflé dish with half the clarified butter and then dust it with half the Parmesan. Chill the dish until this firms up. Repeat with the remaining butter and Parmesan, tipping out the excess cheese. Chill the dish again.

To make the soufflé, melt the butter in a small saucepan, stir in the flour and cook the roux for a couple of minutes. Take off the heat and very gradually incorporate the milk. Return the sauce to the heat and bring to the boil, stirring. Simmer over a low heat, stirring frequently, for 4 minutes. Stir in the grated Cheddar. Remove the pan from the heat and season with salt, pepper and nutmeg. Allow the sauce to cool for a few minutes and then beat in the egg yolks. Transfer the mixture to a large bowl.

Preheat the oven to 220°C, fan oven 200°C, gas 7. Whisk the egg whites in another large bowl until stiff. Fold a couple of spoonfuls into the sauce to lighten it. Then fold in the remaining whisked egg whites, half at a time. Pour the soufflé mixture into the prepared dish; scatter the Parmesan evenly over the surface and immediately place in the oven, giving it plenty of headroom. Bake for 5 minutes, then turn the oven down to 170°C, fan oven 160°C, gas 3 and cook for a further 20–25 minutes. Do not open the door for the first 20 minutes. The soufflé should ideally be baveuse or slightly wet in the centre on serving, so act on the side of caution. Serve immediately.

Spinach, Garlic and Goat's Cheese Soufflé

Enjoy this soufflé on its own with a green salad to follow.

Serves 4
1 head of garlic
1 tablespoon olive oil
Sea salt, black pepper
75 g unsalted butter
100 g Parmesan cheese, freshly grated
350 g spinach leaves, picked over and washed
50 g plain flour
300 ml milk
4 large organic eggs, separated, plus 3 extra egg whites
Freshly grated nutmeg
75 g semi-mature goat's cheese, crumbled

Preheat the oven to 150°C, fan oven 140°C, gas 2. Slice the top off the head of garlic to reveal the cloves and place in a small ovenproof dish. Drizzle over the olive oil, season and roast for 1 hour. Remove and leave to cool, then squeeze out the garlic flesh from the cloves and coarsely mash, using a fork.

Melt 25g of the butter. Swill the inside of a 20cm soufflé dish with the melted butter, dust with a third of the Parmesan and chill until required.

Place the spinach in a large saucepan with just the water that clings to the leaves after washing. Cover the pan and steam over a gentle heat until the spinach collapses. Drain in a sieve and press out all excess water. Once it is cool enough to handle, turn the spinach on to a board and chop, using a large knife. Squeeze out as much water as possible using your hands.

Melt the remaining 50g butter in a small saucepan and stir in the flour. Cook the roux for a minute or two, then remove it from the heat and gradually blend in the milk using a wooden spoon. Return the sauce to the heat and bring to the boil, stirring. Simmer over a low heat for 4 minutes, stirring frequently. Remove from the heat and leave to cool for several minutes, then beat in the egg yolks and season with salt, pepper and nutmeg. Stir in the garlic, chopped spinach, another third of the Parmesan and the goat's cheese. Spoon the mixture into a large bowl.

Preheat the oven to 220°C, fan oven 200°C, gas 7. Whisk the egg whites in another large bowl until stiff, and then fold them into the soufflé base, a third at a time. Transfer the soufflé mixture to the prepared dish and sprinkle over the remaining Parmesan. Immediately place in the oven, giving it plenty of headroom. Bake for 5 minutes, then turn the oven down to 170°C, fan oven 160°C, gas 3 and bake for a further 25 minutes. Do not open the door for the first 20 minutes. The soufflé should emerge domed and golden, slightly runny and frothy in the centre. Serve at once.

A soufflé of which the late, great Arnold Bennett would have approved.

Serves 4

For the dish

25 g unsalted butter, softened
25 g flat-leaf parsley, finely chopped

Soufflé

150 ml white wine
350 g undyed smoked haddock fillet
300 ml milk
  1 bay leaf
    Sea salt, black pepper
 50 g unsalted butter
 40 g plain flour
  ¼ teaspoon finely grated lemon zest
  1 teaspoon Dijon mustard
  4 medium organic eggs,
    separated, plus 3 extra
    egg whites
  2 tablespoons freshly grated
    Parmesan cheese

Liberally grease a 20cm soufflé dish with the softened butter, using your fingers. Scatter over the chopped parsley pressing it into the butter, then chill until required.

Bring the wine to the boil in a medium saucepan and reduce it to a couple of tablespoons; pour into a small bowl or jug and reserve. Place the haddock in the same saucepan, cutting it in half to fit if necessary. Add the milk, bay leaf and a grinding of black pepper. Bring to a simmer then put the lid on the pan, leaving a small gap for steam to escape, and poach over a low heat for 4 minutes. Drain off and reserve the cooking liquid, and discard the bay leaf. Once the fish is cool enough to handle, flake it on a plate using your fingers, making sure you remove any stray bones.

Preheat the oven to 220°C, fan oven 200°C, gas 7. To make the sauce, melt the butter in the cleaned saucepan and add the flour. Cook the roux for a minute or two, allowing it to seethe and turn floury in appearance. Remove the pan from the heat and very gradually beat in the haddock milk and the wine. Return to the heat and allow the sauce to splutter over a very low heat for 5 minutes, stirring almost constantly. Stir in the lemon zest and mustard and leave to cool for a few minutes.

Pour the sauce base onto the egg yolks in a large bowl, whisking to combine them. Stir in the flaked fish and taste for seasoning. Whisk the egg whites in another large bowl until they are stiff. Lightly fold them into the sauce base, a third at a time. Pour the soufflé into the prepared dish and scatter over the Parmesan. Immediately place in the oven, giving it plenty of headroom. Bake for 5 minutes, then turn the oven down to 170°C, fan oven 160°C, gas 3 and cook for a further 20–25 minutes. Do not open the door for the first 20 minutes. The soufflé should still be a little runny in the centre. Serve it straightaway.

Croque Monsieur

The only time you are ever likely to encounter a Croque Monsieur of any merit, oozing a nutty Gruyère from its crisp buttery crumb and laced with enough Dijon to set the pulse racing, is if you make it at home. Eat it with a stack of white linen napkins close-by, it's a pleasantly greasy affair.

Serves 2
4 slices coarse-textured white bread, such as pain de Campagne, 1cm thick
Unsalted butter, for spreading
200 g Gruyère cheese, thinly sliced
2 to 4 slices honey-roast ham
Dijon mustard

Spread both sides of the bread with butter. Cover two of the slices with a layer of Gruyère, then a layer of ham, smear over some mustard and cover with another layer of Gruyère. Close the sandwiches with the top layers of bread. They can be prepared to this point in advance.

Heat two frying pans over a high heat for several minutes, or one large one if it can hold both sandwiches. Non-stick frying pans are ideal. Place the sandwiches in the pans, turn the heat down to medium-low and cook for 4–5 minutes each side until golden on the outside and oozing melted cheese. Cut the toasted sandwiches into 4 triangles and arrange on plates with the cut edges showing.

Wild Mushroom Torte

This is something like a softly set quiche with a thin shell of toasted Parmesan in lieu of pastry, and a wild mushroom filling.

Serves 6
50 g unsalted butter
150 g Parmesan cheese, freshly grated
4 tablespoons extra virgin olive oil
2 shallots, peeled and finely chopped
800 g mixed wild and cultivated mushrooms, trimmed and finely sliced
Sea salt, black pepper
225 ml double cream
3 tablespoons chopped flat-leaf parsley
2 medium organic eggs, plus 1 egg yolk, whisked

Preheat the oven to 200°C, fan oven 190°C, gas 6. Use a knob of butter to grease a 20cm cake tin with a removable base and dust it with some of the Parmesan.

You will need to cook the mushrooms in 4 batches. Heat a quarter of the butter with a tablespoon of oil in a large frying pan. Add a quarter of the shallots and once they soften, add a quarter of the mushrooms. Fry, stirring frequently, until they soften and start to colour, seasoning towards the end. Transfer to a bowl and cook the remainder in the same way. Once all the mushrooms are cooked, transfer half of them to a food processor and work to a textured purée. Combine with the other mushrooms in a large bowl. Stir in the cream, chopped parsley, beaten eggs, half the Parmesan and some seasoning.

Turn this mixture into the prepared tin, scatter over the remaining Parmesan and bake for 35–40 minutes until golden on the surface and set. We like the torte best about 10 minutes out of the oven, though it can also be eaten at room temperature. Run a knife around the side of the tin and remove it. Serve the torte in wedges.

Very post-theatre, tagliatelle alla carbonara demands just enough sleight of hand to continue the dramatics after the curtain's come down. It also makes a great Sunday brunch with a jug of Bloody Mary.

Serves 4
1 tablespoon extra virgin olive oil
10 g unsalted butter
225 g unsmoked back bacon, rind and fat removed, sliced into thin strips
4 tablespoons white wine
450 g dried green and yellow egg tagliatelle
3 large organic eggs
75 g Parmesan cheese, freshly grated, plus extra to serve
3 tablespoons chopped flat-leaf parsley
Sea salt, black pepper

Place the oil and butter in a frying pan, add the bacon and fry until it turns crisp at the edges. Add the wine and cook for 1 minute, then remove from the heat.

Bring a large pan of salted water to the boil and add the pasta, stir to separate it and cook until just tender. Lightly beat the eggs in a large bowl. Stir in the Parmesan and the parsley and season well. Drain the tagliatelle, though not too thoroughly, and rapidly toss into the egg and cheese mixture. Quickly reheat the bacon, and tip the entire contents of the pan into the pasta. Toss to mix and taste for seasoning. Serve straightaway on warmed plates, scattered with more Parmesan.

Tagliatelle with Butter and Parmesan

Almost taboo in our cholesterol-correct society, this is a celebration of butter in all its glory. Here it fuses with grated Parmesan and the liquid that clings to the pasta into a velvety sauce that subtly coats every strand. It's the Italian equivalent of eating a hot buttered crumpet so lavishly buttered it trickles down your chin.

Serves 4
350 g dried egg tagliatelle
100 g Parmesan cheese, freshly grated, plus extra to serve
100 g unsalted butter, softened
Sea salt, black pepper

Bring a large pan of salted water to the boil, add the tagliatelle and give it a stir to separate out the strands, then cook until it is just tender.

Drain the pasta into a colander over the sink, and then immediately return it to the saucepan while there is still some water trickling off. This is all-important in creating a creamy emulsion. Toss half the cheese and then half the butter and some seasoning into the pasta. Once they have melted enough to coat the strands, toss in the remaining cheese and butter, turning the pasta several times to coat it thoroughly. Serve on warmed plates with additional Parmesan at the table.

Midnight Spaghetti

A lounge-lizard's pasta that can be mustered at a moment's notice when the assembled company is starving. Approaching midnight it always fits the bill. By way of forethought keep a packet of spaghetti in the cupboard, and a large chunk of Parmigiano Reggiano.

Serves 2
225 g dried spaghetti
   4 tablespoons extra virgin olive oil
   3 garlic cloves, peeled and finely chopped
   2 teaspoons finely chopped medium-hot red chilli
   3 tablespoons finely chopped flat-leaf parsley
      Sea salt, black pepper
      Freshly grated Parmesan, to serve

Bring a large pan of salted water to the boil. Add the spaghetti, stir to separate the strands and cook until just tender. Have your olive oil, garlic and chilli at the ready in a small saucepan. Start heating it as you drain the pasta. Tip the pasta into a sieve, but don't drain too thoroughly, and return to the pan. The moment the garlic starts to fry, toss the chilli mixture into the drained spaghetti. Toss in the parsley and season with plenty of salt and pepper. Serve with lots of grated Parmesan.

Variations
Pasta with chilli and garlic
Leave out the parsley.

Pasta with garlic and oil
Leave out the parsley and chilli.

Spaghetti Puttanesca

Born in the slums of Naples and named after a tart, this is the high stiletto of pasta sauces with attitude to match.

Serves 4
400 g dried spaghetti
  3 tablespoons extra virgin olive oil
  2 garlic cloves, peeled and finely chopped
  6 salted anchovies in oil, sliced
400 g can chopped tomatoes
  1 dried red chilli, finely chopped
  1 heaped tablespoon capers, rinsed
110 g mixed green and black olives, pitted and sliced
  2 heaped tablespoons chopped parsley
  Sea salt
  Freshly grated Parmesan, to serve (optional)

Bring a large pan of salted water to the boil. Add the spaghetti, stir to separate the strands and cook until just tender. At the same time, heat the olive oil in a frying pan over a medium heat, add the garlic and anchovies and cook for 1 minute, mashing the anchovies to a paste. Add the tomatoes and chilli and simmer for about 7 minutes until the sauce is glossy and thickened, stirring occasionally. Stir in the capers, olives and parsley and cook for 1 minute longer.

Drain the pasta, but not too thoroughly, and return it to the saucepan. Add the sauce and toss well. Taste for seasoning and add a little salt if necessary. Serve straightaway, with the lightest sprinkling of Parmesan if required.

Spaghetti with Bottarga

Bottarga is the preserved roe of a tuna or red mullet; both types are pressed and salted whole, but they are quite different. Tuna bottarga in accordance with the size of the fish is some 30cm in length. Rather beautiful, it has a granite sheen where fine crystals of sea salt cling to its papery skin. The roe of the mullet is Lilliputian by comparison, smooth and glossy, and burnt orange right through to the inside. Mullet roe, with its savour of sea urchins, is that much subtler than the anchovy-tinge of tuna roe, but either will do. This is one of the simplest ways of serving bottarga, the beauty of it—aside from the sheer ease of preparation—being that there is nothing to detract from its flavour. If using mullet rather than tuna, you might like to step up the amount to allow for its delicacy.

Serves 4
12 tablespoons extra virgin olive oil
  2 heaped teaspoons finely chopped red chilli
  Juice of 1 lemon
  6 tablespoons finely chopped flat-leaf parsley
  Sea salt, black pepper
200 g bottarga, skin removed and grated
400 g dried spaghetti

Bring a large pan of salted water to the boil. Combine the oil, chilli, lemon juice, parsley and pepper in a large bowl, and gently mix in the bottarga. Add the spaghetti to the boiling water, stir to separate the strands and boil until cooked but firm to the bite. Drain into a sieve and leaving it quite wet, tip into the dressing. Toss and add a little salt if needed. Serve at once on warmed plates.

Spaghetti with Lemon

Deceptive in the innocence of its appearance, this is clean, sharp and richly flavoured with lemon and Parmesan. The cry is for a crisp green salad to follow.

Serves 4
350 g dried spaghetti
 75 ml white wine
    Finely grated zest of 3 lemons
200 ml crème fraîche
    Juice of ½ lemon
100 g Gruyère or Emmental
    cheese, grated
    Sea salt, black pepper
    Freshly grated Parmesan,
    to serve

Bring a large pan of salted water to the boil, add the spaghetti and stir to separate the strands. Cook until just tender. In the meantime, put the wine and lemon zest in a small saucepan, bring to the boil and reduce by half.

Once the spaghetti is just tender, drain it into a colander, but not too thoroughly, then return it to the saucepan. Toss with the reduced wine mixture, the crème fraîche, lemon juice and grated Gruyère or Emmental. Season liberally and cook over a high heat for a minute or two until the sauce thickens enough to coat the pasta. Serve straightaway, scattered with freshly grated Parmesan.

Angel Hair Pasta with Tomato and Basil Sauce

A simple fresh tomato sauce to make in quantity late summer when tomatoes are at their sun-ripened best. It's an all-singing, all-dancing basic that won't shame a plate of pasta if the only other addition is grated Parmesan. Equally it can be used as the starting point for other sauces.

Serves 4–6
Fresh tomato sauce
1.6 kg plum tomatoes, halved
  1 heaped teaspoon sea salt
  1 teaspoon caster sugar
100 g unsalted butter
  4 tablespoons extra virgin olive oil

Pasta
  1 tablespoon extra virgin olive oil
  6 garlic cloves, peeled and sliced
  2 handfuls basil leaves, shredded
450 g fresh angel hair pasta
    Sea salt, black pepper
    Freshly grated Parmesan,
    to serve

To make the sauce, put the tomatoes in a saucepan, cover and cook over a low heat for 20 minutes until they collapse, pressing them down after 5 minutes to release some of the juices. Pass through a sieve or mouli-legumes and return to the pan. Add the remaining ingredients and simmer very gently, uncovered, for a further 50–60 minutes until reduced and thickened.

Bring a large pan of salted water to the boil for the pasta. Heat the olive oil in a saucepan and sweat the garlic until nicely aromatic. Add the basil, which should wilt instantly, then add the tomato sauce, bring to a simmer and cook for 10 minutes.

Add the pasta to the boiling water, stir to separate the strands and cook until just tender.

Drain the pasta, though not too thoroughly, and toss with the tomato sauce. Season with salt and pepper to taste. Divide between warmed plates and serve straightaway, with freshly grated Parmesan.

Penne and Roasted Vine Tomatoes with Black Olives

Roasting tomatoes on the vine intensifies their sweetness, and here their caramelised roasting juices act as a dressing for the pasta. Toss and serve this warm or almost cool. It is still good eaten cold like a pasta salad, although it doesn't stand endless hanging around.

Serves 4
650 g small tomatoes on the vine
4 tablespoons extra virgin olive oil
1 tablespoon balsamic vinegar
  Sea salt, black pepper
200 g dried penne or other
  tubular pasta
150 g black olives, pitted
  Few shredded basil leaves

Preheat the oven to 250°C, fan oven 240°C, gas highest setting. Arrange the tomatoes in a roasting tray so they fit snugly in a single layer. Drizzle over half the olive oil and the balsamic vinegar and season with salt and pepper. Roast for 10 minutes by which time the tomatoes will be soft, the skins burst and the stalks blackened.

Once the tomatoes are cool enough to handle, pop them off the stalks leaving them intact as far as possible. The easiest way to do this is to pinch the very top by the calyx. Pile these up at one end of the roasting tray. Pour the remaining olive oil into the tray and blend it with the roasting juices.

Bring a large pan of salted water to the boil. Add the pasta, stir to separate the pieces and cook until it is just tender. Drain it into a sieve, run cold water through it and leave to cool for about 5 minutes.

Add the penne to the roasting tray and gently toss with the tomatoes and dressing, the olives and basil. Sprinkle over a little more sea salt and serve.

Variations
Serve the tomatoes and their juices with fresh ricotta as an appetiser, either with croûtons or on bruschetta.

Add a few fine strips of salted anchovies in oil to the salad.

Toss some cooked borlotti beans into the salad.

Toss some torn rocket leaves and strips of avocado into the salad.

Penne with Prosciutto

This is another deceptively simple pasta sauce with a great deal of character. The prosciutto casts its aromatic magic into the frying pan as it crisps, flavouring the crème fraîche in a way you don't expect. You can use Parma, San Daniele, Serrano or Bayonne ham, in other words any air-dried ham.

Serves 4
350 g dried penne
 50 g unsalted butter
125 g prosciutto, sliced into strips
150 g crème fraîche
      Sea salt, black pepper
100 g Parmesan cheese, freshly
      grated, plus extra to serve

Bring a large pan of salted water to the boil. Add the penne, give it a stir to separate the pieces and cook until tender. Meanwhile, melt the butter in a small saucepan over a medium heat. Separating the pieces of prosciutto, add them to the pan and cook until they colour and begin to crisp, stirring frequently. Add the crème fraîche and some seasoning and simmer for a few minutes until the butter and cream emulsify.

Drain the pasta without being too thorough and return it to the saucepan. Add the sauce and toss, and then mix in the grated Parmesan. Serve straightaway, with extra Parmesan on the table.

Penne with Mussel and Saffron Sauce

The intense salty juices shed by mussels as they steam open are well employed in a sauce for coating pasta. The texture of these shellfish too is very much at home with the comforting pudginess of penne.

Serves 6
  2 kg mussels in shells
150 ml white wine
  3 leeks, trimmed
 25 g unsalted butter
300 ml double cream
 30 saffron threads, ground and
      infused with 1 tablespoon
      boiling water
  1 teaspoon plain flour
  1 teaspoon unsalted butter
600 g dried penne
  2 large handfuls flat-leaf parsley
      leaves, coarsely chopped
      Sea salt, black pepper

To clean the mussels, wash them in two changes of cold water, pull off the beards and remove any barnacles with a blunt knife. Discard any that are damaged or that do not close when sharply tapped.

Bring the wine to the boil in a large saucepan, add the mussels and cover the pan with a lid. Cook over a high heat for 5 minutes until the mussels open, shaking the pan or stirring the shellfish to circulate them halfway through. Once the mussels are cool enough to handle, set a quarter aside and shell the remainder. Put them all in a bowl and splash over a little of the mussel liquor to keep them moist.

Pour the remaining mussel juices into a saucepan, discarding the last little gritty bit. Cook until reduced to a quarter of the volume.

Cut the leeks into thin strips, 5–7cm long. Melt the butter in a large saucepan, add the leeks and sweat until they relax and turn translucent, taking care that they don't colour. Add the cream and the saffron and cook until it thickens. Mix the flour and butter together to form a paste, or beurre manié. Add the beurre manié in pieces to the sauce together with the mussel juices and simmer for a couple of minutes; the sauce should thicken a little. You can prepare everything to this point in advance.

To serve, bring a large pan of salted water to the boil. Add the penne, give it a stir to separate the pieces and cook until tender. Reheat the sauce, stir in the parsley and then add the mussels to heat through. Drain the pasta, toss with the sauce and adjust the seasoning. Serve straightaway.

Buckwheat Noodles with Gorgonzola and Rocket

Buckwheat noodles are the acceptable form of wholemeal pasta. Marrying their slightly sour and gritty disposition with the slithery likes of mascarpone softens them around the edges. Once you have assembled your ingredients this takes all of 10 minutes to cook. As well as Italian pasta, you can use Oriental buckwheat or soba noodles.

Serves 4
125 g mascarpone
300 g dried buckwheat noodles
200 g Gorgonzola cheese, diced
   Knifetip of cayenne pepper
  1 tablespoon extra virgin olive oil
  2 garlic cloves, peeled and
     finely chopped
175 g rocket leaves
     Sea salt, black pepper
     Freshly grated Parmesan,
     to serve

Bring a large pan of salted water to the boil for the pasta. Put the mascarpone in a bowl set over a saucepan containing 4–5cm of simmering water. Add the pasta to the boiling water and cook according to pack instructions until it is just tender.

A few minutes before the pasta will be cooked, add the Gorgonzola and cayenne pepper to the mascarpone; it needn't melt completely. When you think the pasta is almost ready, heat the olive oil in a large frying pan, add the garlic and once it sizzles add the rocket leaves and toss until they wilt, seasoning them with salt and pepper.

Drain the pasta, but not too thoroughly, and return it to the pan.

Add the Gorgonzola sauce and rocket, separating the rocket leaves with a fork to distribute them evenly. Season with salt and pepper and serve at once, scattered with plenty of Parmesan.

Rigatoni with Spinach and Ricotta

A recipe courtesy of jewellery designer Dinny Hall's mother. Clearly a perfectionist, she insists the spinach must be baby, the ricotta ultra fresh, the pasta organic, a light olive oil, Pecorino rather than Parmesan, and pepper coarsely ground with a pestle and mortar.

Serves 4
  1 scant tablespoon vegetable oil
  1 scant tablespoon sesame oil
 40 g pine nuts
275 g dried rigatoni (ideally organic)
  2 tablespoons olive oil
  8 spring onions, trimmed and
     sliced, including green parts
225 g baby spinach leaves
     Sea salt, black pepper
     Freshly grated nutmeg
250 g tub ricotta cheese
     Freshly grated Pecorino, to serve

Heat the vegetable and sesame oils in a small frying pan, add the pine nuts and toast until evenly golden, then remove them to a bowl using a slotted spoon. Bring a large pan of salted water to the boil, add the rigatoni, stir and cook until just tender.

Meanwhile, for the sauce, heat the olive oil in a large saucepan over a medium heat. Add the spring onions and sweat for several minutes until they begin to colour and turn crispy. Add the spinach and toss until it wilts, seasoning with salt and pepper. Add a good grinding of nutmeg, then tip in the ricotta, turn the heat to low and stir until the sauce is smooth, creamy and warmed through. Drain the pasta, but not too thoroughly, then tip it into the sauce and stir to coat. Toss in the pine nuts and serve scattered with Pecorino.

Rigatoni all'Amatriciana

A sauce that relies on a tin of chopped tomatoes, lots of bacon and onions, and a chilli or two to spice it up. In other words the kind of staple you can hope to have the wherewithal to cook when you haven't had time to shop for dinner. Rigatoni and penne are natural shapes to choose; spaghetti and tagliatelle are also contenders.

    Serves 4
    3 tablespoons extra virgin olive oil
    3 onions, peeled, halved and sliced
    2 small dried chillies,
        finely chopped
    250 g unsmoked streaky
        bacon, diced
    400 g can chopped tomatoes
    ½ teaspoon dried oregano
    300 g dried rigatoni or penne
    30 g unsalted butter
    50 g Parmesan cheese, freshly
        grated, plus extra to serve

Bring a large pan of salted water to the boil for the pasta.

Heat 2 tablespoons of the oil in a large frying pan over a fairly low heat. Add the onions with the chillies and cook for about 15 minutes, stirring constantly, until they are golden and silky. You will need to do this slowly to ensure the onions caramelise evenly.

At the same time, heat the remaining tablespoon of olive oil in another frying pan over a medium-low heat and cook the bacon until it is golden and beginning to crisp, stirring occasionally. Using a slotted spoon, add the bacon to the onions. Add the chopped tomatoes and oregano. Simmer the sauce for a few minutes until it is thick.

Towards the end of cooking the sauce, add the pasta to the boiling water and give it a stir to separate it. Cook until the pasta is just tender, drain it and return to the pan. Add the sauce and toss, then stir in the butter and Parmesan. Serve at once, with extra Parmesan at the table.

Rigatoni with Courgettes and Feta

A chunky plateful of pasta with garlicky fried courgettes and feta, which turns soft and creamy with the warmth of the rigatoni.

    Serves 3
    6 tablespoons extra virgin olive oil
    500 g courgettes, trimmed and cut
        into 1cm thick slices
    250 g dried rigatoni
    3 garlic cloves, peeled and
        finely chopped
        Juice of ½ lemon
        Sea salt, black pepper
    200 g feta cheese
    4 tablespoons coarsely chopped
        flat-leaf parsley
        Freshly grated Parmesan,
        to serve

Bring a large pan of salted water to the boil for the pasta. About 10 minutes later, heat half the olive oil in a large frying pan over a medium heat. Add the courgettes and sauté for 12–15 minutes, turning occasionally, until they are deep golden on both sides. Put the pasta on to cook about halfway through cooking the courgettes, giving it a stir to make sure it doesn't stick together.

Thirty seconds before the courgettes finish cooking, add the garlic and stir. Remove the pan from the heat, pour over the lemon juice and season with salt and pepper. Drain the pasta, but not too thoroughly, and return it to the pan. Add the contents of the frying pan and toss. Coarsely crumble in the feta, add the parsley and remaining olive oil, and toss again. Serve straightaway, scattered with freshly grated Parmesan.

This lasagne is best made during the hot summer months when flavourful tomatoes are plentiful. It is a million miles away from the towering creation of meat and béchamel, which can be wonderful in the hands of a sympathetic cook but all too often isn't. There's enough fresh tomato sauce and melted mozzarella here to take centre stage.

Serves 6

Tomato sauce

1.3 kg beefsteak tomatoes
3 tablespoons extra virgin olive oil
1 onion, peeled and finely chopped
4 garlic cloves, peeled and finely chopped
2 tablespoons tomato purée
75 ml red wine
1 bay leaf
2 thyme sprigs
1 teaspoon caster sugar
Sea salt, black pepper

Lasagne

230 to 250g dried egg lasagne
3 buffalo mozzarella cheeses, 350g in total, diced
75 g Parmesan cheese, freshly grated
8 large basil leaves, torn in half
1 tablespoon extra virgin olive oil

To make the sauce, cut a cone from the top of each tomato and remove the core. Plunge the tomatoes into a pan of boiling water for 20 seconds, then refresh in cold water and slip off the skins. Coarsely chop the tomatoes. Heat the olive oil in a medium saucepan over a moderate heat. Add the onion and sweat for a few minutes until soft and translucent. Add the garlic and stir it around, then add the tomatoes, the tomato purée, the wine, bay leaf and thyme. Bring to a simmer then cook over a low heat for 30 minutes, stirring occasionally. Discard the herbs. Beat the sauce to a slushy purée using a wooden spoon. Add the sugar and season with salt and pepper.

Preheat the oven to 190°C, fan oven 180°C, gas 5. Select a 28cm by 20cm by 6cm baking dish (or one with similar dimensions) and cover the base with some of the tomato sauce. Add a layer of lasagne, cover this with tomato sauce, scatter over some mozzarella and Parmesan and dot with a couple of the torn basil leaves. Repeat these layers using the remaining ingredients; you should have 4 layers of pasta in all. Finish with tomato sauce and cheese, omitting the basil from this top layer. Drizzle a tablespoon of olive oil over the surface and cover with foil. You can prepare the lasagne to this point in advance, and chill it for up to 12 hours until you need it.

Bake the lasagne in the oven for 20 minutes, then remove the foil and bake for a further 25 minutes until the top is golden and bubbling. If necessary, give it a few minutes under the grill. Serve straightaway.

Red Wine Risotto

As well as cloaking the rice with a lustrous vermilion emulsion, wine creates a delectably unctuous texture, in much the same way as squid ink. It isn't of great import to use any particular red wine as by the time you've simmered and flavoured the risotto with lashings of Parmesan the finer nuances are going to be eclipsed.

Serves 4
1 bottle of red wine
100 g unsalted butter
1 onion, peeled and finely chopped
300 g risotto rice (Carnaroli or Vialone Nano)
450 ml strong, seasoned fresh chicken stock
110 g Parmesan cheese, freshly grated, plus a little extra to serve
Sea salt, black pepper

Bring the wine to the boil in a small saucepan; keep it simmering over a very low heat, half covered. Melt half the butter in a large heavy-based saucepan over a medium heat, add the onion and sweat for several minutes until glossy and relaxed. Add the rice and stir for a minute until translucent. Start to add the red wine a ladleful or two at a time, at no stage should the rice be drowned in liquid. Bring the stock to the boil; keep it at a simmer. Once all the wine has been absorbed, add the stock, again a ladleful at a time. The risotto should take 25–30 minutes to cook in total.

Stop cooking the risotto while the rice is on the moist side and still slightly resistant to the bite. Stir in the Parmesan and remaining butter and taste for seasoning. Serve straightaway on warm plates, scattering with extra Parmesan.

Saffron Risotto

To maximise the combined charm of saffron's golden hue and its honeyed scent, a risotto is best prepared with saffron liquor made by infusing threads in a little boiling water, plus a sachet of powdered saffron which casts the deepest dye. This is one of the finest risottos of all. If you have tired of serving it alone, try it as a bed for grilled mullet or sea bass, adding just enough Parmesan to sharpen its wits, but not the full heady hit.

Serves 4
About 30 saffron threads
1.2 litres well seasoned fresh chicken or vegetable stock
100 g unsalted butter
1 onion, peeled and finely chopped
300 g risotto rice (Carnaroli or Vialone Nano)
150 ml white wine
1 sachet powdered saffron (0.125g)
100 g Parmesan cheese, freshly grated, plus extra to serve
Sea salt, black pepper

Put the saffron threads in a bowl with 1 tablespoon boiling water and leave to infuse for 30 minutes. Bring the stock to the boil in a small saucepan and keep it simmering at the back of the hob. Heat half the butter in a heavy-based saucepan over a medium heat. Add the onion and sweat for several minutes until glossy and softened. Add the rice and stir for a minute or two until it is translucent. Add the wine, saffron liquor and powdered saffron. Once this is absorbed, start adding the stock a ladleful at a time, at no stage should the rice be flooded. The risotto should take 20–25 minutes to cook once you start to add the liquid.

Remove from the heat while the rice grains still have some bite, leaving the risotto on the sloppy side. Stir in the Parmesan and remaining butter. Taste and adjust the seasoning if necessary. Serve on warmed plates sprinkled with a little extra Parmesan.

Risotto with Roast Chicken and Gravy

Gravy juices soaking into a risotto are so good it's worth roasting a chicken especially.

Serves 4–5

Chicken

1.6 kg free-range oven-ready chicken
50 g unsalted butter
Juice of 1 lemon
Sea salt, black pepper

Risotto

1.2 litres fresh chicken stock
50 g unsalted butter
1 onion, peeled and finely chopped
300 g risotto rice (Carnaroli or Vialone Nano)
150 ml white wine
100 g Parmesan cheese, freshly grated
1 tablespoon each finely chopped tarragon, flat-leaf parsley and chives

Preheat the oven to 200°C, fan oven 190°C, gas 6. Place the chicken in a roasting tin; smear the butter all over its surface, pour over the lemon juice and season with salt and pepper. Roast for 50 minutes or until tender.

Five minutes before the chicken will be cooked, start making the risotto. Season the stock, bring it to a simmer in a small pan and keep it simmering on the back of the hob. Heat all but a knob of the butter in a heavy-based saucepan over a medium heat. Add the onion and sweat for several minutes until it is glossy and soft. Add the rice and stir for a minute or two until it turns translucent.

When the chicken is cooked, loosely cover with foil and leave to rest on the hob for 20 minutes while you finish cooking the risotto. Add the wine to the rice and once this has been absorbed, start to add the stock a ladleful or two at a time, at no stage should the rice be flooded. The risotto should take 25–30 minutes to cook in total.

Start carving the chicken a few minutes before the risotto is ready. Tip any juices inside the bird back into the roasting tin and gently reheat. Finally stir the Parmesan, herbs and remaining butter into the risotto and taste for seasoning. Serve the risotto with the chicken, spooning the gravy over and around the edge of the rice.

Risotto with Fontina

A risotto that will appeal to those who like sea urchins and the briny insides of oysters. Soft skeins of molten Fontina coated with raw egg yolk course over the surface of the rice as you break the membrane.

Serves 4
1.2 litres seasoned fresh
   chicken stock
50 g unsalted butter
 1 onion, peeled and finely chopped
300 g risotto rice (Vialone Nano
   or Carnaroli)
150 ml white wine
100 g Parmesan cheese, freshly
   grated, plus extra to serve
   Sea salt, black pepper
150 g Fontina cheese, cut into
   1cm dice
 4 organic egg yolks

Bring the stock to the boil in a small pan, and keep at a simmer. Melt all but a knob of the butter in a large heavy-based saucepan. Add the onion and cook for a few minutes until glossy and relaxed, then add the rice and stir until translucent. Pour in the wine and once this has been absorbed, start to add the stock, a ladleful or two at a time. Wait for each addition to be absorbed before adding more.

Take off the heat while the rice still has a certain resistance and the risotto is quite sloppy, more so than usual. It should take a total of about 30 minutes to cook. Add the knob of butter and Parmesan. Check the seasoning. Stir in the Fontina, cover the pan and leave for 3 minutes for the cheese to melt. Spoon on to warmed plates or bowls, make a well in the centre and drop in an egg yolk. Serve at once, with more Parmesan for those that want it.

Lemon Risotto

A really flavourful homemade broth is needed for this risotto.

Serves 4
1.2 litres seasoned chicken or
   vegetable stock
50 g unsalted butter
 1 onion, peeled and finely chopped
 1 garlic clove, peeled and
   finely chopped
300 g risotto rice (Vialone Nano
   or Carnaroli)
125 ml dry vermouth
   Finely grated zest of 2 lemons
 2 tablespoons lemon juice
50 g Parmesan cheese,
   freshly grated
 2 tablespoons double cream
100 g Emmental cheese, grated
 3 tablespoons finely chopped
   flat-leaf parsley, plus extra
   to serve
   Sea salt, black pepper

Bring the stock to the boil in a medium saucepan and keep it at a gentle simmer. Melt the butter in a large saucepan. Add the onion and garlic and sweat for a few minutes until softened, without colouring. Add the rice and cook for 1 minute until it turns translucent and is coated with butter. Pour in the vermouth. Once this has been absorbed, add the stock a couple of ladlefuls at a time. At no stage should the risotto be flooded. Stir from time to time, not constantly.

Remove the pan from the heat while the risotto is a touch too moist and the rice still just firm. Stir in the lemon zest and juice, then the Parmesan and cream. Finally add the Emmental, parsley and a generous grinding of black pepper. Check the seasoning and serve at once, scattered with extra parsley.

Venetian Peas and Rice

There are few better ways of enjoying the first peas of the season than in this half-soup half-risotto. Only fresh will do, ready-shelled at a push.

Serves 4
50 g unsalted butter
 1 small onion, peeled and chopped
275 g shelled fresh peas (about 900g
   unpodded weight)
200 g risotto rice (Vialone Nano
   or Carnaroli)
150 ml white wine
 1 litre fresh vegetable stock
   Sea salt, black pepper
70 g Parmesan cheese,
   freshly grated
 4 tablespoons coarsely chopped
   flat-leaf parsley, plus extra
   to serve

Heat the butter in a large saucepan, add the onion and cook until it is lightly coloured. Add the peas and rice and stir for a minute or two. Now add the wine, stock and seasoning. Bring to a simmer, cover and cook for 15 minutes or until the rice is tender. Stir in the Parmesan and parsley and adjust the seasoning.

Ladle into warmed bowls and scatter with a little extra parsley. Ideally serve straightaway, although this is more accommodating than a risotto and will sit for a few minutes if you're not quite ready to eat.

Not long ago, the only way you could prepare a risotto with squid ink was to buy in a job lot of this cephalopod and operate with a scalpel to remove the ink sacs. It also involved living off squid for weeks to come. An ink sac is a precious thread-like innard a centimetre long and to achieve a dramatically dark and syrupy risotto requires a great number. Civilisation has since spread to fashionable fishmongers, delicatessens and food halls and sachets of ink are now at least as common as squid itself. If you don't feel like going to town with scallops, which should be as plump as a pin cushion, then briefly sautéed squid will do nicely as a substitute.

Serves 4
8 shelled scallops
1 to 1.1 litres strong fish stock
65 g unsalted butter
1 small onion, peeled and
   finely chopped
300 g risotto rice (Vialone Nano
   or Carnaroli)
150 ml white wine
6 sachets of squid ink (3 teaspoons)
   Sea salt, black pepper
   Extra virgin olive oil, for frying
2 heaped tablespoons freshly
   grated Parmesan
   Squeeze of lemon juice
150 ml whipping cream,
   lightly whipped
   Finely chopped flat-leaf parsley,
   to serve

To prepare the scallops remove the gristle at the side and the tough skirt that runs around the edge which will come away with the coral. Cut off the skirt where it joins the coral and discard, reserving the corals.

Heat the stock in a small saucepan and keep it just below a simmer at the back of the hob. Heat 50g of the butter in a large heavy-based saucepan. Add the onion and sweat over a low heat until it is translucent and soft; it must not colour. Add the rice and cook for 1 minute. Pour in the wine and cook until it has been absorbed, then add the squid ink. Start to add the simmering stock a couple of ladlefuls at a time. At no stage should the risotto be flooded. The risotto will take about 25 minutes to cook. Season halfway through and stop cooking once the rice is tender, leaving it on the moist side. It will continue to absorb moisture as you finish off and serve it.

As the risotto is finishing cooking, heat two cast-iron frying pans on a high heat. Brush the scallops and their corals with olive oil and season them. Sear on each side for 1½–2 minutes, turning them with a palette knife; they should remain faintly transluscent in the centre.

To finish the risotto, stir in the Parmesan, remaining butter, the lemon juice, and lastly the whipped cream; adjust the seasoning. Serve the risotto on warmed plates with the scallops in the centre and sprinkled with a little parsley.

Mussels with Tomato and Chorizo

Mussels are not averse to garlicky nibs of chorizo. This recipe is from the late Mark Malloy, whose wife continues to welcome guests to their country house hotel Tonlegee, in the heart of Ireland's horse racing country, south of Dublin. As with most mussel dishes you will need some crusty bread alongside, and a spoon and fork for implements.

Serves 6

1.8 kg mussels in shell
200 g can chopped tomatoes
Large pinch of saffron threads (about 25)
175 ml white wine
100 g chorizo sausage, thinly sliced and cut into fine strips
2 garlic cloves, peeled and finely chopped
Freshly ground black pepper
Handful of chopped chervil or flat-leaf parsley

To clean the mussels, wash them in a sink of cold water, then pull off the beards and scrape off any barnacles. Discard any that are damaged or that do not close when sharply tapped. Wash them again in clean water and place in two large saucepans. Combine the tomatoes, saffron, wine, chorizo and garlic in a bowl and season with pepper. Pour this over the mussels. You can prepare to this point in advance, but refrigerate unless you intend to cook within 30 minutes.

To cook, put tight-fitting lids on the saucepans and place over a high heat for about 5 minutes until the mussels open up, shaking the pan or stirring occasionally. Serve the mussels and liquor in warmed bowls, scattered with a little chervil or parsley.

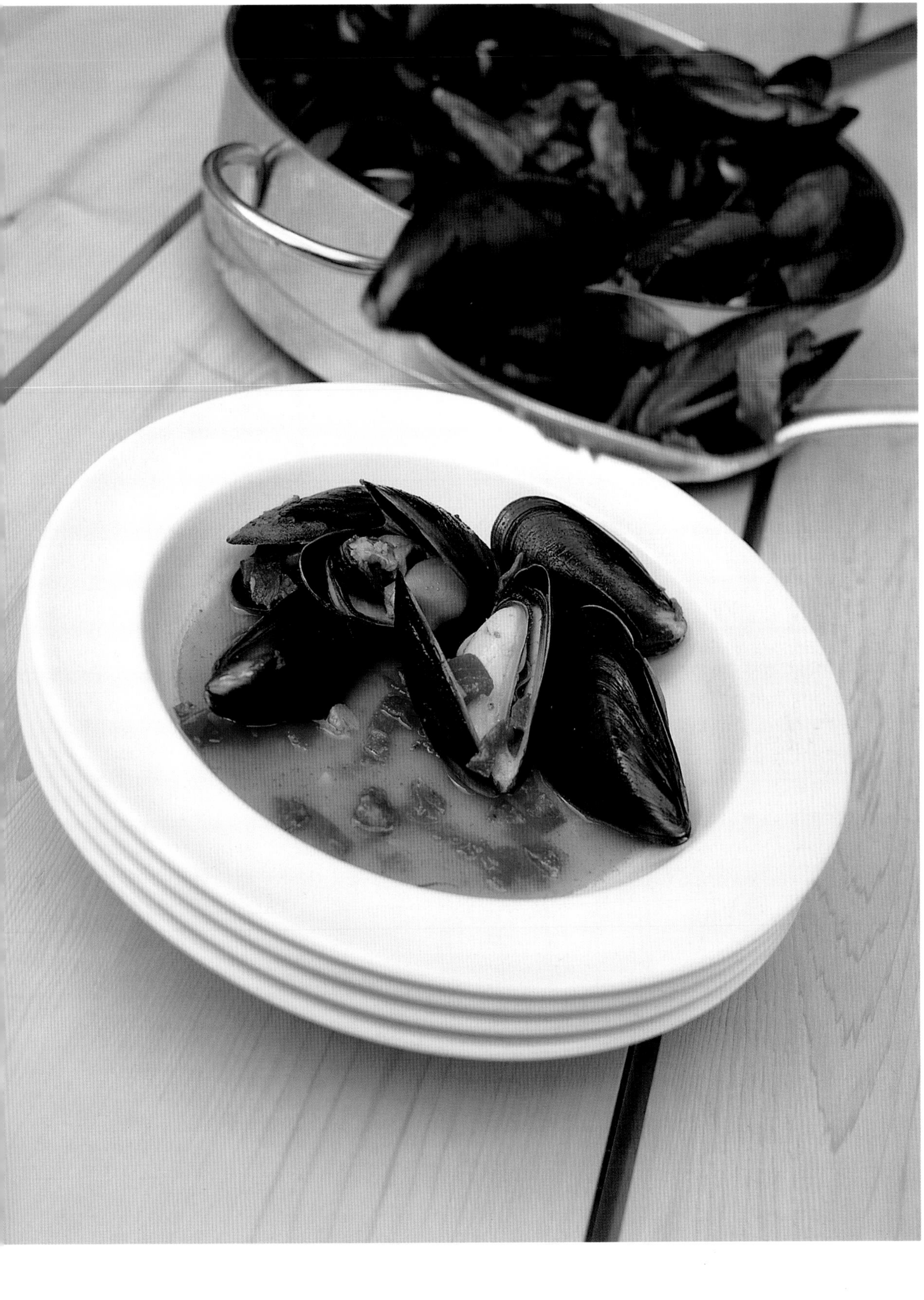

Saffron Mussels

In our opinion the finest mussels of all are the tiny dark orange bouchots which visitors to Normandy are privileged to be able to feast on during their stay. These are grown ranged up wooden poles in the sea, which are part of the landscape along much of the Norman coastline. If you find a good supply of mussels, then nurture it. Serve these mussels with a warm baguette and unsalted butter.

Serves 2
15 saffron threads
1 kg mussels in shell
2 shallots, peeled and finely chopped
125 ml dry white wine
3 heaped tablespoons crème fraîche
1 teaspoon beurre manié (equal quantities of plain flour and unsalted butter blended together)

Put the saffron threads in a bowl, add 1 tablespoon boiling water and set aside to infuse for 30 minutes.

Clean the mussels (see page 102). Put them in a large saucepan with the shallots and wine. Cover with a tight-fitting lid and place over a high heat for 3–4 minutes, shaking once or twice, by which time the mussels should have opened. Decant the juices into a small pan, leaving the mussels in the covered pan. Boil the juices vigorously to reduce by half, then add the crème fraîche and saffron. Stir in the beurre manié and simmer for a further 2–3 minutes until you have a thin creamy sauce. Transfer the mussels to a large bowl, pour over the sauce and toss. Serve at once in large warm bowls.

Salad of Langoustines and Green Beans with Fines Herbes

Fines herbes is as classically French as a string of onions, a complex scent that courses through some of France's more elegant fare. It is a blend of freshly chopped parsley, tarragon, chervil and chives. The quantities of these components can vary. As tarragon is very pungent, it should not account for more than one part, assuming there are two parts of chervil and three each of parsley and chives. Chervil is the most delicate herb within the mix. If you can grow it then do, it's a wonderful herb, like soft-leafed parsley with hints of aniseed. And if it does elude you in supermarkets and greengrocers don't despair, you can still make an effective blend with the other three. Equally, if langoustines prove hard to find you can use any large prawn.

Serves 4
1 beefsteak tomato
180 g fine green beans, topped and tailed
40 g vermicelli rice noodles
450 g langoustines in shell, cooked
1 shallot, peeled and finely chopped

Dressing
1 heaped teaspoon Dijon mustard
2 teaspoons cider or white wine vinegar
4 tablespoons single cream
Pinch of caster sugar
Sea salt
3 tablespoons finely chopped fines herbes

Bring a large pan of salted water to the boil. Cut out the core from the tomato, plunge it into boiling water for 20 seconds and then into cold water. Peel and quarter the tomato, discarding the seeds, and dice the flesh. Keeping the water on the boil, add the beans and cook for 3–4 minutes leaving them slightly resistant to the bite. Drain and refresh them in cold water then remove, pat dry and place in a salad bowl. Put the noodles in a bowl, pour on boiling water to cover and leave for 5 minutes, then drain and refresh them under cold water. Add them to the beans and toss to mix.

To shell the langoustines, pull off the head, then pinch the sides together to break the spines across the belly. Open out the shell and remove the langoustine flesh in one piece. Slit it in half vertically and scrape out the dark intestine and the orange sac.

To make the dressing whisk the mustard, vinegar, cream, sugar and a little salt together, then stir in the herbs. Toss the green beans, rice noodles and shallot with the dressing, then carefully mix in the langoustines and the tomato. The salad will keep for an hour at room temperature. If you want to prepare it further in advance, assemble the component parts and toss them with the dressing closer to serving.

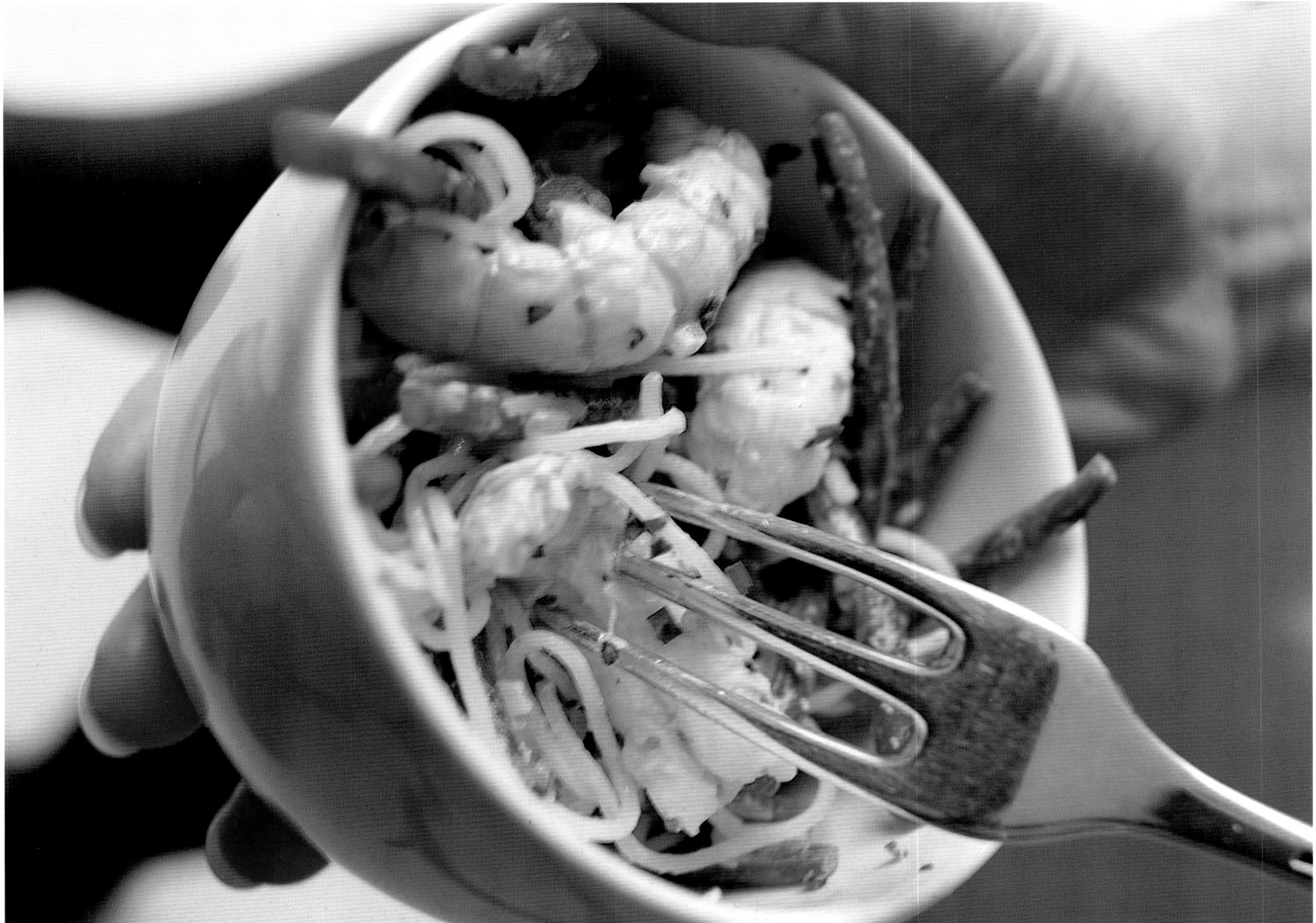

Scallop and Bacon Brochettes with Saffron Mash

Combining a shellfish of such elevated piscatorial standing as scallops with swine seems louche. There again, oysters angelically ride the same path to great acclaim.

Serves 4

Mash

175 ml milk
30 saffron threads
900 g waxy potatoes, such as Charlotte, peeled
125 ml double cream
50 g unsalted butter
Sea salt, black pepper
2 tablespoons extra virgin olive oil

Brochettes

8 slices of unsmoked streaky bacon, rind and excess fat removed
12 large scallops, shelled
½ lemon
Extra virgin olive oil, for brushing

For the mash, put the milk and saffron threads in a small saucepan, bring to the boil, then remove from the heat and set aside to infuse. Bring a large pan of salted water to the boil, add the potatoes and cook for 20 minutes or until tender. Drain and pass through a mouli-legumes back into the pan. Alternatively press the potatoes through a sieve.

Add the cream, butter and some seasoning to the saffron milk, and heat until the butter melts. Beat this liquor into the potatoes a third at a time, then add the olive oil and taste to check the seasoning.

For the brochettes, heat the grill. Lay the bacon rashers on the grill pan grid and grill both sides until the fat just turns translucent and the meat colours pink, then cool.

Prepare the scallops by removing the gristle at the side and the tough skirt that runs around the edge. This will come away with the coral. Cut off the skirt where it joins the corals and reserve them. Rolling up the bacon rashers as you go, thread 3 scallops and their corals and 2 bacon rolls, on to each of four 20cm skewers, alternating them.

Heat a ridged griddle on a medium-low heat. Brush the brochettes on all sides with olive oil and lightly season them. Grill for 6 minutes, turning occasionally. Squeeze a few drops of lemon juice over the brochettes. If necessary re-warm the mash while the brochettes are cooking. Spoon the mash on to warmed plates and place the brochettes on top.

Warm Salad of New Potatoes and Oysters

Native oysters, however lauded by those who know their crustacea, are simply too puny for this salad. It is the cushioned lobes of the Pacific oyster that are called for. This is a good salad for novices. The texture of the oysters is offset by the sweet mealiness of the potatoes, and they are cooked just long enough to be on the firm side of wobbly—definitely not alive. A gentle olive oil is essential.

Serves 4
900 g medium new potatoes, scrubbed or peeled
24 Pacific oysters
1½ tablespoons Champagne or white wine vinegar
Sea salt, black pepper
6 tablespoons extra virgin olive oil
3 heaped tablespoons chervil leaves, coarsely chopped

Bring a large pan of salted water to the boil, add the potatoes and cook until tender. Drain and leave to cool for 5 minutes.

While the potatoes are cooking, shuck the oysters (see page 038). Pick over the meat and strain the juices into a small pan, discarding the last bit of gritty liquor. Bring to the boil and reduce by half. To make the dressing, put the vinegar in a bowl with some seasoning, then whisk in the olive oil.

To serve, slice the potatoes and arrange on 4 dinner plates. Poach the oysters in the reduced liquor for 30 seconds each side then place on top of the potatoes. Add the dressing to the oyster juices and spoon over the salad. Scatter over the chervil and serve straightaway.

Grilled Squid with Lemon and Chilli

The secret of grilling squid at home is to get your griddle seriously hot in order to brand the flesh in the short time permitted before it starts to toughen. This means procuring squid that are at least as long as your hand, with pouches thick enough to slit open and score with the tip of a knife, without being cut through. Chilli is squid's natural dancing partner, added here to devilish effect.

Serves 2
450 g squid (see above)
2 to 3 large handfuls of rocket leaves, or assorted salad leaves to include rocket
Extra virgin olive oil
Squeeze of lemon juice
Black pepper

Dressing
½ teaspoon finely grated lemon zest
1 tablespoon lemon juice
1 medium-hot red chilli, deseeded and finely chopped
Sea salt
2 tablespoons extra virgin olive oil

First clean the squid. Tug the tentacles away from the pouch to separate them. Pull off the wings and with them the transparent porphyry-coloured film covering the pouch. Remove the hard pen from inside the pouch and as much of the insides as you can. Slit the pouch open from top to bottom, open it out and scrape off any residual white matter. Score the flesh in a criss-cross pattern at 1cm intervals using the sharp tip of a knife, and set aside. Cut the tentacles off the body just above the eyes. Rinse and pat dry.

Heat your griddle on a high heat. For the dressing, combine the lemon zest and juice, chilli and some salt in a bowl and whisk in the oil. Place the salad leaves in a bowl and toss with a little olive oil to coat them, a squeeze of lemon juice and the lightest sprinkling of sea salt.

Brush the squid on both sides with oil, season with salt and pepper and cook for 3 minutes, turning halfway through this time. As you cook the second side it should curl up, and be striped with gold on the outside. Place the squid on warm serving plates, spoon over the dressing and serve at once, accompanied by the salad.

Kedgeree

The morning after a May Ball, when dinner is a distant memory, the sky is streaked with the illuminated greys and blues of dawn, and you are starving in an unnatural way is the time to appreciate a kedgeree.

Serves 4
25 g unsalted butter
 1 teaspoon ground coriander
 1 teaspoon ground cumin
 ¼ teaspoon turmeric
250 g basmati rice
   Sea salt, black pepper
450 g smoked haddock fillet
125 ml milk
125 ml double cream
 2 tablespoons coarsely
   chopped coriander
   Lime wedges, roast nuts, raisins
   and mango chutney, to serve

Melt the butter in a medium saucepan. Add the spices, stir, then add the rice and cook for 1 minute until it is translucent. Add 450ml water and 1 teaspoon sea salt. Bring to the boil and simmer for 9 minutes. Cover with the lid, remove from the heat and leave to steam in the residual heat for 15 minutes.

In the meantime, put the smoked haddock, milk, cream and some pepper in a large saucepan. Bring to a simmer, cover and cook over a moderately low heat for 5 minutes; effectively the fish will steam. Lift out the fish and, when cool enough to handle, flake it. Return the fish to the juices in the pan and gently reheat.

Fluff the rice with a fork, then toss with the haddock and juices. Adjust the seasoning and stir in the coriander. Serve with lime wedges, nuts, raisins and chutney.

Jansson's Temptation

Named after an elusive Swede whose name changes from Jansson to Jonsson to Janzon, followed up by 'frestelse' which is Swedish for temptation. In turn, as a missionary in the nineteenth century he is said to have founded a sect in Illinois which forbade eating for pleasure, though Jansson yielded to this dish. He is also incarnated as a Swedish chef. Elsewhere he's been cited as a gourmet opera singer who tempted friends after performances with this late night snack.

Serves 4
 1 Spanish onion, peeled and halved
900 g waxy potatoes
 15 g unsalted butter
 15 salted anchovies in oil, plus
   2 teaspoons of the oil
300 ml double cream
150 ml vegetable stock
   Black pepper

Preheat the oven to 220°C, fan oven 200°C, gas 7. Finely slice the onion into half moons. Peel the potatoes and cut into very thin chips. Grease a large gratin dish, which should hold the vegetables to a depth of 5cm, with the butter. Lay half the potatoes in the dish. Scatter over the onions, then the anchovies and top with remaining potatoes. Press down with your hand.

Mix together the cream and stock, and season with pepper. Pour this liquid over the potatoes, to half-cover them. Spoon the anchovy oil over the potatoes. Cover with foil and bake for 30 minutes. Remove the foil and bake for another 20–30 minutes until the top chips are golden and crisp, and those underneath are tender.

This Normandy fish pie boasts seriously rich mash, succulent flakes of haddock, and the luxury of a few scallops and prawns thrown in. Aside from its obvious gustatory charm the real joy of a fish pie is that you can prepare it well in advance and pop it into the oven half an hour before you want to eat.

Serves 6
800 g haddock fillets, with skin
250 ml milk
  1 bay leaf
    Sea salt, black pepper
250 g scallops
  60 g unsalted butter
  50 g plain flour
150 ml dry cider
150 g crème fraîche
  1 heaped teaspoon Dijon mustard
200 g shelled raw prawns
  1 tablespoon small capers, rinsed

Mash
1.5 kg maincrop potatoes, peeled,
    and halved if large
100 g crème fraîche
  50 g unsalted butter
  2 large egg yolks

Place the haddock fillets in a large saucepan. Pour on the milk, tuck in the bay leaf, season and bring to a simmer. Cover with a lid, leaving a gap for the steam to escape, and cook on a low heat for 4 minutes. Take off the heat and leave until the fish is cool enough to handle. Strain the cooking liquor into a bowl and reserve. Flake the fish coarsely, discarding the skin. If any additional liquid is given out now, throw it away. Pull off the white gristle at the side of the scallops and remove the surrounding skirt. Cut off and reserve the corals. Slice each scallop into 2 or 3 discs.

To make the béchamel, melt the butter in a medium non-stick saucepan, add the flour and allow the roux to seethe for a minute. Very gradually work in the cider, followed by the fish cooking liquor, then the crème fraîche and mustard. Bring to the boil, stirring constantly, and simmer over a very low heat for 10 minutes, stirring occasionally. If any butter separates out, stir vigorously to reincorporate. Taste to check the seasoning.

Fold the haddock, scallops, prawns and capers into the béchamel. Turn into a 35cm oval gratin dish or other 2.5 litre capacity ovenproof dish that affords a large surface and leave it to cool. (Cooling helps prevent the potato from sinking in when you layer it on top.)

To prepare the mash, bring a large pan of salted water to the boil, add the potatoes and cook until tender. Drain them into a colander and leave the surface moisture to evaporate for a minute or two. Pass the potatoes through a mouli-legumes or a sieve back into the pan. Heat the crème fraîche with the butter and some seasoning and beat this into the mash, then beat in the egg yolks.

Spoon the mash over the top of the pie filling; smooth the surface and then fork into furrows. You can cover and chill the pie at this point for up to 48 hours until required, but it will then take a little longer to cook.

To cook, preheat the oven to 190°C, fan oven 180°C, gas 5 and bake the pie for 35–40 minutes until crusty and golden on the surface.

Smoked Haddock, Leek and Gruyère Quiche

Homemade pastry is ever a fine thing, but failing the energy shop-bought will do nicely. The important matter is the marriage of haddock with eggs and cream and Gruyère. This is a main-course tart, more lunch than dinner. A tomato salad alongside would be ideal.

Serves 6

Pastry

225 g plain flour
Pinch of sea salt
150 g unsalted butter, chilled and diced
1 medium egg, separated

Filling

450 g undyed smoked haddock fillet
1 bay leaf
250 ml milk
Black pepper
40 g unsalted butter
450 g trimmed leeks, sliced
250 ml double cream
2 large organic eggs, plus 2 extra yolks
200 g Gruyère cheese, grated

To make the pastry, place the flour and salt in a food processor, add the butter and work to a fine crumb-like texture; a couple of quick bursts should do it. Incorporate the egg yolk, and then with the motor running trickle in just enough cold water for the dough to cling together into lumps. Transfer the pastry to a large bowl and bring it together into a ball using your hands. Wrap the pastry in clingfilm and chill for at least 1 hour.

Preheat the oven to 190°C, fan oven 180°C, gas 5. Knead the pastry gently until it is pliable. Roll it out thinly on a lightly floured surface and use to line a 23cm tart tin, 4cm deep, with a removable base. The pastry is quite durable and shouldn't tear as you lift it. Press into the corners of the tin and trim the top edge, using a knife. Reserve the trimmings to patch the pastry case after it is baked. Prick the base with a fork and line it with a sheet of foil, tucking it over the top edge. Now weight it with baking beans—dried beans or chickpeas will do.

Bake the case for 15 minutes, then remove the foil and baking beans. If any of the side has shrunk more than it should, patch with a little of the reserved pastry. Remember a tart can only be filled as far as the lowest point of the side. Brush the base and sides of the case with egg white, then bake for another 10 minutes until it is lightly coloured. This glaze helps to seal the pastry and prevent the custard from soaking into it.

Cut the haddock fillet in half (to fit the pan). Place in a saucepan, skin-side down. Tuck in the bay leaf; pour on the milk and season with pepper. Bring to a simmer, cover with a lid, leaving a gap for the steam to escape, and poach gently for 5 minutes. Lift out the fish, reserving the milk. Once the fish is cool enough to handle, flake it. Melt the butter in a frying pan, add the leeks, season and sweat over a low heat for about 10 minutes, until they are soft.

Whisk together the cream, eggs, extra yolks and seasoning in a bowl, then add the reserved milk and half the cheese. Scatter the flaked haddock and leeks evenly over the base of the tart. Give the egg and cream mixture a quick whisk and pour into the tart case. Scatter over the remaining cheese and bake for 35–40 minutes until set and golden. Remove the side of the tin and leave the tart to stand on its base for 10 minutes. While it is best eaten hot, this quiche does reheat successfully. (You would need to cover it with foil and reheat in the oven for about 20 minutes.)

Poached Salmon with Sauce Verte

However hackneyed, poaching salmon is one of the finer fates for this king of the river, its flesh rendered supremely succulent and moist, on the naked side of cooked. But never formally poached—its backbone adorned with cucumber slices and squeezy mayonnaise. Apart from regarding the fish kettle as the prima donna of all saucepans and a waste of space, salmon look so much more enticing if poached coiled embryonically within a large preserving pan or saucepan, a linen teatowel for a sling.

Under 2kg is small for a salmon —you wouldn't find many fishermen flaunting their prowess —but it's the ideal size for 6 or 8 people, and the flesh of a small fish is that much more delicate. Steamed or boiled small waxy new potatoes—tossed in unsalted butter and scattered with sea salt —are the ideal complement.

Serves 6
1 bottle of white wine
1 carrot, thinly sliced
2 celery sticks, thinly sliced
1 leek, trimmed and thinly sliced
    Sea salt
1 small salmon, about
    1.8kg, cleaned

Sauce verte
25 g spinach leaves
25 g watercress
1 small handful of chives
1 small handful of tarragon leaves
150 g crème fraîche
    Squeeze of lemon juice

For the poaching liquor, put the wine, carrot, celery, leek and 3 tablespoons sea salt in a large saucepan. Measure the maximum height of the fish and add water to the pan to this depth, which should ensure the fish will be fully immersed. Cover and bring to a rolling boil.

If you like, remove the head from the salmon. Place the fish on a teatowel in an upright position, curved to fit the pot. Gather up the corners of the teatowel and pin them with a safety pin. Lower the salmon into the boiling liquid and once it comes back to the boil, cover with a tight-fitting lid, remove from the heat and leave it for several hours to cool. The salmon will be at its best if you lift it out when the water is lukewarm; you can leave it overnight but for our taste it's a bit overcooked after this length of time.

To make the sauce, bring a large pan of salted water to the boil, add the spinach and watercress and blanch for 30 seconds. Drain them in a sieve, refresh under cold running water and squeeze out as much liquid as possible. Turn on to a board and chop together with the herbs. Put the crème fraîche in a bowl, stir in the spinach and herb mixture, season with salt and add the lemon juice.

Once the fish is ready, lift it onto a plate, undo the pin and carefully slip the teatowel from underneath it. Drain off any liquid that collects on the plate. Using a knife, lift off the skin and remove the fatty core running down the spine. Loosen the salmon flesh from the spine in large fillets and place on cold plates, removing any visible bones. Serve the fish with the sauce.

Sea Bass roasted with Lemon and Thyme

If destined to be eaten at room temperature, cool, fillet and douse the sea bass with the sauce, leaving it to steep a while.

Serves 4
1 sea bass, about 1.2kg, gutted and scaled, head on
10 tablespoons extra virgin olive oil
Sea salt, black pepper
1 lemon, sliced
1 beefsteak tomato, sliced crossways
1 onion, peeled and sliced crossways
2 red chillies
10 soft-leafed or lemon thyme sprigs, plus 1 heaped teaspoon thyme leaves
75 ml sweet white wine
Squeeze of lemon juice

Preheat the oven to 220°C, fan oven 200°C, gas 7 and heat the grill. Score the fish at 2cm intervals, brush with oil and season inside and out. Grill for 4–6 minutes each side until blistered and coloured.

In a baking dish that will hold the fish, lay half the lemon, tomato and onion slices overlapping in a row, and season. Place the fish on top and put the chillies and thyme sprigs in the cavity. Overlap the remaining lemon, tomato and onion slices on top, and season. Pour the wine and 6 tablespoons olive oil over the fish. Roast for 15 minutes.

Turn the vegetables and flavourings into a sieve over a small pan and press to extract the juices. Stir in the remaining thyme and oil, adjust the seasoning and add lemon juice to taste. Reheat gently, without boiling. Fillet the fish and serve with the sauce poured over.

Sea Bass baked in Salt

There is considerable awe surrounding the magnificence achieved here with just two ingredients. The salt paste encasing the sea bass bakes to a hard shell that lifts off like an Anthony Gormley body cast. The flesh is not only perfectly cooked and succulent but also perfectly seasoned too. You may even decide the sauce is superfluous.

Serves 6
1.5 kg fine-grain sea salt
2 sea bass, each about 1kg, gutted but not scaled

Red wine shallot sauce
3 shallots, peeled and finely chopped
3 thyme sprigs
425 ml red wine
225 g unsalted butter, diced
Sea salt, black pepper

Preheat the oven to 240°C, fan oven 230°C, gas 9. Tip the salt into a large bowl, pour over 425ml water and stir until the salt is uniformly wet. Lay a sheet of foil on the base of a baking tray large enough to hold the sea bass side by side. Scatter over half the salt, levelling it into an even layer. Lay the sea bass on the salt, top to toe, and cover with the remaining salt, leaving the head and tail uncovered. Bake for 30 minutes by which time the fish should be just cooked.

Meanwhile, make the sauce. Place the shallots, thyme and wine in a small saucepan. Bring to the boil and reduce until syrupy and only a few tablespoons remain; this will take 20–30 minutes. Discard the thyme sprigs. To finish the sauce, gradually whisk in the butter, working on and off the heat as necessary. At no point should the sauce simmer; season it about halfway through.

When you take the fish from the oven, lift off the upper crust of salt and carefully transfer the fish to a serving plate. Fillet by cutting along the backbone with a sharp knife and easing the fillet off. It makes life easier to leave the skin in place although you can't eat this. Serve the fish fillets with the sauce spooned over.

Eating   Shellfish and Whole Fish

Gigot of Monkfish

There are lots of buttery pan juices here, and bread performs the task of mopping that much more enthusiastically than potatoes.

Serves 4
1 kg monkfish, cut from the belly
75 g unsalted butter, softened
8 salted anchovies in oil, rinsed and chopped
1 teaspoon finely chopped rosemary
1 teaspoon finely grated lemon zest
Black pepper
6 slices of Parma Ham
Juice of ½ lemon

To prepare the monkfish, pull off the skin and slice off any grey membrane. Use your finger to loosen the cartilaginous spine on either side and pull it out as far as you can. Cut to remove it entirely, leaving you with two long fillets.

Preheat the oven to 200°C, fan oven 190°C, gas 6. Cream together 50g of the butter, the chopped anchovies, rosemary, lemon zest and some pepper. Spread this along the fillets where the bone lay. Holding the fillets together, wrap the Parma ham around them. Tie securely with string by knotting the string around one end and winding the reel down the length of the fillet, then knotting the loose end.

Place the gigot in a small ovenproof frying pan. Dot with the remaining butter and pour over the lemon juice. Roast for 25–30 minutes, basting halfway through. Cut the string along the top of the monkfish using a pair of scissors. Slice and serve on warm plates with the pan juices.

Monkfish à l'Americaine

Juicy virgin-white medallions of monkfish in a rich tomato sauce specked with tarragon and parsley —with chunks of fried bread on the side—is one of the finer fates for this ugly swollen-headed brute from the deep.

Serves 4
900 g monkfish
800 g beefsteak tomatoes
5 tablespoons extra virgin olive oil
5 shallots, peeled and sliced
1 garlic clove, peeled and finely chopped
1 tablespoon tomato purée
Sea salt, black pepper
1 teaspoon caster sugar
150 ml white wine
300 ml strong fish stock
2 tablespoons brandy
1 tablespoon chopped tarragon leaves
2 tablespoons chopped flat-leaf parsley

Croûtes
Extra virgin olive oil, for frying
16 to 20 slices of French bread, 1.5cm thick

Slice the monkfish off the bone and run a sharp knife between the skin and the flesh, removing the grey membrane. It's very important that none of this membrane remains as it contracts and toughens on cooking. Cut the fillets into generous slices, about 4cm thick.

Cut a cone from the top of each tomato to remove the core. Plunge the tomatoes into a pan of boiling water for 20–30 seconds, then refresh in cold water, remove and slip off the skins. Roughly cut up the tomatoes.

Heat the olive oil in a large sauté pan or heavy-based saucepan. Add the shallots and garlic and sweat over a medium heat until they are soft. Turn the heat up, add the monkfish and cook briefly on both sides to seal, then remove it to a plate. Add the tomatoes, tomato purée, seasoning, sugar, wine and fish stock to the pan. Bring to the boil and simmer for 30 minutes. Stir frequently, mashing up the tomatoes until the sauce is rich and thick. Taste to check for seasoning. You can prepare the stew to this point in advance.

While the sauce is cooking, prepare the croûtes in batches. Heat a 4–5mm depth of oil in a frying pan. Add a single layer of French bread slices and fry on both sides until golden and crispy. Drain on kitchen paper and cook the remainder, replenishing the oil as necessary. The croûtes should have the consistency of traditional British fried bread, chewy on the outside and soft within.

To finish the stew, add the monkfish to the simmering sauce along with the brandy and cook for 5 minutes. Ladle into warmed shallow soup bowls and scatter with the herbs. Serve accompanied by the croûtes.

Charmoula-grilled Halibut

Long ago when Bruno Loubet cooked in a Magreb-inspired restaurant near the Groucho club, he coated his sea bream with charmoula before grilling it. The cooking time of your fillet will depend on its thickness. Give it a gentle prod and if it seems too giving, then subject it to a little longer under the grill.

Serves 4
4 halibut fillets, each about 180g, with skin

Charmoula
4 tablespoons extra virgin olive oil
2 tablespoons lime juice
3 shallots, peeled and finely chopped
1 teaspoon finely chopped red chilli
1 garlic clove, peeled and finely chopped
1½ teaspoons ground cumin
1 heaped teaspoon finely chopped rosemary
Sea salt, black pepper

To serve
Lemon wedges

Combine all the ingredients for the charmoula in a bowl. Score the halibut skin at 2cm intervals then lay the fillets in a shallow dish. Spoon the charmoula over the fish and leave to marinate in the fridge for at least 1 hour, ideally overnight.

Preheat the grill. Scrape the marinade off the fish and reserve. Season the fish and grill skin-side up for 5 minutes until beginning to colour and crisp. Turn and grill the flesh side for 2–3 minutes. Place skin-side up on warmed plates and spoon over some of the marinade. Serve with lemon wedges.

Plaice à la Meunière

Plaice tends to be eclipsed by its rich relation, the Dover sole, but it deserves better. At its freshest, plaice is milky and sweet, and here you can wallow in its pleasures following with a lightly dressed green salad.

Serves 2
100 g unsalted butter
2 plaice fillets, each 175–225g, with skin
Plain flour, for coating
Sea salt, black pepper
2 lemon quarters
2 teaspoons finely chopped flat-leaf parsley

Gently melt the butter in a small saucepan, and then remove from the heat. Preheat a non-stick frying pan over a high heat. Season the flour with sea salt on a plate. Dip the plaice fillets into the flour to coat them, then brush liberally with the melted butter. Lay one plaice fillet flesh-side down in the frying pan, turn the heat down and cook for 3 minutes, then turn and cook the skin side for 3 minutes. Slip the plaice fillet on to a warm plate and cover with foil to keep warm while you cook the second fillet.

While the plaice is cooking, return the butter to a medium-low heat and stir frequently until the milky solids turn into fine golden particles. It should have the appearance of clear yellow butter with paprika in the bottom. Immediately pour into a bowl.

Once the fish fillets are cooked, spoon the butter over them and squeeze over the lemon juice. Season with salt and pepper and sprinkle over the chopped parsley.

This is one of the most tantalising ways of roasting a chicken and a garlic lover's dream. The bird is cooked surrounded by whole garlic cloves that, as well as scenting the chicken flesh, emerge meltingly soft and creamy. Any potato from roast to mash or gratin dauphinoise will do alongside, and some watercress or other salad to mop up the garlicky juices afterwards.

Serves 4
4 heads of garlic
1.6 kg oven-ready free-range chicken
50 g unsalted butter
Sea salt, black pepper
Juice of 1 lemon

Preheat the oven to 190°C, fan oven 180°C, gas 5. Slice the top and bottom off the heads of garlic, separate out the cloves and peel them. Tuck several cloves inside the chicken's cavity with half of the butter. Place the chicken in a roasting dish and smear the remaining butter over the skin. Season with salt and pepper and pour over the lemon juice. Roast the chicken for 30 minutes, then scatter the garlic cloves around the bird, basting them and the chicken with the juices. Roast for a further 25 minutes.

Loosely cover with foil and leave to rest in a warm place for 20 minutes. Tip any juices inside the bird back into the roasting dish and gently reheat these and the garlic cloves. Carve the chicken and serve on warmed plates with the roasted garlic cloves, spooning the pan juices over.

Butter-roasted Herbed Chicken

A classy bird, and nothing less than you would expect from the fabulous Patricia Wells whose hallmark is fare that is both elegant and homely at the same time. It's almost better served cold than hot, after the scent of the herbs has permeated the flesh. Bear this recipe in mind for a picnic, a cold roast chicken on the rug is as welcome as a bottle of wine chilling in the stream.

Serves 4
1 lemon
Sea salt, black pepper
1.6 kg oven-ready free-range chicken with giblets
1 bunch of fresh thyme
75 g unsalted butter, softened
5 tablespoons finely chopped mixed herbs (chervil, tarragon, chives, parsley)

Preheat the oven to 220°C, fan oven 200°C, gas 7. Roll the lemon back and forth on a work surface to soften it and then pierce it about 20 times with a sharp skewer. Season the chicken cavity with salt and pepper and place the giblets, lemon and thyme inside.

In a bowl, mix 50g of the butter with the herbs and ½ teaspoon each of salt and pepper. Starting at the neck end, slip your fingers beneath the skin to loosen it over each breast. Then insert the herb butter and pat the skin back into place, spreading the butter out evenly over the chicken breasts. Rub the remaining butter over the skin and season well.

Lay the chicken on one side on a rack in a roasting dish and roast for 20 minutes. Turn the chicken on to the other side and roast for another 20 minutes. Reduce the heat to 190°C, fan oven 180°C, gas 5. Turn the chicken breast-side down with the head end tipped downwards and roast for a further 15 minutes. Transfer the chicken in this position to a warmed platter, season and cover loosely with foil. Turn the oven off leaving the door ajar and rest the chicken inside for 10–30 minutes.

Place the roasting dish on the hob and simmer the juices for 2–3 minutes until they are almost caramelised, scraping up the sticky bits on the bottom. Discard any excess fat and add several tablespoons of cold water. Simmer for 3–4 minutes, then strain the sauce and serve with the chicken.

Note

If the chicken is to be served cold, then use the sauce as a base for a vinaigrette, to dress an accompanying salad. Whisk in ½ tablespoon balsamic vinegar together with a squeeze of lemon juice, 2 tablespoons olive oil and 2 tablespoons groundnut oil.

Olive Oil Roast Chicken

Minimal roast chicken needs no more than a sprinkling of sea salt and pepper. Here a film of olive oil is smeared over to crisp the skin, a few aromatics inside to scent the juices. You will end up with a small quantity of flavourful light gravy. If the call is for a river of gravy, simply add extra chicken stock after the wine. A good unpretentious chicken to serve with roasted vegetables.

Serves 4
Extra virgin olive oil
1.6 kg oven-ready free-range chicken
Sea salt, black pepper
Few thyme sprigs
1 garlic clove, peeled and smashed
½ onion
4 tablespoons white wine
4 tablespoons chicken stock or water

Preheat the oven to 220°C, fan oven 200°C, gas 7. Pour some olive oil into the palm of your hand and generously coat the chicken skin. Season the bird inside and out. Put the thyme, garlic and onion into the cavity. Place the chicken in a roasting tin and bake for 50–55 minutes until the skin is golden and the juices run clear when the thigh is pierced with a skewer.

Transfer the chicken to a warm plate, tipping out any juices inside the bird into the roasting tin. Turn the oven off and rest the chicken inside with the door ajar for 15 minutes. Skim off the fat from the roasting juices, then add the wine. Simmer to reduce by about half, scraping up all the sticky bits. Add the stock or water and simmer for a minute, then check the seasoning. Carve the chicken and serve with the gravy.

Chicken baked in Salt with Lapsang Souchong

This chicken emerges from the oven in a salt overcoat flecked with black. Lapsang souchong has a tarry taint that originated in days gone by when the tea was laid out to dry on trestle tables covered with old fishing nets. As well as absorbing the scent of tar from the nets it took up the smokiness from the drying fires. By using the tea to cut the salt, the chicken flesh is very subtly smoked. It would take an astute palate in a blind tasting to pick up on the mystery scent. As with fish baked in this fashion, the chicken doesn't lose moisture and so remains beautifully succulent. A good chicken for eating cold with Celeriac Rémoulade (see page 190), or Green Bean Salad (see page 193).

Serves 4
1 kg fine-grain sea salt (two 500g tubs)
4 heaped tablespoons Lapsang Souchong tea leaves
1.6 kg oven-ready free-range chicken

Preheat the oven to 220°C, fan oven 200°C, gas 7 and line a baking tray with foil. Mix the salt and tea leaves together in a large bowl. Add 250ml cold water and mix to a firm, wet paste. Lay half of this on the foil as a base for the chicken, pierce the chicken all over with a knife tip or a skewer and place it on top. Pat the remainder of the salt mixture around the chicken, so it is coated with a cloak, about 7mm thick.

Bake the chicken for 1 hour. Allow to rest in a warm place for 15 minutes then break off the salt crust, which will have dried out. You can serve the chicken straightaway or allow it to cool, carving in the usual fashion.

Paprika Roast Chicken with Grilled Pepper Salad

Paprika enhances the irresistible golden crispness of chicken skin as it roasts. The chicken and peppers hand in hand are so deliciously succulent it seems a shame to spoil the experience with potatoes. Some warm flat bread would be more in line.

Serves 4
1.6 kg oven-ready free-range chicken
25 g unsalted butter, softened
Extra virgin olive oil
Paprika, for dusting

Pepper salad
6 red or yellow peppers
Sea salt
1 garlic clove, peeled
5 tablespoons extra virgin olive oil
1 teaspoon red wine vinegar
1 large or 2 small shallots, peeled and very finely sliced
3 heaped tablespoons coarsely chopped flat-leaf parsley

Start to prepare the pepper salad at least half a day in advance, if not the day before serving. Preheat the oven to 220°C, fan oven 200°C, gas 7. Roast the peppers sitting on a grid or rack for 20 minutes until the skin appears blistered and blackened in patches. Transfer them to a bowl, cover with clingfilm and leave to cool.

Working over a bowl to catch the juices, peel off the roasted pepper skins and remove the core and seeds. Cut or tear each pepper into about 3 wide strips and add them to the bowl with the juices. Scatter over 1 teaspoon sea salt and stir to distribute it. Cover the bowl and leave to marinate in a cool place but not the fridge, for at least 4–5 hours.

To roast the chicken, heat the oven to 220°C, fan oven 200°C, gas 7. Starting at the neck end, slip your fingers beneath the skin to loosen it over each breast. Divide the butter between the breasts, smoothing it under the skin. Pour a little olive oil into the palm of your hand and use to lightly coat the chicken all over. Now liberally dust the breast and legs with paprika and season with salt. Place the chicken in a roasting dish and roast for 50–55 minutes, basting it halfway through.

Transfer the chicken to a plate, cover loosely with foil and leave to rest for at least 15 minutes. We like it warm with the peppers, but as you are serving it with a salad you can leave it to cool if you prefer.

To finish the pepper salad, crush the garlic: finely chop, sprinkle over a little salt and crush to a paste using the flat edge of a knife; or use a garlic press. Whisk the crushed garlic, olive oil and vinegar together in a bowl. Pour the dressing over the peppers and mix together, then toss in the shallot and parsley. Carve the chicken and serve it with the pepper salad.

Mustard Roast Chicken

A good roast to eat with a pile of peppery green leaves. Dijon mustard ensures enviably golden skin, the flesh beneath it butter-basted and succulent.

Serves 4
- 1.6 kg oven-ready free-range chicken
  Sea salt, black pepper
- 1 lemon, pierced all over with a skewer
- 75 g unsalted butter, softened
  Large handful of tarragon or dill leaves, coarsely chopped
- 1 tablespoon Dijon mustard
- 4 tablespoons white wine
- 4 tablespoons chicken stock or water

Preheat the oven to 200°C, fan oven 190°C, gas 6. Season the chicken cavity and pop the lemon inside. In a bowl, mix 50g butter with the herbs and ½ teaspoon each of salt and pepper. Starting at the neck end, slip your fingers beneath the skin to loosen it over each breast. Insert the herb butter and pat the skin back into place, spreading the butter out evenly. Put the chicken in a roasting tin, season and dot with the remaining butter. Roast for 40 minutes, basting every 15 minutes, then brush with the mustard and baste again. Roast for another 15 minutes, until the skin is deep golden.

Transfer the chicken to a plate, tipping any juices into the roasting tin, and rest for 15 minutes loosely covered with foil. Skim off excess fat from the roasting juices and add the wine. Cook to reduce by half, scraping up the sticky bits. Add the stock or water and simmer for 1–2 minutes, check the seasoning. Carve the chicken and serve.

All-in-one Chicken Roast

This has become a favourite way of cooking chicken with potatoes. The potatoes emerge meltingly tender inside, with tops like old-fashioned roast potatoes cooked around the joint, smooth and nicely leathery.

Serves 4
- 1.6 kg oven-ready free-range chicken
- 700 g potatoes, peeled and cut into 5cm pieces
- 5 garlic cloves (unpeeled)
- 3 rosemary sprigs
- 225 ml dry white wine
- 225 ml chicken stock or water
- 25 g unsalted butter
  Sea salt, black pepper

Preheat the oven to 200°C, fan oven 190°C, gas 6. Put the chicken in a roasting tin and surround with the potatoes, tucking the garlic cloves and rosemary between them. Pour 150ml each of the wine and stock or water into the dish. Dot the butter over the potatoes, smearing a little over the chicken. Season generously and roast for 1 hour, basting occasionally.

Transfer the bird to a plate, cover loosely with foil and leave to rest in a warm place for 15 minutes. Loosen the potatoes and move to the middle of the roasting tin; baste and bake for a further 10 minutes.

To make the gravy, transfer the potatoes and garlic to a serving dish, discarding the rosemary. Skim off excess fat in the roasting tin and deglaze with the remaining wine, simmering until it is well reduced. Add the remaining stock or water and cook for a few minutes, then taste for seasoning. Carve the chicken and serve with the potatoes, garlic cloves and gravy.

Roast Poussin with Summer Vegetables in Cider Butter

If you are a gardener, all that toiling bent double and soil ingrained into your fingers finally pays off when you can wander into the garden early evening, drink in hand, and harvest the fruits of your labour. If this is the case, forget the ingredient list below and improvise with whatever sweet young vegetables are good enough to offer up for the pot. The poussin cavities are crammed floor to roof with rosemary and thyme; it's a method that can also be applied to a larger chicken or guinea fowl. The smell that seeps out from the oven is delectable. Try to buy your poussin from a reputable butcher, supermarkets tend to sell intensively reared babes which have little flavour.

Serves 4
4 free-range poussin
2 large handfuls of rosemary and thyme sprigs
25 g unsalted butter, softened
Juice of ½ lemon
Sea salt, black pepper

Cider butter
150 ml dry cider
50 g unsalted butter, diced

Vegetables
25 g unsalted butter
½ teaspoon caster sugar
1 bunch of spring onions (about 8), trimmed to 7cm lengths
150 g young fresh or frozen peas
120 g mangetout, topped and tailed
50 g baby spinach leaves

Preheat the oven to 220°C, fan oven 200°C, gas 7. Stuff the poussin cavities with the herbs until they are spilling out. Place in a roasting dish about 2cm apart to allow the air to circulate. Smear the butter over the skin, pour over the lemon juice and season. Roast for 30 minutes, basting halfway through. Loosely cover the poussin with foil and leave to rest in a warm place for 10 minutes.

About 10 minutes before the chicken will be cooked, start preparing the cider butter and vegetables. Place the cider in a small saucepan with a little salt and cook to reduce to a few tablespoons. Whisk in the butter, on and off the heat, without allowing the sauce to boil.

To cook the vegetables, put the butter, sugar and ½ teaspoon salt in a medium saucepan with 200ml water. Bring to a simmer, then add the spring onions, cover and cook over a low heat for 7 minutes. Add the peas, mangetout and spinach and simmer for a further 3 minutes. Drain the vegetables and toss with the cider butter, gently reheating it first if necessary.

Place the poussin on 4 warmed plates, tipping any juices back into the dish. Skim off excess fat and add the juices to the vegetables. Spoon the vegetables and juices around and over the poussin.

Roast Guinea Fowl with Pistachio and Lemon Crumbs

This is a variation on theme of the inspired grouse and buttered crumb combination, with a few pistachios thrown in. If you want to be generous with the guinea fowl—and they can be mean—roast two birds. Everything can be prepared within an hour, though you may find it more relaxing to prepare the creamed parsnips in advance.

Serves 3–4
Vegetable oil
1.2 kg oven-ready guinea fowl
Sea salt, black pepper
80 g unsalted butter
900 g parsnips, peeled and thickly sliced
225 ml white wine
425 ml chicken stock
3 heaped tablespoons crème fraîche
25 g shelled pistachios (unroasted), finely chopped
25 g white breadcrumbs
Finely grated zest of 1 lemon
1 teaspoon thyme leaves, finely chopped

Preheat the oven to 200°C, fan oven 190°C, gas 6. Pour a little oil into the palm of your hand and rub over the guinea fowl to coat lightly. Place in a small roasting tin, season and roast for 45 minutes.

While the guinea fowl is cooking, make the parsnip purée. Melt two thirds of the butter in a large saucepan on a medium heat. Add the sliced parsnips and sweat for 5–8 minutes until they appear translucent and begin to colour, stirring frequently. Pour in 150ml of the wine and cook until it is well reduced and sticky. Add a third of the chicken stock, bring to a simmer then cover the pan and cook on a low heat for 15 minutes. Transfer the parsnips to a blender and purée with another third of the chicken stock, the crème fraîche and some seasoning. Depending on the size of your blender you may need to do this in two goes.

Melt the remaining butter in a frying pan over a medium heat. Add the pistachios and breadcrumbs and sauté, stirring constantly, until they are crisp and golden. Drain on kitchen paper, then transfer to a bowl and toss in the lemon zest, the thyme and a little seasoning.

Once the bird is cooked, transfer it to a warm plate, tipping any juices inside back into the roasting tin. Cover with foil and leave to rest in a warm place for 15 minutes. In the meantime, make the gravy. Pour off as much of the fat as possible from the tin. Heat the pan on the hob, add the remaining wine and cook until this is well reduced and syrupy. Pour in the remaining stock and simmer for several minutes until amalgamated. Taste for seasoning.

Reheat the creamed parsnips and carve the guinea fowl. Place a mound of creamed parsnip on each warmed plate and place the guinea fowl on top. Strain the gravy and serve this and the pistachio crumbs separately at the table.

Guinea Fowl roasted with Rosemary and Garlic

The flavour of a guinea fowl is something like a chicken aspiring to be a pheasant. As such it is that much stronger in personality, and enjoys the company of those two old roués rosemary and garlic. Try serving this with Spiced Sweet Potatoes (see page 170).

Serves 3
1 head of garlic, broken into cloves
1.2 kg oven-ready guinea fowl
50 g unsalted butter, softened
5 rosemary sprigs, 5–7cm long
Juice of 1 lemon
Sea salt, black pepper

Preheat the oven to 200°C, fan oven 190°C, gas 6. Peel 2 garlic cloves and cut into long thin slivers. Make a number of incisions in the guinea fowl breasts and legs and insert the garlic slivers. Smear the butter over the bird. Tuck a sprig of rosemary in between each leg and breast. Put the remaining garlic cloves into the cavity, along with 2 rosemary sprigs.

Place the guinea fowl in a roasting dish. Pull the leaves off the remaining rosemary sprig and scatter over the bird. Pour over the lemon juice and season with salt and pepper. Roast for 45 minutes, basting halfway through. By the end the skin should be golden and crispy. Cover the guinea fowl loosely with foil and leave to rest in the roasting dish for 15 minutes.

Remove the bird to a plate, tipping any juices back into the dish. Reheat the juices while you carve. Serve the guinea fowl on warm plates. Strain the pan juices, give them a stir and spoon over the meat to serve.

Chicken, Spinach and Lemon Pie

A chicken pie with a golden glazed lid of pastry is one of the finer sights of the domestic hearth, and this one tastes as good as it looks.

Serves 4
1 head of garlic
10 free-range chicken thighs
Sea salt, black pepper
1 tablespoon extra virgin olive oil
3 heaped tablespoons flour
150 ml white wine
4 thyme sprigs
1 lemon
15 g unsalted butter
250 g young spinach leaves
125 ml double cream
500 g puff pastry
1 organic egg yolk, mixed with 1 tablespoon milk, to glaze

Slice the top and bottom off the head of garlic using a sharp knife and separate the cloves, then slit the skins and slip them off the cloves. Season the chicken thighs with salt and pepper. Heat the olive oil in a large saucepan or sauté pan, add half the chicken thighs and fry, turning, until coloured on all sides. Transfer to a plate with a slotted spoon. Fry the remaining chicken thighs in the pan, adding the garlic cloves towards the end, so they soften without colouring.

Return all the chicken to the pan, sprinkle with the flour and turn the chicken to coat it. Stir in the wine, which will thicken as it blends with the flour, and let this seethe for a minute. Pour in 225ml water and stir until the sauce is smooth. Add the thyme, 2 long strips of finely pared lemon zest, and some seasoning. Bring to a simmer, cover and cook over a low heat for 30 minutes, stirring once.

While the chicken is cooking, melt the butter in a frying pan, add the spinach and toss until it wilts, then drain in a sieve, squeezing out as much water as possible using the back of a spoon.

Transfer the cooked chicken thighs to a bowl. Once they are cool enough to handle, discard the skin and remove the chicken from the bone, then cut into shreds. Discard the thyme sprigs and lemon zest from the sauce. Stir in the cream, add a generous squeeze of lemon juice and adjust the seasoning. Stir the spinach and chicken into the sauce and leave to cool to room temperature.

Preheat the oven to 220°C, fan oven 200°C, gas 7. Roll out two thirds of the pastry thinly on a lightly floured surface and use to line a deep 1.7 litre pie dish. Spoon in the chicken and spinach filling. Roll out the remaining pastry, brush the pastry rim with eggwash and position the lid. Trim the pastry lid, leaving a good 1cm for shrinkage, reserving the trimmings. Press the edges together with a fork, and trim them again to tidy if you like.

Brush the top of the pie with eggwash. Cut out some leaves from the pastry trimmings, mark veins using the tip of a sharp knife, then position the leaves on top of the pie and brush with eggwash. Bake in the oven for 45–50 minutes until the pastry is crisp and golden. Serve straightaway.

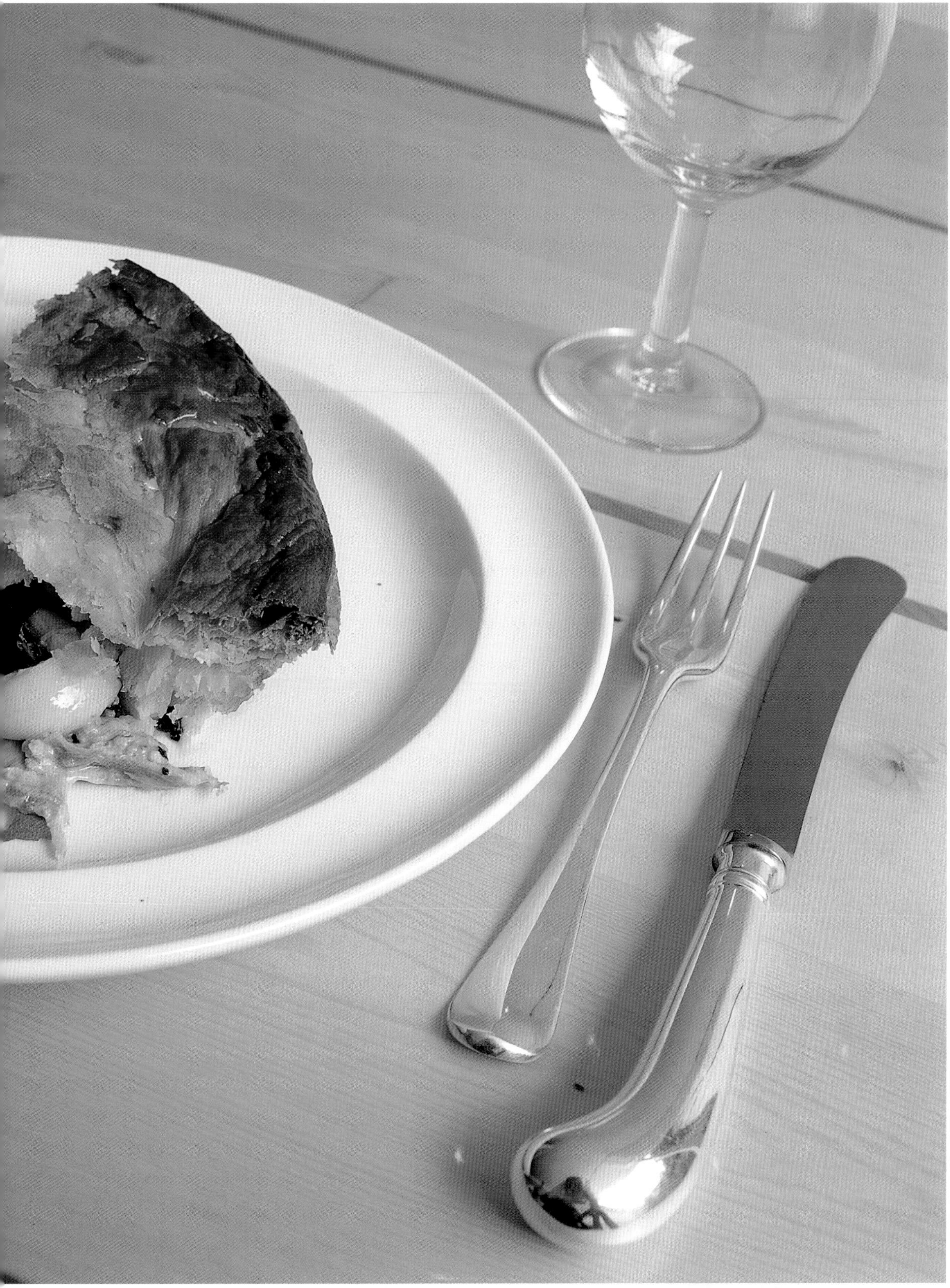

Chicken and White Wine Stew with Gremolata

Like all good stews this is awash with rich soupy juices and full of hidden treasures like bacon, celery and tomato. Gremolata may sound like a female goblin, when in fact it is a blend of parsley, garlic and lemon zest, equally at home beside a pan-fried chicken breast as scattered over a stew.

Serves 4

3 tablespoons extra virgin olive oil
100 g unsmoked streaky bacon, rind removed and sliced
1 large onion, peeled, halved and sliced
1 celery heart, trimmed and sliced
1 garlic clove, peeled and finely chopped
Sea salt, black pepper
1.1 kg free-range chicken pieces (thighs and drumsticks)
½ tablespoon plain flour
300 ml white wine
300 ml chicken stock
230 g can chopped tomatoes
3 red chillies
2 rosemary sprigs

Gremolata

½ garlic clove, peeled and finely chopped
2 tablespoons coarsely chopped flat-leaf parsley
Finely grated zest of 1 lemon

Heat 2 tablespoons of olive oil in a flameproof casserole over a medium heat. Add the bacon, onion, celery and garlic and sweat for about 10 minutes.

In the meantime, season the chicken pieces. Heat the remaining tablespoon of oil in a frying pan and then tip out the excess. Fry the chicken, in batches if necessary, over a high heat until coloured on both sides. Add them to the casserole. Sprinkle over the flour and stir to coat the chicken pieces and vegetables.

Pour over the wine, stock and chopped tomatoes and add some seasoning. Tuck the whole chillies and rosemary sprigs in between the chicken pieces. (The chillies are included simply to flavour the stew, it's important that they don't break otherwise they will release their fiery heat.) Bring the liquid to a simmer, then cover the casserole and cook gently for 30 minutes.

Turn the chicken pieces and cook uncovered for a further 30 minutes. Meanwhile, mix together the ingredients for the gremolata in a small bowl. Skim off any fat from the surface of the stew and remove the chillies and rosemary. Serve the stew with the gremolata scattered over.

'Guinea' Coq au vin

Just to prove that anything chicken can do guinea fowl can do better, here's a favourite classic, replete with button mushrooms and baby onions. You'll need something for mopping up all the rich red juices, some warm crusty bread. The red wine needn't be anything special— cheap, cheerful and with plenty of character. This is a casserole that reheats well, with the added advantage if you allow it to cool completely that you can scrape off any fat that has collected on the surface. If you buy your guinea fowl from a butcher, talk him into jointing it for you.

Serves 3
1 tablespoon vegetable oil
1.2 kg guinea fowl, jointed into
   8 pieces
   Sea salt, black pepper
75 g unsmoked streaky bacon, rind
   removed and sliced
1 heaped tablespoon flour
600 ml red wine
150 ml chicken stock
1 bay leaf
2 thyme sprigs
10 g unsalted butter
100 g baby onions, peeled
100 g button mushrooms, stalks
   trimmed if necessary
   Coarsely chopped flat-leaf
   parsley, to serve

Preheat the oven to 180°C, fan oven 170°C, gas 4. Heat the oil in a flameproof casserole over a medium-high heat (Use a casserole that will hold the guinea fowl pieces snugly in a single layer.) Season the guinea fowl with salt and pepper and fry them in the casserole, in batches if necessary, until coloured on both sides. Transfer to a bowl.

Add the bacon to the casserole and fry, stirring, until it just begins to colour. Return the guinea fowl to the casserole, sprinkle over the flour and cook, turning the pieces, for about 1 minute. Pour over the red wine and chicken stock, and add the bay leaf and thyme. Heat the liquid until it just begins to bubble, then put the lid on the casserole and cook in the oven for 50 minutes, basting the guinea fowl halfway through.

On removing the casserole from the oven, melt the butter in a small frying pan over a low heat. Add the onions and fry, turning them frequently, for about 7 minutes. Add the mushrooms and cook for a further 3 minutes until they are all softened and lightly golden. Meanwhile, carefully skim off any fat from the surface of the casserole. Stir in the mushrooms and onions. Serve on warm plates, sprinkled with parsley.

Devilled Drumsticks

Drumsticks conveniently present a protruding knuckle to serve as finger food, but they are the last ingredient to economise on. Aside from the importance of flavour and texture, the sheer water content of inferior poultry will prevent chicken drumsticks from emerging from the oven coated in a thick sticky goo. This should be every bit as salty and concentrated as the residue from a roast. The chilli sauce should be the Thai variety, which is not overly fiery.

Makes 12
12 free-range chicken drumsticks

Marinade
6 tablespoons groundnut oil
3 tablespoons tomato ketchup
3 tablespoons Worcestershire
   sauce
2 heaped teaspoons Dijon mustard
3 teaspoons chilli sauce
1 tablespoon dark brown sugar
1½ teaspoons sea salt
2 tablespoons white wine vinegar
   Juice of 1 lemon
1 tablespoon grated ginger
1 tablespoon minced garlic

Combine all the ingredients for the marinade in an airtight container that will hold the chicken. Add the drumsticks and coat thoroughly. Leave to marinate in the fridge overnight, basting once.

Preheat the oven to 230°C, fan oven 220°C, gas 8. Lay the chicken drumsticks on a rack over a baking tray and spoon over a little of the marinade. Roast for 25–30 minutes until the drumsticks are deep golden and caramelised at the edges. Serve hot or cold.

Lemon Chicken in Paper with Straw Potatoes

This is chicken and chips of a kind that emerge steamy and scented from their paper casing. One joy is the texture retained by the potatoes—silky on the outside but retaining a certain bite within. Lemon, garlic and parsley complete the picture. Follow with a green salad.

Serves 4
600 g large new potatoes
4 free-range chicken breasts, with skin
Extra virgin olive oil
Sea salt, black pepper
Finely grated zest of 1 lemon
1 garlic clove, peeled and finely chopped
2 tablespoons chopped parsley
75 g unsalted butter
4 tablespoons lemon juice

Preheat the oven to 190°C, fan oven 180°C, gas 5. Peel the potatoes and cut into matchsticks, 5mm square and about 7cm long; set aside in a bowl of cold water. Heat a cast-iron frying pan over a medium heat. Lightly coat the chicken breasts with olive oil and season. Add to the pan and colour on both sides.

Cut four 37cm squares of baking parchment and lay out on the work surface. Divide the potatoes between them, piling them in the centre. Season and mix in the lemon zest, garlic and parsley. Dot with the butter, place the chicken breasts on top and drizzle over the lemon juice. To seal the packages, pleat the long edges together, then fold in the sides. Place folded-side up on a baking tray and bake for 30 minutes. The potatoes will remain slightly firm and be coated in a lemony butter.

Pot-roast Chicken with a Watercress Sauce

As a recommendation for its ability to perform under extreme conditions, this recipe began life in a gite in France. Predictably enough the gite had a plastic garden table in lieu of a dinner table that rocked and contorted every time you sliced a baguette, a gas oven that drowned out all conversation and left you wondering whether you'd get through the night, just the one serrated knife and a melamine chopping board. But experiences like that reaffirm what we all know, that you can produce extraordinarily good food with very little in the way of equipment, even if it is frustrating. As long as your chicken is of good character, your watercress a fat, glossy bunch, your crème fraîche as sour, yellow and alive with likeable bacteria as it should be, you can't go far wrong.

Serves 4
1.6 kg free-range chicken
Vegetable oil
Sea salt, black pepper
2 bay leaves
3 thyme sprigs
150 ml white wine
150 ml chicken stock or water
1 heaped teaspoon beurre manié (equal quantity of flour and butter mashed together)
1 bunch of watercress, about 100g, trimmed and chopped
3 tablespoons crème fraîche

Preheat the oven to 190°C, fan oven 180°C, gas 5. Coat the chicken with oil and season it. Heat a frying pan, add the chicken and colour it on all sides, then place it breast-side up in a large flameproof casserole. Add the herbs, the wine and stock or water, bring this to a simmer, then cover and cook in the oven for 55 minutes. Check it halfway through cooking and if it appears to be drying out add another 50–100ml water. Uncover the chicken and leave it to rest in the pan for 15 minutes. Remove the chicken to a plate, pouring any juices inside back into the pan.

Carve the chicken into hearty chunks. Skim any excess fat off the juices in the pan and remove the herbs. Bring back to the boil, add the beurre manié in tiny pieces and stir until it has melted. Stir in the watercress and the crème fraîche and taste for seasoning. Allow this to heat through and serve poured over the chicken.

Guinea Fowl Fricassée with Young Vegetables

The vegetables are young and sweet, and cosseted separately from the bird, only making its acquaintance at the very end in a creamy broth. If you buy your guinea fowl from a butcher then you can prevail upon him to do the jointing—hacking up birds is best left to the professionals.

Serves 4
1.5 kg guinea fowl, jointed into 8 pieces
Groundnut oil
Sea salt, black pepper
200 ml dry cider
4 tarragon sprigs
4 small turnips, about 5cm across
175 g carrots
1 bunch of slim spring onions, (about 8)
25 g unsalted butter
Pinch of caster sugar
100 g young fresh or frozen broad beans
150 g crème fraîche

Heat a large flameproof casserole over a high heat. Brush the guinea fowl pieces all over with oil and season with salt and pepper. Fry them in the casserole in two batches to colour on both sides; remove the pieces as they are ready. Return all the guinea fowl to the casserole. Add the cider, which will boil instantly, and tuck in the tarragon sprigs. Cover and cook on a very low heat for 45 minutes.

In the meantime, prepare the vegetables. Trim, peel and quarter the turnips. Trim and peel the carrots, and unless they are very young, slice them diagonally into 1cm thick slices. Trim the spring onions and cut off the dark green parts so they are about 7cm in length. Finely slice and reserve a couple of tablespoons of the green parts for garnishing. Melt the butter in a medium saucepan. Add the carrots, turnips, sugar, a pinch of salt and 150ml water. Bring to a simmer, then cover and cook over a low heat for 7 minutes. Add the spring onions and broad beans and cook for a further 3 minutes.

Once the guinea fowl is cooked, remove the pieces to a bowl and cover to keep warm. Simmer the juices over a high heat until visibly rich, reducing them by about half. Add the crème fraîche and simmer for a minute longer, then taste for seasoning. Strain the vegetables, add them to the sauce and return the guinea fowl to the pan. Serve the fricassée on warmed plates scattered with the sliced green spring onion.

Glazed Duck

A perfectly plain roast duck, glazed and golden. Delicious served with salads. If you are after some gravy, try to buy a duck with its giblets, and proceed as for Giblet Gravy, (see page 219).

Serves 2–3
2 tablespoons honey
2 tablespoons brandy
Sea salt, black pepper
2 kg oven-ready duck

Preheat the oven to 200°C, fan oven 190°C, gas 6. Blend the honey and brandy together in a bowl. Season the duck all over and place it breast-side up on a roasting rack, over a roasting tray which contains a mug of boiling water. Don't pierce the duck skin.

Roast the duck for 20 minutes, then turn it over, baste the top with half of the glaze and roast for another 25 minutes. Turn breast-side up again, baste with the remaining glaze and give it a final 20 minutes. If at any point the sugars in the glaze appear to be burning at the edges of the roasting pan, add a little more boiling water. Rest the duck in a warm place for 15 minutes before carving.

Grilled Marinated Quail

The author of these quail is the quizzically ironic Fergus Henderson, proprietor chef of St. John in Smithfield. He describes quail as 'a rather maligned bird, that quite enjoys a certain firmness in handling'. Henderson recommends serving these with a 'spirited aioli' (see recipe on page 210). You may find it more relaxing to cook these birds outside where the smoke emitted in rendering them perfectly succulent isn't a concern. An indoor griddle is good for half the number specified. They make a fine match for Savoury Lentils (see page 167).

Serves 6
12 quails
Sea salt

Marinade
1 tablespoon finely chopped thyme
1 tablespoon finely chopped garlic
1 tablespoon finely chopped
   medium-hot red chilli, deseeded
200 ml extra virgin olive oil
   Black pepper

Snip out the quails' backbones (not the breastbone) using scissors; if possible, get your butcher to do this for you. Press down with the palm of your hand to flatten the birds spatchcock fashion. Combine the thyme, garlic and chilli with the oil and some pepper. Place the quail in a large shallow container and smear the marinade over them. Cover and leave to marinate in the fridge overnight.

Season the quail with salt and cook them flesh-side down on a medium-low griddle for 12 minutes, then turn and cook on the other side for 10 minutes. Alternatively cook the quail on a barbecue.

Char-grilled Chicken with Roasted Chilli and Thyme Glaze

If you are planning on eating outdoors, you cannot do better than change tack from chicken breasts to spatchcock poussin that grill to an especially sticky finger-licking finish. These small chickens —opened out at the breastbone and flattened like butterflies—can be allowed the necessary space to spread themselves on an outside grill. As to spatchcocking your poussins, you do have to split them to within a few millimetres of the breastbone with a kung fu stroke of a cleaver. Much easier, ask your butcher to do it for you.

Serves 6
6 free-range chicken breasts, with
   skin, or spatchcock poussin

Roasted garlic
6 heads of garlic
   Few thyme sprigs
4 tablespoons olive oil
   Sea salt, black pepper

Glaze
4 plum tomatoes, halved
1 red chilli
2 tablespoons extra virgin olive oil
2 teaspoons soft thyme leaves
1 teaspoon clear honey

To serve
Lemon wedges
Watercress

For the roasted garlic, preheat the oven to 150°C, fan oven 140°C, gas 2. Cut the top off each head of garlic to reveal the cloves and place them in a shallow baking dish. Tuck the thyme sprigs between the heads of garlic. Pour over the olive oil, season and cover with foil. Place the plum tomatoes, cut-side up, and the chilli beside the garlic

and bake for 1¼ hours. Baste the garlic every so often and remove the foil for the last 30 minutes.

To prepare the glaze, combine the olive oil, thyme leaves, honey and seasoning in a small bowl. Remove the seeds from the roast chilli. Put the chilli and tomatoes in a food processor and work to a purée. Pass through a sieve into the bowl containing the oil and honey mixture, and blend together.

Heat a ridged iron griddle, and heat the oven to 190°C, fan oven 180°C, gas 5. Season the chicken breasts or poussin and grill skin-side down for 7 minutes until the skin is nice and golden. Turn and grill the other side for 3 minutes. Place skin-side up in a roasting dish or on a baking tray and smooth the glaze over the skin. Cook in the oven for about 8 minutes. If necessary reheat the garlic in the oven; it should be warm rather than hot, as the cloves will be squeezed out using fingers.

Serve the chicken with the roasted garlic and some of its oil. Accompany with lemon wedges and watercress.

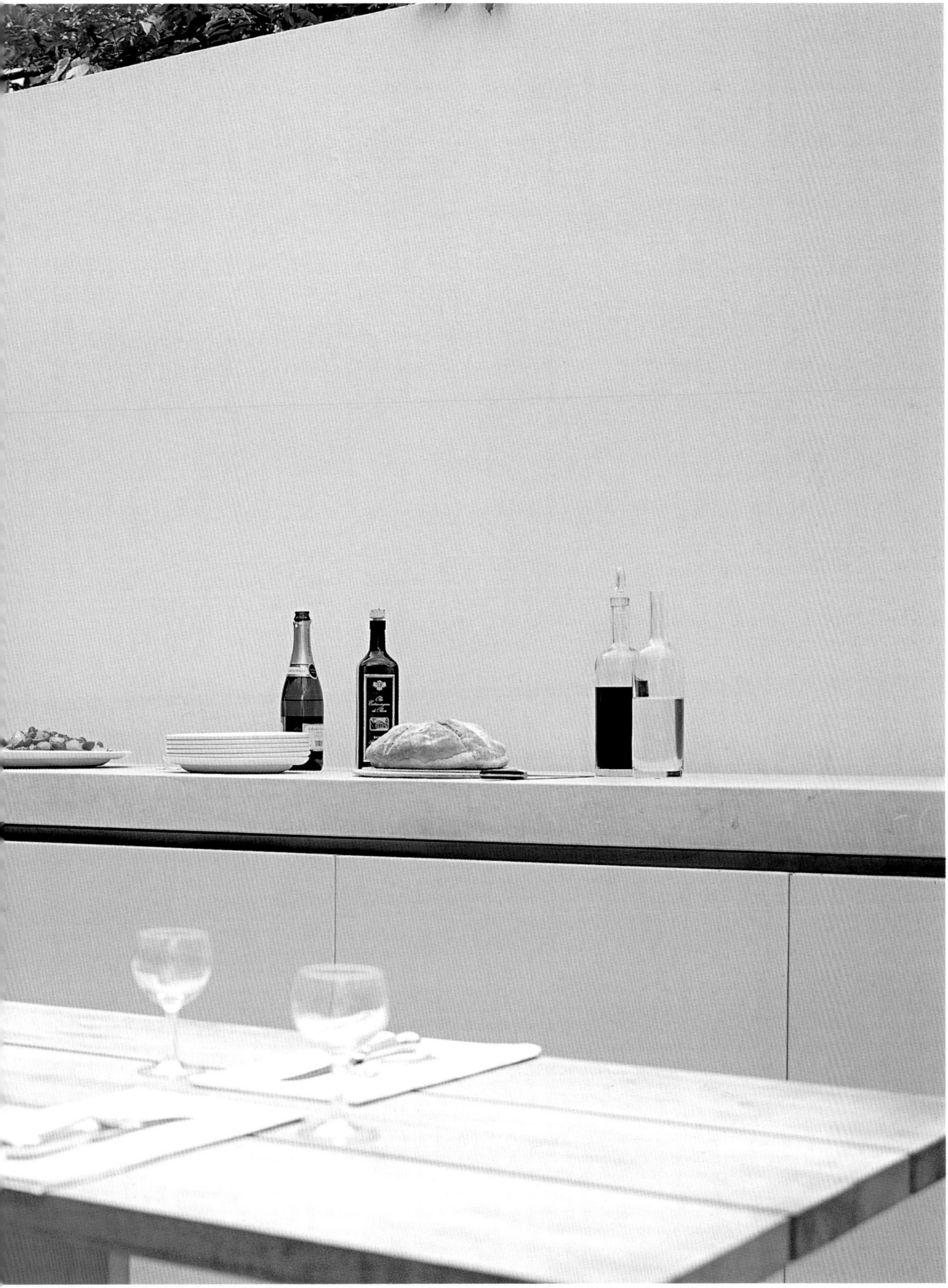

Parmesan-grilled Chicken Breasts

Chicken breasts wrapped in Parma ham, smothered with mascarpone and sprinkled with Parmesan before being shown a hot grill.

Serves 4
- 4 free-range chicken breasts, skinned
- 1 large organic egg
- Sea salt, black pepper
- 75 g fresh white breadcrumbs
- 3 tablespoons extra virgin olive oil
- 4 slices of Parma ham
- 2 tablespoons mascarpone
- 25 g Parmesan cheese, freshly grated

Remove the tendon from the thin inner fillet of each chicken breast. Whisk the egg in a shallow bowl with some seasoning; place the breadcrumbs in another shallow bowl, again seasoning them. Dip the chicken breasts first into the beaten egg and then into the breadcrumbs. Do this twice; pressing the crumbs into the flesh to ensure they adhere.

Heat the oil in a large frying pan on a medium heat. Fry the chicken, in two batches, for 4 minutes each side until evenly golden, scraping out any loose crumbs from the pan in between. Once cooked, transfer to a shallow gratin or other ovenproof dish. Cover loosely with foil while you cook the rest. Heat the grill towards the end of frying.

Lay a slice of Parma ham over the top of each breast, spoon the mascarpone down the centre and scatter the Parmesan on top. Place under the grill for a few minutes until the Parmesan is golden and the mascarpone is melted and sizzling. Serve at once.

Chicken Breasts Escoffier

If you have ever secretly harboured a craving for chicken nuggets, this is the socially acceptable take. It was originally the inspiration of the late great Escoffier and reinterpreted by Alice Waters in California. Both are advocates of the 'faite simple' school of cookery, which here involves elegantly slim chicken escalopes dipped in butter, coated in breadcrumbs and fried until crisp in more butter. The final gesture is a drizzle of butter and a few succinct drops of lemon juice.

Serves 4
- 225 g unsalted butter
- 2 large free-range chicken breasts, skinned
- Sea salt, black pepper
- 100 g fresh breadcrumbs
- 250 g cherry tomatoes
- Lemon wedges, to serve

To clarify the butter, gently melt it in a saucepan. Skim off the surface foam and decant the clear yellow liquid, discarding the milky residue in the bottom.

Slice the chicken into two long escalopes and remove the tendons. Fold the inner fillets to the side so they are evenly thick, and season the chicken breasts. Place half the clarified butter in a shallow dish and scatter the breadcrumbs on a plate. Dip the chicken breasts in the butter to coat both sides, then pat them in the breadcrumbs to form a crust. Set aside for 10 minutes.

Heat half the remaining butter in a cast-iron frying pan over a medium heat. When hot, put the chicken breasts in the pan and season with salt and pepper.

Reduce the heat to medium-low and sauté for 4–5 minutes each side; the crust should be a rich golden brown.

Heat the remaining butter in a small saucepan. Transfer the chicken breasts to warm plates and add the tomatoes to the frying pan. Turn the heat up and cook for 1–2 minutes tossing and seasoning them. Drizzle the hot melted butter over the chicken breasts and place the cherry tomatoes alongside. Serve with the lemon wedges.

Chicken Breasts in Vinaigrette with Pine Nuts and Raisins

There is something sweet, sour and Magreb about this, which makes it a summer thing. Time it with a spell of good weather and serve with a Classic Tomato Salad (see page 182) if you like.

Serves 4
150 ml white wine
300 ml chicken stock
    Sea salt, black pepper
4 free-range chicken breasts, skinned
50 g pine nuts
30 ml white wine vinegar
1 bay leaf
½ cinnamon stick, about 5cm long
½ teaspoon caster sugar
6 tablespoons extra virgin olive oil
25 g raisins
    Small handful of green or opal basil leaves, roughly torn

Pour the wine into a small saucepan, bring to the boil and reduce to a couple of tablespoons. Add the stock, season and bring back to the boil. Add the chicken breasts pressing them down so they are submerged, and once the liquid is simmering again, cover and cook gently for 5 minutes. Remove from the heat and leave to cool in the saucepan.

Preheat the oven to 190°C, fan oven 180°C, gas 5. Lay the pine nuts out in a baking dish and toast them in the oven for 8–10 minutes until lightly golden.

Remove the cooled chicken from the pan and reserve 150ml of the liquid in the pan (save the rest for soup). Slice the chicken breasts and arrange on a plate. Add the wine vinegar, bay leaf, cinnamon stick and sugar to the reserved liquid.

Bring to a simmer and cook for 10 minutes. Pour into a bowl, discarding the bay leaf and cinnamon, and allow to cool. Season the chicken, scatter over the pine nuts and raisins and pour the cooled liquid and olive oil over it. Scatter over the basil to serve.

Moroccan Chicken Salad with Preserved Lemon

If you are not already a fan of Moroccan preserved lemons, one taste and you will wonder why you haven't made their acquaintance sooner. Like capers and olives they cast an intense magic in the most minute quantity. In fact only a small amount is ever needed. Most of us don't keep these to hand, and if this is the case and shops fail you, follow the steps below for almost instant preserved lemons.

Serves 6
6 free-range chicken
  breasts, skinned

Poaching liquor
850 ml chicken stock
  1 cinnamon stick, about 7cm long
  6 cardamom pods
  ⅓ teaspoon coriander seeds
  8 black peppercorns
  ¼ teaspoon ground ginger
  ½ teaspoon sea salt

Dressing
 30 saffron threads
  ¾ preserved lemon, soaked in
    water for 30 minutes
  8 tablespoons extra virgin olive oil
  1 medium-hot red chilli, seeds
    removed and finely chopped
  6 tablespoons coarsely
    chopped coriander

Put all the ingredients for the poaching liquor in a large saucepan and bring to the boil. Cover and simmer over a low heat for 10 minutes. Add the chicken breasts, which should be submerged by the liquid. Turn the heat up and bring back to the boil, then cover and poach over a low heat for 4 minutes. Remove from the heat and leave the chicken to cool and marinate overnight.

To assemble the dish, put the saffron threads in a bowl, add 1 tablespoon boiling water and leave to infuse for 30 minutes. Remove the chicken from the poaching liquor and slice it thickly across the grain. Place in a shallow dish. Cut the preserved lemon into thin segments discarding any pips, then slice finely.

Pour the olive oil and infused saffron liquid over the chicken and add the lemon and chilli. (You shouldn't need to add salt, as the preserved lemon provides enough.) Gently toss the chicken to coat in the dressing. Cover and leave in a cool place until required. Toss the chopped coriander into the salad just before serving.

Preserved lemons
To prepare your own preserved lemons, incise the skin of 6 lemons into quarters. Place in a saucepan that holds them snugly in a single layer. Add 4 tablespoons sea salt and just enough water to cover. Boil for 30 minutes, then transfer to a jar or bowl, making sure the lemons are covered by the liquid. Leave to steep for several days.

God made one side of a T-bone steak larger than the other, demanding either a small appetite or a certain largesse from one of two diners. There again, he was at least kind enough to divide it into sirloin and fillet, his and hers.

Serves 2
25 g unsalted butter
1 tablespoon groundnut oil
Sea salt, black pepper
1 T-bone steak, about 650g, 2cm thick
100 g shallots, peeled and thinly sliced crossways
90 ml Madeira

Heat the butter and oil in a 25cm frying pan over a medium heat. Once the butter foam begins to subside, season the steak and add to the pan. Fry for 3–5 minutes each side to cook it medium-rare. There should be a degree of give in the flesh when you press it; cook for a little longer if it feels overly soft. Transfer the steak to a warm plate and leave to rest for 5 minutes, covering with foil to keep warm.

Meanwhile, add the shallots to the frying pan and cook for about 3 minutes, stirring occasionally until soft and starting to caramelise. Tip out any excess fat from the pan, add the Madeira to deglaze and simmer for a few minutes more until sticky and reduced. Taste and season the sauce if necessary. Divide the steak into sirloin and fillet, cutting it off the bone. Serve with the sauce spooned over.

The rank salty pungency of good Roquefort doesn't come cheap, but its charm spreads itself far and wide, here dripping in buttery rivulets down a thick slab of fillet steak.

Serves 4
1 tablespoon groundnut oil
4 fillet steaks, each about 175g, 2cm thick
Sea salt, black pepper
50 g unsalted butter, diced
3 tablespoons port

Roquefort butter
40 g Roquefort, crumbled
60 g unsalted butter, softened
Generous dash of Tabasco

To serve
Watercress

First make the Roquefort butter. In a bowl, blend the cheese and butter with the Tabasco. Form into a sausage shape on a piece of clingfilm and roll it up, smoothing it into a cylindrical shape by twisting the ends. Chill until required.

Heat the oil in a large frying pan over a medium heat. If your frying pan isn't large enough to hold all the steaks then heat two pans, adding a tablespoon of oil to each one. Season the steaks with salt and pepper. Add to the pan(s) and cook for 3 minutes, then add the butter, which will fizzle. Immediately turn the steaks and cook for 3 minutes on the other side.

Preheat the grill. Transfer the steaks to a warm plate to rest for a few minutes, covering with foil to keep warm.

Add the port to the pan to deglaze and once it stops seething, cook for a moment longer scraping up any caramelised bits on the bottom. Add any juices given out by the steak during resting.

Place the steaks on warm plates, spooning over the sauce, and dot each with a couple of slices of Roquefort butter. Flash the plates under the grill until this begins to melt. Place a pile of watercress on the side of each plate and serve.

Glossy watercress and a pan of sautéed potatoes are the most desirable accompaniments here.

Serves 2
2 sirloin steaks, each about 200g
Vegetable oil

Garlic butter
1 garlic clove, peeled
Sea salt, black pepper
50 g unsalted butter, softened
1 tablespoon finely chopped parsley
1 shallot, peeled and finely chopped
1 teaspoon brandy

Prepare the garlic butter in advance. Either purée the garlic in a press, or chop it on a board and sprinkle with salt then crush to a paste. Blend together with the remaining ingredients in a bowl, and chill until needed.

Heat a frying pan over a medium-high heat for several minutes. When it is hot, brush the steaks on both sides with oil, season with salt and pepper and add to the pan. Fry for 2 minutes each side to cook them medium-rare, there should be a degree of give in the flesh when you press it. Cook for a little longer if it feels very soft. Transfer to a warm plate and leave to rest for 5 minutes, covering with foil to keep warm. Meanwhile, preheat the grill.

Place the sirloin steaks on warm plates, spooning over any juices given out while resting, and dot with dollops of garlic butter. Flash the plates under the grill until the butter melts to leave soft mounds of parsley.

Steak 'au Poivre'

In our experience, most recipes for steak 'au poivre' do ignite your palate, but this one is different, having abandoned black peppercorns in favour of milder green ones pickled in brine. They don't cling to the steak in quite the same fashion, but just enough adhere to provide the right piquancy. A pile of salad leaves will temper things nicely, and some sautéed potatoes.

Serves 2
2 tablespoons green peppercorns in brine, rinsed
2 fillet steaks, each about 175g, 2cm thick
Sea salt
1 tablespoon extra virgin olive oil
25 g unsalted butter, diced
Generous dash of brandy

Coarsely chop the peppercorns on a board and spread them into a thin layer. Season the steaks with salt and press each side into the peppercorns to sparsely coat. Heat the olive oil in a frying pan over a medium heat. Add the steaks and cook for 3 minutes, then add the butter, which will fizzle. Immediately turn the steaks and cook for 3 minutes on the other side. Don't expect the peppercorns to cling in quite the same way as black and white ones, any that fall off will turn nicely golden and crunchy. Transfer the steaks to a warm plate to rest for a few minutes, and keep warm.

Standing well back in case it ignites, add the brandy to the pan. Once this stops seething, cook it for a moment longer scraping up any caramelised bits on the bottom. Serve the steaks with the juices spooned over.

Turkish Lamb Kebabs with Garlic Yoghurt

These are perfect for an outdoor grill or picnic. As well as the provocative scent of meat sizzling on the grill, they can be eaten held in hand which does away with the need for plates, knives and forks.

Serves 4
½ deboned leg of lamb, about 750g
4 small tomatoes
100 g shallots, peeled, and halved if large
Black pepper

Marinade
2 teaspoons cumin seeds
1 dried red chilli
3 tablespoons extra virgin olive oil
Finely grated zest of 1 lemon
3 garlic cloves, peeled
Sea salt

Garlic yoghurt
1 garlic clove, peeled
225 g Greek yoghurt
1 tablespoon lemon juice

To serve
4 pitta breads
4 large handfuls of lamb's lettuce or mixed salad leaves
Groundnut oil, for dressing
Squeeze of lemon juice
4 lemon wedges

To prepare the marinade, grind the cumin seeds and dried chilli to a coarse powder using a pestle and mortar. In a large bowl, blend the ground spices with the olive oil and lemon zest. Either purée the garlic in a press, or chop it on a board and sprinkle with salt then crush to a paste using the flat edge of a knife. Whisk the garlic into the marinade.

Trim the lamb of any fat, then cut into 3cm cubes. Add the lamb to the marinade and toss to coat. Cover and leave to marinate in the fridge for at least 2 hours, preferably overnight, turning it once.

For the garlic yoghurt, purée the garlic as above, and then blend it in a bowl with the yoghurt, lemon juice and a little salt (if you haven't used any in crushing the garlic). Cover and chill until required.

Thread the lamb, whole tomatoes and shallots on to four 20cm skewers, alternating the vegetables with two cubes of meat. You should have one tomato and a couple of shallots (or shallot halves) on each skewer. Heat a ridged griddle on a medium-low heat. Brush the vegetables with any excess marinade and season the kebabs with salt and pepper. Grill for 5 minutes each side, about 20 minutes in total.

In the meantime, heat the oven to about 180°C, fan oven 170°C, gas 4 and warm the pitta breads for the last 5 minutes of the kebab cooking time. Or toast them briefly on each side on an outdoor grill if using. Place the salad leaves in a bowl and toss with just enough groundnut oil to coat. Squeeze over a few drops of lemon juice, scatter with a few flakes of sea salt and toss again.

Place a pile of salad leaves on each plate, with a kebab on top and spoon over the garlic yoghurt. Accompany with lemon wedges. Halve the warm pitta breads and serve alongside.

If you had to name the all-time favourite British dish—the one that expatriates lie around dreaming of —this would have to be it. But forget the baloney about serving it with Champagne—stick to claret.

Serves 6

2 tablespoons groundnut oil

3 shallots, peeled and
  finely chopped

1 large or 2 small carrots, peeled
  and thinly sliced

1 leek, trimmed, halved and
  thinly sliced

2 celery sticks (preferably inner
  ones), trimmed and thinly sliced

1 bay leaf

2 thyme sprigs

750 g minced lamb

150 ml red wine

2 tablespoons tomato ketchup

1 teaspoon Worcestershire sauce
  Sea salt, black pepper

Mash

1.3 kg maincrop potatoes, peeled
  and halved or quartered if large

120 g unsalted butter, diced, plus an
  extra knob

3 tablespoons milk

Heat the oil in a large saucepan, add the vegetables and herbs and sweat over a low heat for about 8 minutes until glossy and tender. Add the mince, turn the heat up and cook, stirring, until it colours and separates. Add the red wine, tomato ketchup, Worcestershire sauce and some seasoning. Bring to a simmer and cook over a low heat for 15 minutes.

At the same time, prepare the mash. Either steam the potatoes or cook in boiling salted water until tender. Drain them into a sieve or colander and leave for a minute or two to allow the surface moisture to evaporate. Pass the potatoes through a mouli-legumes or a sieve back into the pan. Add the 120g butter, and once this has melted, stir in the milk and plenty of seasoning.

Skim any excess fat off the surface of the mince and discard the herbs. Transfer to a shallow ovenproof dish, measuring about 20 by 30cm. Spread the potato over the meat and fork the surface into a criss-cross of furrows. You can prepare the pie to this point in advance; cover and refrigerate until required.

Preheat the oven to 190°C, fan oven 180°C, gas 5. Dot the surface with butter and cook for 30–35 minutes until the mashed potato is crisp and golden.

Hamburgers

It seems far too obvious to state that great hamburgers rely on great meat. Yet one of the ironies of modern times is that increasingly the only way to a decent hamburger is to make one at home. We can blame this on the nature of mince, the perfect material for cheapskates to bulk out with anything and everything that takes their fancy, and they do. There is a fine dividing line—in reality a yawning cavern—between 'fine mince', and 'fine meat, minced.' It is the latter you want, which makes it more important than ever to visit the butcher. The best burgers are made with meat containing about 20–25% fat, so pass over the very leanest mince and go for one specked with white that will be nicely succulent once it's cooked.

Then there are the coals, essential in trying to create that flame-grilled flavour and sizzling golden outside that captures the juices inside. A barbecue does a fine job, and failing that a ridged griddle will sear and singe the meat nicely. Finally there are hamburger buns, which belong to that special breed of bread you can squish between your fingers to a solid pap. It's worrying how good this slightly sweet bread can taste wrapped around your burger, especially if it has sesame seeds on top. Beyond this any roll with a close crumb and a flimsy crust will do.

Serves 4

Burgers

450 g best minced beef
1 tablespoon finely
   chopped shallots
   Sea salt, black pepper

To serve

4 hamburger buns, slit in half
½ red onion, peeled, halved and
   thinly sliced
8 cocktail gherkins, sliced
   English mustard
   Tomato ketchup
½ beefsteak tomato, sliced

Mix together the mince, shallots and seasoning in a bowl. If you want perfectly shaped burgers, then mould the mince a quarter at a time inside a 10cm pastry cutter with smooth edges. Or, if you are happy with something more rustic, form the meat into balls using your hands, and then flatten these between your palms. Bear in mind that the burgers will shrink and fatten when you grill them. If you like you can make them in advance, then cover and chill until needed.

Heat a ridged griddle over a medium-low heat and cook the burgers for 4–5 minutes on each side. Either toast the buns on the griddle or under an ordinary grill. Combine the sliced onion and gherkins. Place a burger in each of the buns. Smear with some mustard and then plenty of tomato ketchup. Lay a slice of tomato on each burger and season, then scatter over some sliced onion and gherkin. Serve straightaway.

Middle Eastern Lamb Burgers

Lamb burgers greedily lap up the taste of the Levant—the charmed scents of cumin, coriander and cinnamon. Pop them into warm envelopes of pitta bread with a tomato, herb and olive salad relish.

Serves 4

Burgers

450 g best minced lamb
1 tablespoon finely
   chopped shallots
2 garlic cloves, peeled and
   finely chopped
2 teaspoons ground cumin
1 teaspoon ground coriander
1 teaspoon ground cinnamon
¼ teaspoon ground allspice
   Sea salt, black pepper

To serve

1 beefsteak tomato, skinned and
   cut into strips
1 large handful each of coriander
   and flat-leaf parsley sprigs
50 g black olives, pitted and halved
   Squeeze of lemon juice
4 pitta breads

Put all the burger ingredients in a bowl and mix thoroughly. Shape a quarter of the mixture at a time into a ball, then flatten to a burger 10cm in diameter. You can make these in advance, then cover and chill them.

Warm the oven to 180°C, fan oven 170°C, gas 4, and either heat a ridged griddle over a medium-low heat or a conventional grill to high. Combine the tomato, herbs, olives and lemon juice in a bowl; season. Cook the burgers for 4–5 minutes each side, putting the pitta bread into the oven to warm after the first side is cooked. Slit open the pittas and place a burger in each one with some of the salad. Serve at once.

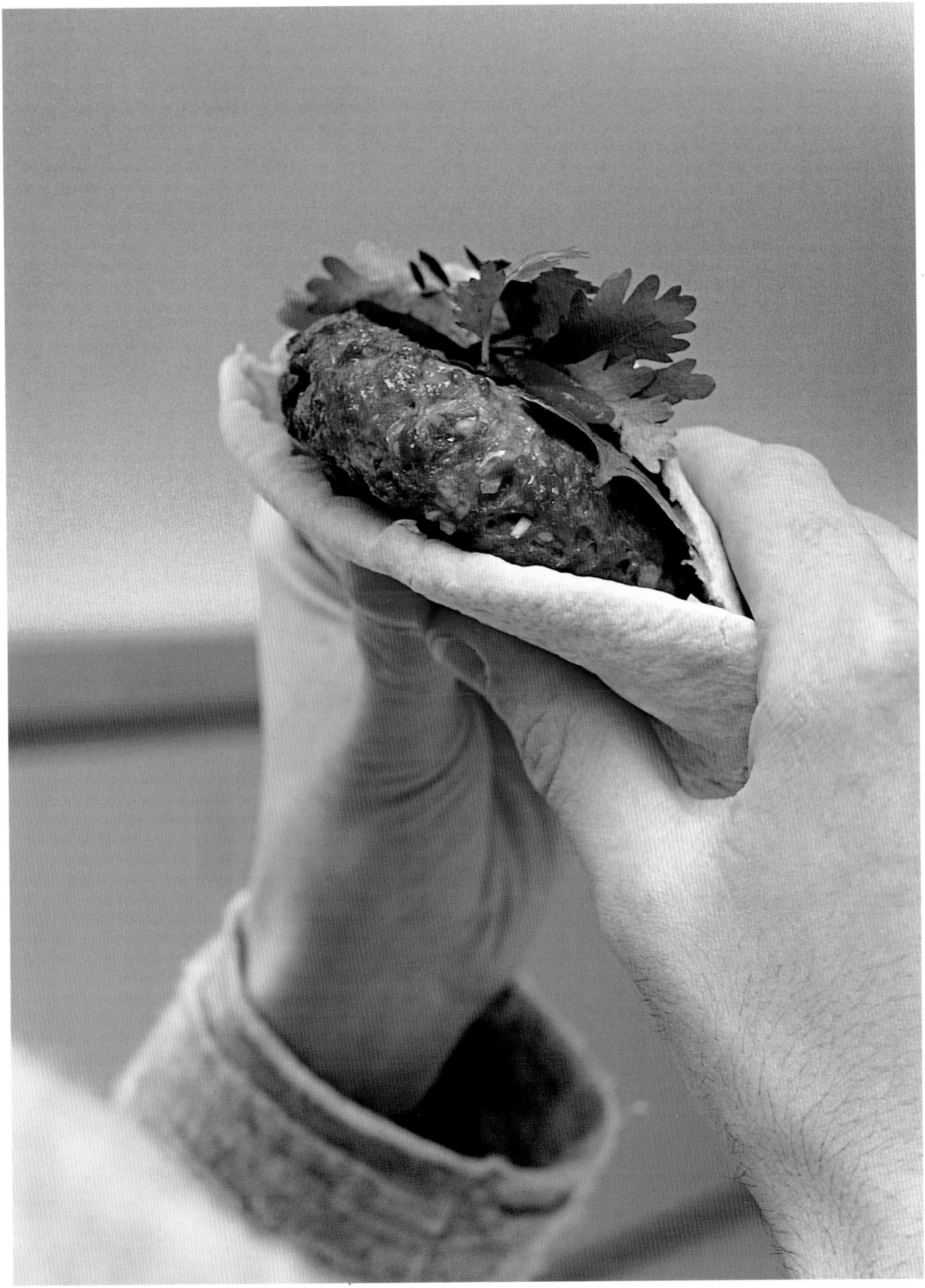

Pot-roasted Leg of Lamb with Black Olives

Alluring in a Provencal way and best enjoyed on its own, with perhaps some braised courgette flowers or roasted peppers afterwards. The lamb is beautifully succulent and tender. Even after 2 hours in a low oven, it's still pink in the centre.

Serves 6
3 tablespoons olive oil
2.7 kg leg of lamb
1 large onion, peeled, halved and sliced
2 tablespoons brandy
10 garlic cloves (1 head), peeled
1 beefsteak tomato, skinned, seeded and cut into strips
12 to 15 thyme sprigs, tied in a bundle with string
150 ml red wine
Sea salt, black pepper
180 g black olives (preferably Kalamata), rinsed and pitted

Preheat the oven to 170°C, fan oven 160°C, gas 3. Heat the olive oil in a large oval casserole and brown the lamb on all sides, then remove. Add the onion to the casserole and cook until it begins to caramelise. Return the lamb. Heat the brandy in a ladle and ignite, then pour over the lamb. Add the garlic, tomato, thyme, half the wine and some seasoning. Cover and cook in the oven for 1 hour, turning the leg halfway through.

Add the remaining red wine and the olives to the casserole and return to the oven for a further 1 hour. Take out of the oven and leave to rest for 15 minutes. Transfer the lamb to a plate and carve. Skim off the surface fat from the cooking liquor and discard the thyme. Serve the lamb with the olives and cooking liquor.

Roast Lamb 'Persillade'

An Eastertime celebration of lamb, not of the extortionate new season babes that have rarely seen a blade of grass and can be all too lacking in character, but rather of yearling sheep—hogget or hogs as they are fondly known. Come March or April, last year's late lambs from the north of England make superbly tender eating, with a rich rounded flavour and red flesh, having been grass-fed throughout their lives.

Serves 6
Sea salt, black pepper
1.8 to 2kg leg of lamb
1 head of garlic, broken into cloves

Persillade
1 heaped tablespoon finely chopped parsley
1 teaspoon finely chopped garlic
25 g breadcrumbs
1 teaspoon olive oil

Preheat the oven to 230°C, fan oven 220°C, gas 8. Season the lamb all over. Place the unpeeled garlic cloves in the middle of a roasting dish to form a bed for the joint and lay the lamb, lower side up, on top. Roast for 16 minutes per 500g to cook medium-rare, turning the meat halfway through cooking.

In the meantime, toss the ingredients for the persillade together in a bowl. About 8 minutes before the end of the roasting time, coat the top and sides of the lamb with the persillade, and return to the oven to colour. If you are planning on making gravy (see page 218), then transfer the roast to another baking dish before applying the persillade. Cover the joint with foil and leave it to rest in a warm place for 20 minutes before carving.

Roast Lamb with Flageolet Bean Gratin and Vine Tomatoes

Flageolet beans are demurely French, and most greengrocers in France sell them loose which is a good indication that they are nice and fresh. If they prove elusive, haricot or cannellini beans can be used in lieu.

Serves 6
Flageolet bean gratin
225 g dried flageolet beans, soaked overnight
2 garlic cloves, peeled
1 shallot, peeled and sliced
2 celery sticks, trimmed and sliced
1 large carrot, trimmed, peeled and sliced
1 bay leaf
120 g crème fraîche
Sea salt, black pepper
50 g breadcrumbs
4 heaped tablespoons freshly grated Parmesan cheese
25 g unsalted butter, melted

Lamb and gravy
2.2 kg leg of lamb
3 garlic cloves, peeled
25 g unsalted butter, softened
2 shallots, peeled and sliced
Few rosemary sprigs
75 ml red wine
1 scant teaspoon redcurrant jelly

Tomatoes
400 g small tomatoes on the vine
1 tablespoon groundnut oil
1 scant tablespoon balsamic vinegar

Preheat the oven to 180°C, fan oven 170°C, gas 4. Place the beans in a medium flameproof casserole and add sufficient water to cover by 5cm. Bring to the boil, then drain and return the beans to the casserole. Cover with water as before, this time adding the garlic,

vegetables and bay leaf. Bring to the boil, cover the casserole and cook in the oven for 50–60 minutes until the beans are tender. Drain them into a sieve discarding the bay leaf; remove some of the vegetables too, if you like, but this isn't essential. Reserve 200ml of the cooking liquor for the gravy. Return the beans to the casserole and mix with the crème fraîche and plenty of seasoning. Toss the breadcrumbs and Parmesan in a bowl with the melted butter and some seasoning, and scatter over the beans. The gratin can be prepared to this point in advance; cover and chill until required.

Preheat the oven to 220°C, fan oven 200°C, gas 7. Make incisions all over the top fatty side of the lamb, about 1cm deep. Slice the garlic, halve the slices lengthways and press into the incisions. Smear the butter over the joint and season. Lay the shallots and rosemary in the centre of a roasting tin that will hold the joint quite snugly (with the knuckle if you have it). Place the lamb on top and pour 75ml water into the tin. Roast for 17 minutes per 500g for medium-rare meat, or 20 minutes per 500g if you like it medium cooked. For a smaller joint of about 1.3kg, increase the time by 3 minutes per 500g. Twenty minutes before the end of the roasting time, put the gratin in the oven to cook for 30 minutes.

Transfer the lamb to a serving plate, cover with foil and leave to rest in a warm place for 20 minutes. Discard the knuckle and skim off any excess fat from the pan juices. Pour in the wine and

cook on the hob until well reduced, scraping up all the sticky bits on the bottom. Add the redcurrant jelly and mash this into the juices, then pour in the reserved bean cooking liquor and simmer for several minutes. Taste for seasoning.

Ten minutes into resting the lamb remove the gratin and cover with foil to keep warm. Turn the oven up to 250°C, fan oven 240°C, gas highest setting. Arrange the tomatoes in a roasting dish so they fit snugly in a single layer. Drizzle over the oil and balsamic vinegar, and season them. Roast for 10 minutes, by which time the tomatoes will be soft, the skins will have burst and the stalks blackened. For ease, serve them with the calyx attached, removing it as you eat.

Reheat the gravy if necessary, and strain it into a jug. Carve the lamb tipping any juices given out into the gravy jug. Serve on warmed plates with the gratin and tomatoes, accompanied separately by the gravy.

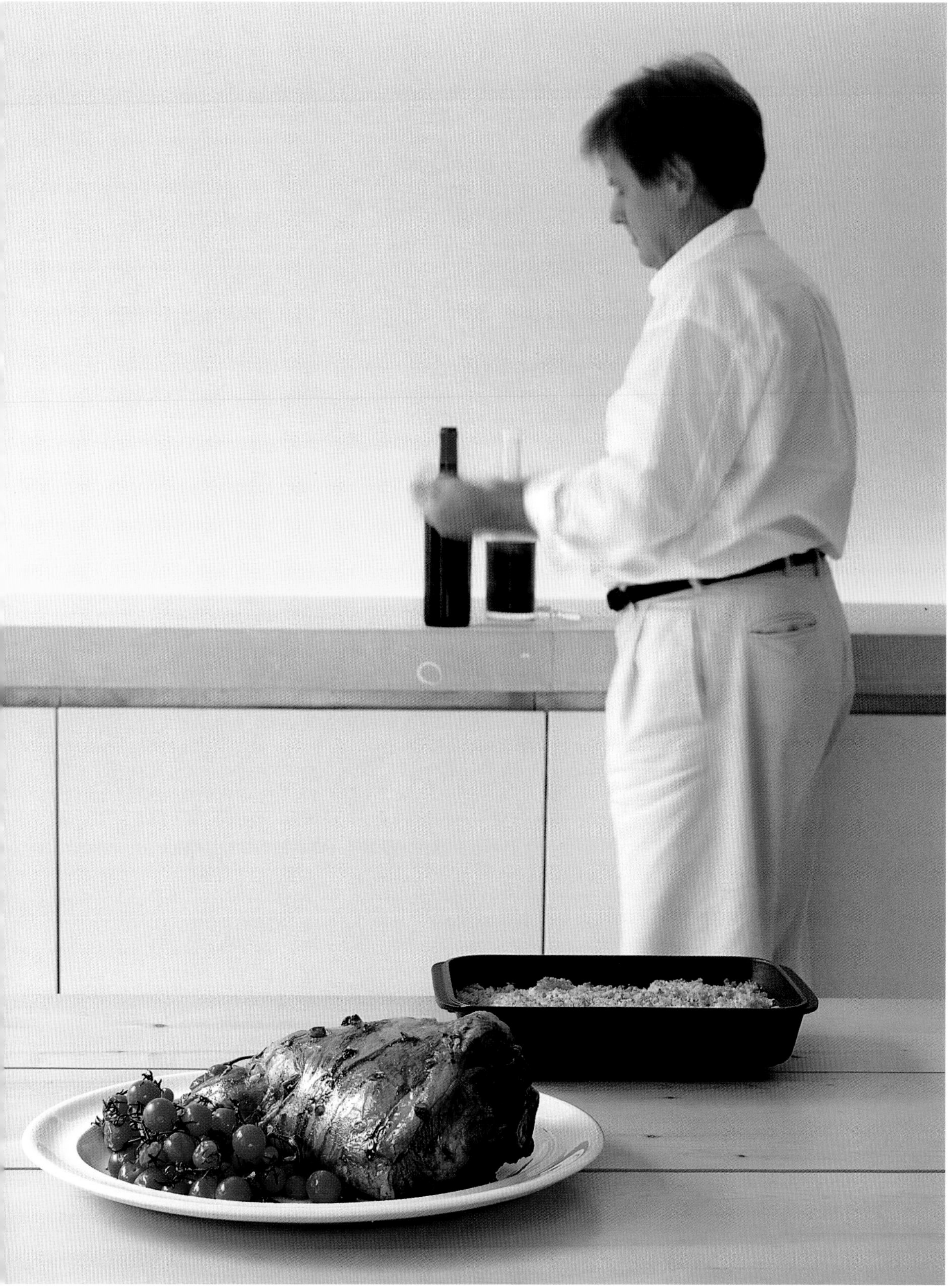

Roast Rib of Beef with Yorkshire Pudding

On top form this is one of the ultimate celebration lunches. So long as you have access to a good butcher there is no reason why the rib that graces your Sunday table should be any less than superlative. As this joint takes up most of the oven, mash is preferred to roast potatoes here. Equally it's less of a last-minute dash to make the Yorkshires in advance and reheat them to serve. The fiery nasal bite of fresh Horseradish Sauce (see page 214) completes the picture.

Serves 6
1 oven-ready 3-bone rib of beef
½ teaspoon plain flour
½ teaspoon English
  mustard powder
75 ml port
½ teaspoon Dijon mustard
175 ml beef stock
  Sea salt, black pepper

Take your joint out of the fridge an hour before roasting to bring it to room temperature. Preheat the oven to 250°C, fan oven 240°C, gas highest setting. Place the rib, fat-side up, in a roasting tin that holds it snugly. Sift the flour and mustard together, then dust over the fat using a fine-mesh sieve.

Roast the joint for 20 minutes, then turn the oven down to 190°C, fan oven 180°C, gas 5. Allow 14 minutes per 500g for rare meat; 17 minutes per 500g for medium-rare. We don't recommend cooking beef well done as it will toughen with prolonged cooking. Baste the joint every 20–30 minutes.

Transfer the beef to a serving plate, cover loosely with foil and leave to rest for 20 minutes in a warm place. In the meantime cook the Yorkshire puddings, or reheat them if baked ahead (see below).

Skim off any excess fat from the roasting juices. Add the port and cook on the hob for a few minutes until well reduced, scraping up all the sticky bits on the bottom. Stir in the Dijon mustard, then thin the gravy with the beef stock and simmer for several minutes. Check the seasoning. Carve the roast and add any juices given out during the process of carving to the gravy. Serve with the Yorkshire puddings.

Yorkshire puddings
110 g plain flour, sifted
½ teaspoon sea salt
2 medium organic eggs
150 ml milk
150 ml water
  Dripping, lard or vegetable oil,
  for greasing

Place the flour, salt, eggs, milk and water in a blender and blend until smooth and creamy. (Alternatively you can use a hand-held electric whisk.) Leave the batter to rest for 30 minutes.

Preheat the oven to 220°C, fan oven 200°C, gas 7. Liberally grease or oil two 12-hole bun or muffin tin trays and place in the oven to heat up for 10 minutes. Either re-whisk or blend the batter, two-thirds fill the greased tins and bake for 15–20 minutes until golden and risen.

Note

If preferred, you can cook the Yorkshire puddings ahead. Return to the oven 5 minutes before serving to heat through, putting the plates in to warm at the same time.

Roast Haunch of Venison with Gravy and Glazed Chicory

The stuff of which Sunday lunches are made. To go the whole hog serve this with the trimmings of your heart's desire—roast, mash potatoes, or Yorkshire pud and horseradish. We don't take as much notice of venison as we should, it is an animal that appeals to small producers and, as such, tends to be of high quality. The only rule is to either cook it rare, or to braise it very slowly for a long time, anywhere in between and it will be tough as old boots.

Serves 4–6
1.3 kg boned and rolled haunch of venison
Sea salt, black pepper
1 tablespoon vegetable oil

Chicory
1 tablespoon caster sugar
1½ teaspoons sea salt
700 g Belgian chicory heads
25 g unsalted butter

Gravy
1 teaspoon plain flour
150 ml red wine
1 heaped teaspoon redcurrant jelly
200 ml beef stock

To prepare the chicory, bring a large pan of water to the boil and add half the sugar and salt. Trim the brown base of the chicory bulbs, taking off as little as possible so they remain whole, and remove any damaged outer leaves. Boil for 20 minutes, then drain and leave them to cool.

Preheat the oven to 220°C, fan oven 200°C, gas 7. Season the venison joint all over with sea salt and pepper.

Heat the vegetable oil in a roasting tin (or a frying pan), add the venison and fry briefly, turning to colour it on all sides. Transfer to a roasting tin (if necessary). Roast the venison in the oven allowing 17 minutes per 500g if you like your meat medium-rare, or 14 minutes per 500g if you like it seriously rare. Baste the joint often.

Transfer the joint to a plate, cover loosely with foil and leave to rest for 15 minutes in a warm place while you make the gravy and finish the chicory. Squeeze the chicory heads with your hands to remove excess water, then sprinkle with the remaining salt and sugar. Heat the butter in a frying pan and cook the chicory on both sides until nicely caramelised and golden.

Spoon off excess fat in the roasting tin, leaving about a tablespoon. Add the flour and let this seethe for a moment on the hob. Add the red wine and stir, scraping up all the brown sticky bits on the bottom, then cook to reduce by about half. Add the redcurrant jelly, mashing it up to help it dissolve. Now pour in the beef stock and let it simmer for a few minutes while you carve the joint. Check the gravy for seasoning. Serve the venison with the chicory and gravy.

Roast Gammon with Pea Purée

This Slavic line-up should warm the cockles of the coldest heart mid-winter. Given the average summer day it's not inappropriate for that time of year either, and perfectly apt for a blustery outdoor lunch. Even if a serious weekend lunch isn't your intention, this way of roasting ham is to be recommended when you want to eat it cold. Of a weekday we would suggest foregoing poaching the vegetables in the name of ease. In theory, if the gammon is mildly cured, there should be no need to soak it. If in doubt, place it in a bowl or a saucepan, cover with plenty of cold water and leave overnight. It's worth doing this with supermarket gammon even when it says it is ready to roast. Serve with a dollop of fresh Horseradish Sauce (see page 214).

Serves 4–6

1.3 kg uncooked smoked gammon joint, boned and rolled
1 carrot, trimmed and sliced
1 celery heart, trimmed and sliced
1 leek, trimmed and sliced
8 black peppercorns
8 juniper berries
4 cloves
110 g clear honey
3 teaspoons Dijon mustard

Pea purée

350 g yellow split peas
1 bay leaf
1 tomato, halved
1 small onion, peeled and halved
Black pepper

Vegetables

4 carrots, peeled, and halved if long
2 celery hearts, trimmed and quartered lengthwise
25 g unsalted butter

Put the gammon in a saucepan, cover with cold water and bring to the boil. Discard the water and start again with fresh water to cover, this time adding the chopped vegetables, peppercorns, juniper berries and cloves. Bring to the boil, cover and simmer for 45 minutes.

To make the pea purée, put the split peas in a medium saucepan with the bay leaf, tomato, onion and 1.5 litres water. Bring to the boil, then skim off the surface foam. Turn the heat down to low, cover and simmer for 65–75 minutes.

Preheat the oven to 150°C, fan oven 140°C, gas 2. Blend the honey and mustard together in a small bowl. Lift the gammon out of the pan and place in a roasting tin; strain and reserve the stock. Cut off and discard the rind or any paper wrapped around the edge of the gammon, then coat the joint with half the honey mixture and roast for 30 minutes.

Turn the oven up to 220°C, fan oven 200°C, gas 7. Drain off any liquid in the roasting tin and coat the gammon with the remaining glaze. Return to the oven for 10 minutes. Cover the gammon loosely with foil and leave it to rest in a warm place for 15 minutes.

Once the split peas are tender, drain them discarding the bay leaf, and place in a food processor. Add 125ml of the gammon poaching stock, season with pepper (and salt if needed) and reduce to a purée. Return to the saucepan. The purée may seem rather sloppy at this stage but it will firm up by the time you eat.

While the ham is resting, put the carrots and celery in a medium saucepan. Add 2–3 ladlefuls of gammon stock, dot with the butter and season. Bring to the boil, then cover the pan and cook over a low heat for 10 minutes.

Gently reheat the pea purée and carve the gammon. Spoon the pea purée on to warm plates, lay the gammon slices on top and place a carrot and some celery to the side. Spoon a dollop of horseradish sauce over the ham and vegetables and serve.

Shortcrust Pastry

Perfectly acceptable shortcrust can be readily bought, although with a little extra effort you can whizz up something infinitely more delicious at home.

Makes 600g
350 g plain flour
½ teaspoon sea salt
200 g unsalted butter, diced
2 medium organic egg yolks

Place the flour and salt in a large bowl, add the butter and rub it in using your fingertips until the mixture resembles crumbs. (Alternatively, you can do this in a food processor or mixer.) Add the egg yolks, and a few drops of water if needed, to bind the pastry. Bring it together into a ball, wrap in clingfilm and chill for at least 1 hour, or overnight if more convenient. Knead the pastry until smooth and pliable before rolling it out.

Steak and Côtes de Rhône Pie with Mushrooms

As the canny cook knows, a steak pie is one of the more useful vehicles for entertaining on an informal basis, especially when the weather is cold. That and a large pot of mashed potato or buttery steamed potatoes on the stove.

Serves 6
600 g Shortcrust Pastry (see left)
1 organic egg yolk, mixed with 1 tablespoon milk

Filling
4 tablespoons vegetable oil
2 leeks, trimmed and sliced
1 celery heart, sliced
950 g chuck steak, trimmed of fat and diced
2 heaped tablespoons plain flour
90 ml medium sherry
200 ml Côtes de Rhône
200 ml beef stock or water
1 bay leaf
3 thyme sprigs
Sea salt, black pepper
250 g lamb's kidneys, fat removed, and sliced
200 g shiitake or other flavourful mushrooms, sliced

To make the filling, heat 2 tablespoons of the oil in a large saucepan or sauté pan. Add the leeks and celery and sweat over a low heat for about 8 minutes until soft and just beginning to colour, stirring occasionally. Transfer to a bowl, using a slotted spoon. You will need to sear the meat in two goes, turn the heat up, add half the meat to the pan and toss to seal on all sides, then remove and sear the remainder in the same way.

Return the meat and vegetables to the pan, sprinkle with the flour and stir to coat everything thoroughly. Pour over the sherry, wine and beef stock or water, stirring well to make a smooth sauce. Add the herbs and some seasoning. Bring to a simmer, then cover and braise gently over a low heat for 45 minutes, stirring occasionally.

In the meantime, heat half the remaining oil in a frying pan over a medium heat. Add the kidneys and toss to seal them, then remove. Heat the remaining oil in the pan, add the mushrooms and cook, tossing them, until they are soft and coloured, then add to the kidneys. Once the meat is cooked, remove the herbs and check the seasoning, then stir in the kidneys and mushrooms, and leave to cool.

Preheat the oven to 200°C, fan oven 190°C, gas 6. Roll out two thirds of the pastry thinly on a lightly floured surface and use to line a 2 litre pie dish, allowing some to overhang. Don't worry if you have to patch the pastry in places, it won't show once it's cooked. Tip the steak and kidney into the pastry case.

Roll out the remaining pastry for the lid, brush the pastry rim with eggwash and position the lid. Trim the pastry edges, leaving a good 1cm to allow for shrinkage; reserve the trimmings. Press the pastry edges together with a fork. Brush the top of the pie with eggwash. Cut out some leaves from the pastry trimmings, mark veins using the tip of a sharp knife, then position on top of the pie and brush them with eggwash. Bake the pie in the oven for 45–50 minutes until nice and golden. Serve at once.

Meatballs with Marjoram and Pine Nuts in Tomato Sauce

As an accompaniment to these meatballs, warm French bread is a lighter alternative to noodles, depending on appetites.

Serves 4

Meatballs

5 tablespoons extra virgin olive oil
1 onion, peeled and finely chopped
100 g rindless unsmoked streaky bacon, finely diced
3 tablespoons marjoram leaves
700 g minced beef
50 g pine nuts
1 medium organic egg yolk
Sea salt, black pepper

Tomato sauce

1 kg beefsteak or plum tomatoes
3 tablespoons tomato purée
1 tablespoon extra virgin olive oil
2 garlic cloves, peeled and finely chopped
1 dried red chilli, finely chopped
½ teaspoon caster sugar

To serve

250 g pappardelle, or other wide egg noodles
15 g unsalted butter
Freshly grated Parmesan

To prepare the meatballs, heat 2 tablespoons olive oil in a large frying pan over a medium-low heat and add the onion and bacon. Sweat gently, stirring occasionally, for about 5 minutes until soft and cooked through, adding the marjoram for the last 2 minutes. Transfer to a large bowl and leave to cool. Add the minced beef, pine nuts, egg yolk and some seasoning, and work together using a spoon. Shape the mixture into balls, the size of a large walnut, and set aside on a plate.

To make the tomato sauce, bring a large pan of water to the boil and cut out a small cone from the top of each tomato to remove the core. Plunge the tomatoes into the boiling water for 20 seconds, then refresh in cold water. Remove and slip off the skins, then halve and chop the tomatoes. Place them in a bowl with the tomato purée, olive oil, garlic, chilli, sugar and some seasoning. Stir to combine.

Heat 1 tablespoon olive oil in a large frying pan over a medium heat, add half the meatballs and fry, turning, until coloured on all sides. Transfer them to a shallow gratin or other ovenproof dish that holds them in a single layer, adding any pine nuts that have come loose. Cook the remainder in the same fashion. Spoon the tomato sauce over and between the meatballs. The recipe can be prepared to this point up to 24 hours in advance and kept covered and chilled. If refrigerated, bring it back to room temperature before cooking.

Preheat the oven to 190°C, fan oven 180°C, gas 5. Drizzle 1 tablespoon olive oil over the meatballs and bake for 40 minutes until the tips of the tomatoes on the top have started to singe. About halfway through the cooking time, bring a large pan of salted water to the boil. Add the pasta, give it a stir to separate out the strands and boil until just tender. Drain, return to the pan and toss with the butter.

Divide the pasta between warm plates, spooning the meatballs and sauce on top. Serve at once, with a bowl of Parmesan on the table for scattering over.

Saffron Rice

The key to success lies in cooking the rice over the very lowest heat to produce a golden crispy layer on the bottom and fluffy rice above.

Serves 4–6
450 g basmati rice
4 tablespoons groundnut oil
30 saffron threads, ground and infused with 1 tablespoon boiling water
Sea salt
50 g unsalted butter, melted

Put the rice in a large bowl, add cold water to cover generously and leave to soak for 30 minutes. Drain the rice into a sieve and rinse well under the cold tap. Bring a large pan of well salted water to the boil, add the rice, bring back to a simmer and cook for 2 minutes, then drain.

Heat the oil and 3 tablespoons water in a saucepan until sizzling. Tip in the rice and poke several holes in it, using the handle of a wooden spoon. Wrap the saucepan lid in a clean teatowel and position on the pan to seal as tightly as possible. Cook over a medium heat for a couple of minutes, then turn the heat down to its very lowest setting and cook for a further 30 minutes. Stand the pan on a cold surface for a couple of minutes.

Add 2 tablespoons of the cooked rice to the saffron infusion and stir. Having absorbed the liquid, mix this with the rice in the saucepan and check the seasoning. Transfer the rice to a serving plate and drizzle over the melted butter. In the bottom of the pan there will be a layer of golden crispy rice— the best bit to many—break into pieces for those who like it.

A Mixture of Grains and Beans

A peasant stew, not unlike a risotto in consistency, from the hands of the Lebanese cook and food writer Nada Saleh. Cumin plays a major role in scenting it and should ideally be freshly ground. The vegetarian take on this dish is a slick of olive oil and chopped parsley at the end. You can also sauté 225g lean ground meat, preferably lamb, until nicely browned, and add this to the bean mixture at the same time as adding the bulgar wheat—at this point it becomes a variation on chilli con carne.

Serves 4
110 g kidney beans, soaked overnight
110 g haricot beans, soaked overnight
75 g chickpeas, soaked overnight
1.8 to 2 litres water
110 g green or brown lentils,
    picked over
½ tablespoon extra virgin olive oil
280 g onions, peeled and
    finely chopped
110 g coarse bulgar wheat, rinsed
    and drained
1½ teaspoons sea salt
¼ teaspoon black pepper
¼ teaspoon freshly ground
    white pepper
1½ teaspoons ground cumin

To serve
Extra virgin olive oil
Coarsely chopped
flat-leaf parsley

Drain the beans and chickpeas and rinse under cold water. Place them all in a large saucepan with the water. Bring to the boil and boil steadily for 10 minutes. Skim, lower the heat, cover and simmer for 1 hour until the beans and chickpeas are tender.

Add the lentils, oil and onions. Bring back to the boil, cover and simmer for 15 minutes. Add the bulgar wheat, seasoning and cumin. Simmer, covered, for 15 minutes or until everything is tender and you have a stew-like consistency. Check the seasoning and serve in warmed soup bowls, with a drizzle of olive oil and some parsley scattered over.

Bulgar Wheat Pilaf

This pilaf cleverly succeeds in being nutty and textured, as well as light and fluffy. Serve it with soupy casseroles, grilled meat and roasts.

Serves 4
2 tablespoons olive oil
1 small onion, peeled and chopped
225 g bulgar wheat, rinsed in a sieve
150 ml white wine
300 ml chicken stock
    Sea salt, black pepper
1 bay leaf
2 thyme sprigs

Heat the olive oil in a medium saucepan. Add the onion and sweat over a fairly low heat for about 5 minutes, stirring occasionally, until it is soft and beginning to colour. Add the bulgar wheat and stir to coat with oil, then add the wine and chicken stock and season generously with salt and pepper. Bring to the boil and add the herbs. Cover with a tight-fitting lid and cook over a low heat for 10 minutes by which time all the liquid should have been absorbed.

Without removing the lid, turn the heat off and leave the pilaf to stand for 15 minutes, during which time it will dry out further and become increasingly tender. Fluff up with a fork and remove the herbs to serve.

Savoury Lentils

Lentils are combined here with the succulence of fennel and watercress. It would be a shame not to let vegetarians steal the day, even though the lentils are just as good with roasted and grilled meat. Serve with a dollop of young and curdy goat's cheese on top—you'll need about 250g.

Serves 6
3 tablespoons olive oil
4 garlic cloves, peeled, halved and sliced
1 onion, peeled and chopped
3 leeks, trimmed and sliced
3 fennel bulbs, outer sheath and feathery leaves removed, cored and diced
500 g Puy lentils
1.7 litres water
6 thyme sprigs, tied with string
2 bay leaves
    Sea salt, black pepper
3 tablespoons extra virgin olive oil
50 g curly parsley, chopped
2 bunches of watercress (about 150g), roughly chopped

Heat the olive oil in a large saucepan. Add the garlic, onion, leeks and fennel, and sweat until they are glossy and relaxed. Add the lentils and sweat them for a minute or two.

Pour in the water, add the thyme and bay leaves, and bring to a simmer. Cook for 50 minutes, adding a little more water if the mixture appears to dry out. The lentils should form a coherent mass rather than be separate, but short of turning to a mush. Season generously. Just before serving stir in the extra virgin olive oil, chopped parsley and watercress.

Roast Potatoes

To be able to produce good roast potatoes will ensure your reputation as a cook far and wide, guaranteeing that you are never short of guests for Sunday lunch. Everyone loves roast potatoes, as much as— if not more than—chips, and it is difficult to cook too many. Those who are full of roast chicken and couldn't manage one more petit pois can often find room for another roast potato.

Roast potatoes come in various guises. Cooked around a joint in time-honoured fashion, they emerge chewy, bronzed and saturated with the juices from the roast, but we are equally fond of them small and golden, masquerading as a chip. You can roast any type of potato, from big mealy maincrop potatoes to small waxy ones in their skins, with different end results. You can roast them in all manner of ways too— dripping in goose fat, with a light slick of olive oil and smattering of coarse sea salt, or with whole garlic cloves, thyme and bay leaves for company.

Your oven

The criticism so often levelled against fan ovens, that they dry food out as it cooks, is exactly what potatoes like best. Compared to roasting them in an Aga or a gas oven, is the difference between potatoes that struggle to crisp, and ones that are enviably golden all over with meltingly tender insides. Either way, for the best results settle your tray of potatoes on the top shelf, if they go below the roast it will likely steal their thunder.

The potatoes

Having potatoes the right size is a good start, too small and they will be dry inside by the time the outside is crisp, too large and you will bemoan the fact they are all insides and not enough shell. Small to medium potatoes should be halved; anything bigger cut into four or even six depending on their size. If you'll forgive the pedantry, each piece should weigh about 80g.

The fat

Potatoes will absorb almost any amount of butter you throw at them. There is no doubt that if allowed to drink it freely as they roast, you will end up with sensationally good potatoes. More usually, not least in the name of health, we roast them using extra virgin olive oil, which produces some of the crispiest potatoes. However the finest roast tatties of all are cooked in goose fat. It's worth keeping a jar of goose fat in the fridge solely for this purpose. It does at least have an almost indefinite shelf life.

The salt

A coarse-textured sea salt is needed, to enhance the crunchiness of the potatoes as well as season them. Fine-running table salt is a no-no, it either has to be Maldon or a pukka French one.

Crisp Roast Potatoes

Deliciously crisp potatoes to accompany the Sunday roast.

Serves 4
900 g maincrop potatoes
    Extra virgin olive oil
    Sea salt

Preheat the oven to 200°C, fan oven 190°C, gas 6 and bring a large pan of salted water to the boil. Peel and cut up your potatoes. Add to the pan, cook for 8 minutes, then drain into a sieve and leave for a minute or two to dry a little. Return to the pan and shake, tossing the potatoes in the air until they appear textured and floury on the surface. You can be as rough as you like without risk of them breaking up.

Tip the potatoes into a roasting tray and trickle over some olive oil, without drowning them—they certainly shouldn't be sitting in a pool of oil. Scatter over some sea salt. Roast the potatoes for 1 hour, turning them halfway through. They should be evenly golden all over, the colour of a crisp. If you are roasting them at the same time as a joint they may need a little longer than this.

Variations
All-time great roast potatoes
Use 80g melted goose fat in lieu of olive oil.

Butter-basted roast potatoes
First clarify 100g unsalted butter: melt gently, skim off the surface foam, decant the clear yellow liquid and discard the milky residue. Now roast your potatoes as above, but note that the butter should swamp them. Turn and baste the potatoes several times during cooking.

Jacket-roasted New Potatoes

A good choice when you are too busy or tired to do the subaltern's bit of peeling a large pile. These potatoes have all the charm of baked ones, with a glistening oily skin. They are delicious with pretty much everything, but especially with char-grilled and spicy food.

Serves 4
900 g waxy or new potatoes, scrubbed
    Olive oil
6 thyme sprigs
    Sea salt

Preheat the oven to 180°C, fan oven 170°C, gas 4. Bring a large saucepan of salted water to the boil. Add the potatoes and cook for 8 minutes, then drain. Place in a roasting dish and drizzle over some olive oil. Tuck in the thyme sprigs and scatter over some sea salt. Roast the potatoes for 1 hour, stirring them halfway through.

Spiced Sweet Potatoes

Sweet potatoes need the interruption of a few spices, and here spinach is an extra foil. A good accompaniment to roast chicken.

Serves 3
800 g small orange-fleshed
    sweet potatoes
    Extra virgin olive oil
    Sea salt
1 teaspoon cumin seeds
2 teaspoons black mustard seeds
75 g young spinach leaves

Preheat the oven to 200°C, fan oven 190°C, gas 6. Peel the sweet potatoes, quarter them lengthways and cut these pieces in half so you have elongated wedges. Toss the sweet potato wedges in a bowl with enough olive oil to coat, and season with salt.

Heat a roasting tin or a large ovenproof frying pan over a medium high heat. Spread the sweet potatoes over the base of the pan in a single layer and sauté for about 8 minutes until coloured on all sides, turning them now and again. Remove from the heat and toss in the cumin and mustard seeds.

Transfer to the oven and roast for 20 minutes. Scatter the spinach leaves over the sweet potatoes and heat briefly on the hob, tossing gently, until the leaves have wilted.

Pan Haggerty

Made as one large cake in a frying pan, this is crisped on the outside, concealing a pulpy goo of mashed potato and melted Gruyère within. It is surprisingly accommodating towards red meats, especially lamb and grilled steak. Serve it with roast chicken, too.

Serves 6
900 g maincrop potatoes
50 g unsalted butter
2 onions, peeled and
    finely chopped
1 tablespoon vegetable oil
    Sea salt, black pepper
100 g Gruyère cheese, grated

Steam or boil the potatoes in their jackets until they are tender. Drain into a sieve and leave for a minute or two for the surface water to evaporate. Peel the potatoes while they are hot (you can use rubber gloves to avoid burning your fingers), then pass them through the coarse blade of a mouli-legumes, or coarsely grate them. It's very important you do this while they are hot. (Don't use cold leftover potatoes.)

Preheat the oven to 220°C, fan oven 200°C, gas 7. Melt a third of the butter in a large ovenproof frying pan. Add the onions and sweat over a gentle heat for about 5 minutes until they just begin to colour. Mix them with the grated potato in a bowl. Add the oil to the pan with another third of the butter and heat until the butter is melted. Scatter half of the potato and onion mix evenly in the pan and season. Scatter over the cheese, then the remaining potato and onion. Season again and gently press down. Bake in the oven for 10 minutes.

Loosen the potato cake using a palette knife, place a plate over the top of the frying pan and carefully invert the Pan Haggerty on to it. Melt the remaining butter in the frying pan. Slide the potato cake back into the pan to brown the other side, tidying the sides with a palette knife. Return the potato cake to the oven for a further 15 minutes until it is cooked right through and golden on top.

If you are eating it straightaway slide the potato cake on to a warm plate, cut into wedges and serve. Alternatively, you can cook Pan Haggerty up to a couple of hours in advance and reheat it in a preheated oven at 220°C, fan oven 200°C, gas 7 for 15 minutes.

Mashed Potato

For luxurious mash that is creamy and silky, you need to add generous amounts of cream—preferably extra thick or double—and butter. This is the one occasion we like to use a lightly salted Breton butter, which gives mash that much more flavour. If you chance upon an untreated cream, this too will boost its character. Having added cream and butter you need to thin the mash to the ideal consistency with a little milk—it should slop off the spoon rather than sit as a spoonable lump. For a healthier, lower-fat mash, halve the butter and replace the cream with fromage frais.

Type of potato
For smooth, creamy mash, the La Ratte potato is king of the castle and following on from that the more widely available Charlotte. Both have waxy yellow flesh that gives a close-textured purée. Other salad potatoes can be used, but avoid tiny ones which will disappear in the process of being peeled.

The milling
Hand-held mashers have their uses but not for mashed potato. The fine art is down to a mouli-legumes, which mills the potato evenly and lightly. Alternatively, you could also press the potato through a coarse-meshed sieve, but this is harder work. Take care that your potatoes are thoroughly and evenly cooked for sieving, otherwise they can turn gluey.

Reheating mash
While mashed potato can be reheated, it is at its best freshly made. On cooling it tends to firm up, and you may need to add a little more milk when reheating it.

Mash
The correct consistency for mashed potato is a thick purée.

Serves 6

- 1.5 kg waxy potatoes, peeled and cut into even-sized pieces if large
- 50 g lightly salted butter, diced
- 4 generous tablespoons extra-thick double cream
- Sea salt
- Milk

Cook the potatoes in a large pan of boiling salted water until tender. Drain them into a sieve and leave for a few minutes for the surface water to evaporate. Pass the potatoes through a mouli-legumes or sieve back into the pan. Add the butter and cream, and season with sea salt. Gently reheat the mash, adding a drop of milk to achieve the right consistency.

Variations
Olive oil mash
Instead of adding butter, enrich the mash with a few tablespoons of extra virgin olive oil. This is good with char-grilled meat and fish, and roasted vegetables.

Mustard mash
Whisk Dijon mustard to taste into the mash.

Saffron mash
Grind 25 saffron threads, infuse with a drop of boiling milk for 15 minutes and then stir into the finished mash.

Basil mash
Purée a large handful of fresh basil leaves together with 2–3 tablespoons single cream and stir into the mash.

Garlic mash
Slice the top off a head of garlic. Stand in a small baking dish, drizzle with olive oil, dot with butter and season with salt and pepper. Cover with foil and roast at 150°C, fan oven 140°C, gas 2 for 2 hours. Squeeze the soft pulp out of the skins and mash to a paste in a bowl using a fork. Stir this into the prepared mash.

Champ

Potatoes don't come any more Irish than this. Serve with a rare steak, roast beef, with venison or roast lamb. To its credit, champ can be cooked in advance if required and gently reheated to serve.

Serves 6
900 g maincrop potatoes, peeled and cut up
3 bunches of spring onions (about 400g), trimmed
100 g unsalted butter, plus a knob to serve
200 ml double cream
Sea salt, black pepper

Cook the potatoes in a large pan of boiling salted water until tender. In the meantime, cut the spring onions, including the green parts, into 1cm slices. Drain the potatoes into a sieve and leave for a few minutes for the surface water to evaporate, then press them through a mouli-legumes.

Melt the butter in a medium or large saucepan, add the spring onions and sweat for about 5 minutes until soft and silky, stirring occasionally. Add the cream and some seasoning, bring to a simmer and cook for a few minutes until this thickens slightly. Stir the cream and onion mixture into the mashed potato and adjust the seasoning. It should have a nice sloppy consistency. To serve, make a well in the centre of the champ and drop in the knob of butter.

Baked Potatoes

A crisp but tender skin—good enough to eat without further embellishment—and a soft, fluffy inside are the characteristics of a good baked potato. To this end avoid lengthy baking otherwise the skins can become dry and tough.

Type of potato
The big maincrop names—Maris Piper, Desirée and King Edward—possess a robust skin that will turn into a flavoursome chewy jacket, with a soft floury inside. Designated 'baking potatoes' are not so much special varieties as potatoes of a particular size. They should be 225–275g in weight.

Crisping the skin
You can encourage potato skins to crisp by coating them very lightly with olive oil. A sprinkling of coarse sea salt renders them even crispier and brings out the flavour.

Smooth flesh
To ensure soft, creamy insides you need to bake potatoes at a comparatively low temperature. This also allows the pulp to infuse with the scent of the skin.

Filled baked potatoes
Scoring a lid in the top of the potatoes makes it easy to remove the lids and scoop out the soft insides after baking. This potato flesh can then be flavoured to taste and spooned back into the potato skins. When you scoop out the flesh, leave a 1cm thick shell. Once the potatoes have been refilled, you can either reheat them in the oven straightaway or chill them until required and then reheat at 170°C, fan oven 160°C, gas 3 for about 20 minutes to serve.

Perfect Baked Potatoes
Serves 4
4 baking potatoes, scrubbed and dried
Extra virgin olive oil
Coarse sea salt, such as Maldon

Preheat the oven to 170°C, fan oven 160°C, gas 3. Make a shallow cut around the top of each potato with a small sharp knife, for a lid. Place a little olive oil in the palm of your hand; rub your hands together and then over the potatoes, to coat them lightly with the oil. Place them on a baking tray, sprinkle over some sea salt and bake for 1½ hours.

Fillings
For each of these, score a lid before baking (see left) and scoop out the cooked potato into a bowl.

Crushed potatoes
Loosely mash the potato flesh with 5 tablespoons extra virgin olive oil, 2 heaped tablespoons chopped parsley, ½ crushed garlic clove, salt and pepper, and then refill.

Truffle potatoes
Press the potato flesh through a sieve or mouli-legumes. Enrich with butter and double cream, season and add a few drops of truffle oil, or even better some finely diced Perigord truffles. Refill.

Fondue potatoes
Press the potato flesh through a sieve or mouli-legumes, add a knob of butter and season. Spoon half of this into the potato cavities and fill with a mixture of grated Gruyère and Emmental. Replace the lids. Reheat for 20 minutes at 170°C, fan oven 160°C, gas 3.

Sautéed Potatoes

Unless you possess a deep-fat fryer, sautéed potatoes are as close as you will get to chips in the home. Salad or waxy potatoes—cooked skin on—give the best results. Experiment with any type that takes your fancy, be it Charlotte, Pink Fir Apple, or La Ratte. Later into the year you can also use Jersey Royals. Cook the potatoes fully before frying them to ensure meltingly tender insides. Sautéing in a combination of butter and olive oil gives an especially good flavour, but you can vary this. Use all olive oil, or lard or goose fat if you prefer. And sauté the potatoes slowly to allow them to caramelise.

Serves 3–4

600 g salad or waxy potatoes, scrubbed
25 g unsalted butter
1 tablespoon extra virgin olive oil
Sea salt, black pepper
1 garlic clove, peeled and finely chopped
2 tablespoons finely chopped flat-leaf parsley

Bring a large pan of salted water to the boil, add the potatoes, bring back to the boil and cook for about 15 minutes until tender when pierced with a knife. Drain them into a colander, leave to cool and then slice thickly.

Heat the butter and oil in a 25cm frying pan over a low heat. Add the potatoes and sauté for about 20 minutes, turning them every few minutes, until they are evenly golden and crisp. Season a few minutes into cooking, and add the chopped garlic 5 minutes before the end. Sprinkle with the chopped parsley, toss and serve at once.

Variations

Potatoes lyonnaise

Peel and finely slice 2 white onions. Fry gently in 2 tablespoons olive oil, stirring frequently, for 20–25 minutes until evenly golden and sweet. At the very end, season them with salt and pepper, and add 1 teaspoon red wine vinegar. Toss them into the sautéed potatoes and serve straightaway.

Sautéed potatoes for chicken

Boil your potatoes in chicken stock rather than water (it can be used for soup later). These potatoes go especially well with grilled or roast chicken and a dollop of aioli.

Garlic and rosemary fries

Add a handful of unpeeled garlic cloves and a few sprigs of rosemary to the potatoes when you sauté them. Die-hards may like to eat the soft insides of the garlic.

Chilli potatoes

Fry the potatoes with several whole red chillies, removing them at the end.

There are endless variations on theme of this classic, and this version—by design—is nothing like as rich as most. The potatoes are cooked with butter, garlic and thyme until tender, and then given a flourish with a little cream and cheese at the end. Maincrop potatoes like Maris Piper and Desirée are best for this type of gratin, as their starch helps the slices to adhere into a thick cake on baking. The potatoes must be sliced thinly and evenly, although the bottom layers needn't be as neat as the top layer.

Serves 6
50 g unsalted butter
6 maincrop potatoes (about 1.1 kg)
1 garlic clove, peeled and finely chopped
2 teaspoons thyme leaves (optional)
Sea salt, black pepper
4 tablespoons double cream
150 g Gruyère cheese, grated

Preheat the oven to 190°C, fan oven 180°C, gas 5. Clarify the butter: melt it in a small pan, skim off the surface foam, decant the clear liquid and discard the milky solids on the bottom. Peel and slice the potatoes as thinly as possible; you may like to use a mandolin, or a food processor fitted with a fine slicing attachment. Toss the potato slices in a bowl with the clarified butter, garlic, thyme if using, and seasoning. Lay them, overlapping, in a 20cm by 30cm gratin or shallow ovenproof dish of an equivalent size. Cover tightly with foil and bake for about 45 minutes until the potatoes are tender when pierced with a knife.

Turn the oven up to 220°C, fan oven 200°C, gas 7. Drizzle the cream over the potatoes and scatter over the cheese. Return to the oven for 15–20 minutes until the cheese is golden and bubbling. Serve straightaway.

Alternatively, the gratin can be prepared ahead and reheated at 220°C, fan oven 200°C, gas 7 for 20 minutes to serve.

Variations
To accompany lamb, replace the thyme with rosemary.

Butter can be used instead of olive oil.

Step up the garlic by layering the potatoes with fine slivers of it.

Any cheese that melts well can be used in place of Gruyère—it could be Emmental, Fontina or Raclette.

Instead of—or as well as—the layer of grated cheese, scatter over breadcrumbs tossed with melted butter.

The heady scent of extra virgin olive oil, while extraordinary, is also quite heavy—in flavour and texture too. So we prefer to anoint a mixed bowl of salad leaves—cresses, chicory, dandelion, mizuna and the like—with a light splash of lemon juice and groundnut oil. The latter lubricant is sometimes erroneously described as being flavourless. It is indeed very mild and gentle, but also creamy and to its credit allows the flavour of the salad leaves to shine through.

Groundnut oil
Lemon juice
Maldon sea salt

Toss the leaves in a bowl with just enough oil to coat them lightly—you may find it easier to dive in there with both hands. Now add literally a few drops of lemon juice, not even a teaspoon, and a few crystals of sea salt. Toss again and serve straightaway.

Olive Oil and Balsamic Vinegar Dressing

If ever there was an excuse for spending a fortune on estate-bottled oil and an aged balsamic vinegar it can be justified here, where both are fully appreciated in their raw state. For once rocket is the most appropriate leaf, bully enough to hold its own under the weight of both oil and vinegar. Steamed and lightly boiled vegetables are also contenders, and raw crudités.

Extra virgin olive oil
Balsamic vinegar
Maldon sea salt

Drizzle some olive oil over the salad in a bowl and toss using your hands to coat the leaves. Add a succinct splash of balsamic vinegar and a few crystals of sea salt and toss again. Vegetables can simply be anointed on a plate and served.

Caesar Salad Dressing

A Caesar salad has more to do with the dressing than the recipient ingredients despite the wars that wage over what these are. It's a great dressing, even if it's only modestly thrown at a bowlful of sliced Little Gems. We can live without the anchovies but a few croûtons, shallow fried in olive oil, are always welcome.

Serves 4
2 medium organic eggs
½ garlic clove, peeled and chopped
2 tablespoons lemon juice
2 teaspoons Worcestershire sauce
150 ml extra virgin olive oil
Sea salt, black pepper
50 g Parmesan cheese, freshly grated

Bring a small pan of water to the boil and cook the eggs for 1 minute, then remove and cool them under cold running water. Immediately shell the eggs into a blender, scooping out the cooked white that lines the inside of the shells. Add the remaining ingredients, except the Parmesan, and whizz to a pale and creamy emulsion.

To serve your salad, pour over the Caesar salad dressing and lightly mix in the Parmesan.

Salad of Cresses

All cresses share an addictive warming nasal pungency, and this salad plays on the textures and subtly different flavours of the various types. Of them all, watercress remains our choice for a single leaf salad. It does however have to be the bunched variety, scythed by hand when it's mature, and not the weedy stuff you buy in packets.

Serves 4
1 bunch of watercress
2 handfuls of rocket leaves
1 punnet of mustard and cress
Oil and Lemon Dressing (see page 178)

Fill the sink with cold water. Pick over the watercress, discarding any tough stems or yellowing leaves. Nip off the ends of the rocket leaves using your fingers, again discarding any yellowing leaves. Add the watercress and rocket to the sink and give them a good swirl. Carefully lift the leaves out, shaking off as much water as possible.

To dry, place the leaves in a clean teatowel, gather the corners and shake a few times to get rid of any excess water (do this outside). Or lay the leaves on a clean teatowel on the work surface, place another teatowel on top and gently pat dry. Drying the leaves properly after you have washed them is all-important. You can of course use a salad spinner, if you have one.

Place the leaves in a large bowl. Cut the mustard and cress, then toss into the salad. Dress with groundnut oil and lemon (as described on page 178).

Green Salad to serve with Cheese

This salad pays homage to the French custom of serving cheese before pudding, the rationale being that you should go from savoury to sweet and not back again. A small salad does away with the need for all those ghastly crackers, which arrive at a stage of the meal when the last thing you want is a hefty dose of carbohydrate. This is a slightly stronger dressing as befits a selection of cheeses.

Serves 6
Selection of salad leaves, such as watercress, frisée, batavia and lamb's lettuce, for 6 small side salads

Dressing
1½ teaspoons sherry vinegar
Squeeze of lemon juice
½ teaspoon Dijon mustard
Sea salt, black pepper
1 teaspoon finely chopped shallot
½ garlic clove, finely chopped
2½ tablespoons extra virgin olive oil

To make the dressing, whisk the vinegar and lemon juice with the mustard and seasoning in a bowl. Add the shallot, garlic and the oil and whisk to emulsify.

Wash and dry the salad leaves, then place in a bowl. Just before serving, toss with the dressing.

Chicory Salad with Mustard Dressing

A classic French salad that goes hand in hand with Bayonne ham or any other kind of ham, air-dried or otherwise. You may also like to toss some freshly chopped parsley into the salad at the end.

Serves 6
6 heads of Belgian chicory

Dressing
1½ teaspoons red wine vinegar
1 teaspoon Dijon mustard
1 teaspoon grainy mustard
Finely grated zest of
½ lemon (optional)
Sea salt, black pepper
7 tablespoons groundnut oil
1 tablespoon water

To make the dressing, whisk the vinegar with the mustards, lemon zest if using, and seasoning in a bowl. Slowly whisk in the oil and water until you have a creamy emulsion. You can prepare this in advance in which case re-whisk it to emulsify just before serving.

Slice the root end off the chicory bulbs and discard any damaged outer leaves. Separate the chicory leaves, and wash and dry them. Place in a bowl and toss with the dressing.

Rocket and Parmesan Salad

A rare concession to fashion, these are two ingredients that were destined to walk the same path. A fine lunch-on-a-tray is to be had with this salad, the Oven-roasted Tomatoes (on page 186), a selection of goat's cheeses and some thick slices of crusty white bread, toasted on a ridged griddle or barbecue and anointed with olive oil.

Serves 6
Several large handfuls of rocket leaves, enough for 6
40 g Parmesan cheese, finely shaved

Dressing
1 tablespoon lemon juice
¼ teaspoon finely grated lemon zest
Sea salt, black pepper
4 tablespoons extra virgin olive oil

To make the dressing, whisk the lemon juice and zest with some seasoning in a bowl, then incorporate the oil. Place the rocket in a large salad bowl, toss with the dressing and then carefully mix in the Parmesan shavings.

Tomato Salads

Before heaping scorn on the tomatoes that offer themselves up from British soil, a word in their defence. The poor things are ill suited to our clime, struggling beneath moody skies when what they revel in is sunlight that will endow them with sugars, which in turn make them tasty to eat.

Sugar though is only half the battle, acidity is equally important. Just as the tasteless strawberry is brought to life by a squeeze of lemon, so tomatoes need to balance sweet and sour to be truly scintillating. The seeds too, which we all too readily dispense with, are crucial as the surrounding jelly harbours a wealth of acids and volatile flavours. Unless it is absolutely necessary to a recipe, ridding tomatoes of their seeds is a wasteful vanity. And if it is the wrong time of year generally, the best bet will be cherry tomatoes— the smaller they are, the sweeter and more intensely flavoured they will be. One ruse for encouraging otherwise unexciting fruit is to line them up on a wall in the sun before cutting into them.

Classic Tomato Salad

There are endless ways of jazzing this salad up, but none so useful or delicious as the basic. A large chunk of crusty bread is essential for mopping up the juices—there should be plenty. In fact you can leave the tomatoes to bleed for up to an hour by which time you will have a lovely soupy pool to dip into.

Take advantage of the many types of tomato on offer—tiny pert cherries in gold and red, slightly larger ones on the vine, plum, beefsteak and so on—and play on their different characters.

Serves 4
700 g assorted tomatoes
¾ teaspoon sea salt
½ teaspoon caster sugar
6 tablespoons extra virgin olive oil

Cherry tomatoes excepted, cut out the core, then halve, quarter or slice the tomatoes as seems appropriate. Such is the difficulty of cutting these slippery balls, you either need to have a razor sharp blade, or even better a serrated knife.

The next step is to 'bleed' the tomatoes of some of their juices— these have their own acidity and dispense with the need for added vinegar. Place the tomatoes in a large bowl and sprinkle with the salt and sugar. Leave to stand for 30 minutes.

Arrange the tomatoes on a large, shallow rimmed plate, adding any juices that are given out. Pour over the olive oil to serve.

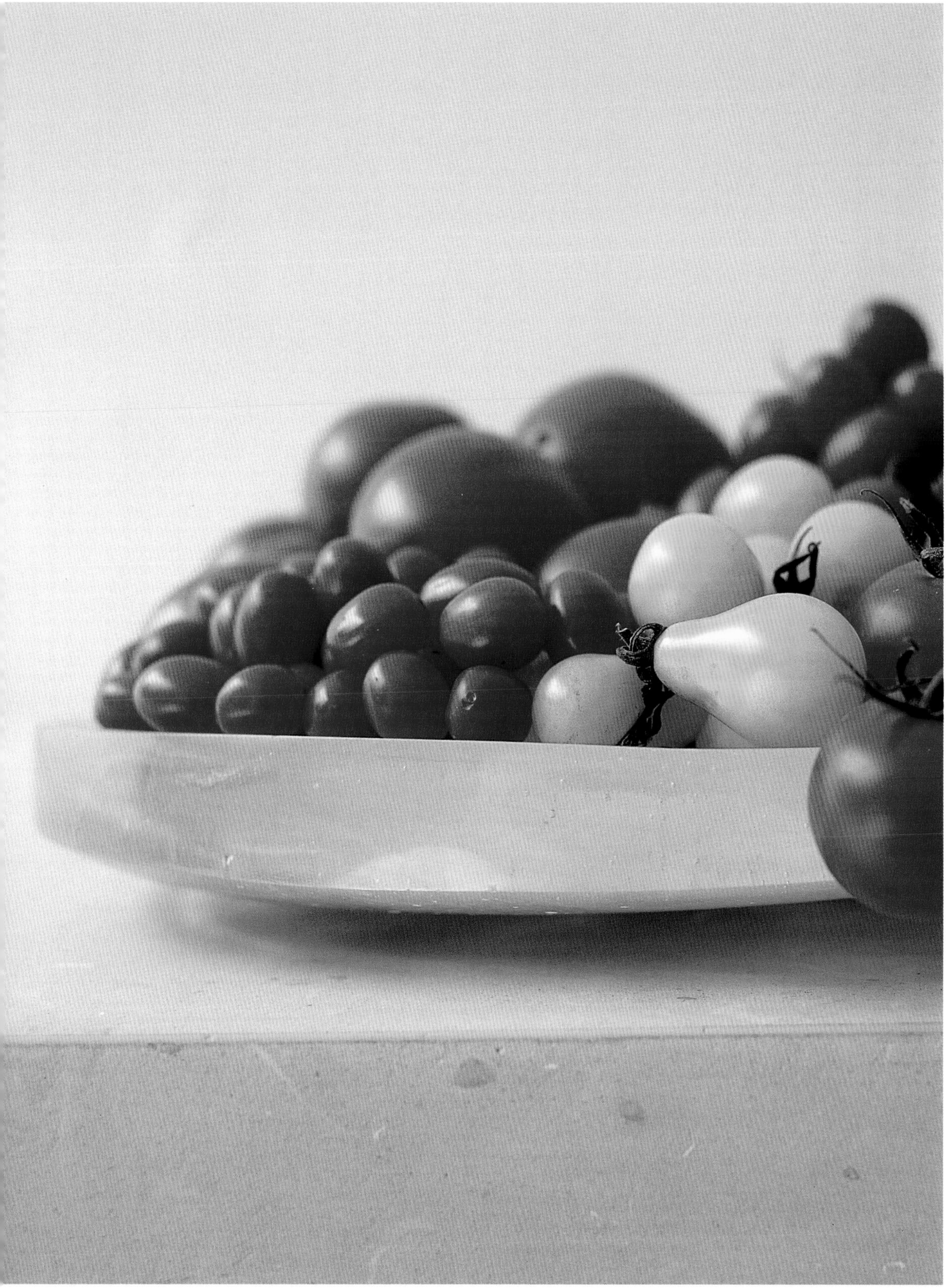

Italian Tomato and Bread Salad

This robust salad is warm weather fare. The rougher and readier your bread the better, and the smaller the capers the more likely they are to explode with flavour.

Serves 2
350 g plum tomatoes
¾ teaspoon sea salt
½ teaspoon caster sugar
50 g day-old crustless white bread
⅓ cucumber
7 tablespoons extra virgin olive oil
¼ red onion, peeled and
   finely sliced
½ tablespoon capers, rinsed
   Few basil leaves, roughly torn
   Black pepper
1 teaspoon red wine vinegar

Bring a pan of water to the boil. Cut out a small cone from the top of each tomato to remove the core. Plunge the tomatoes into the boiling water for 20 seconds, then into cold water. Remove and slip off the skins, quarter and slice into chunks. Place in a bowl, sprinkle over the salt and sugar and leave for 30 minutes to let the juices to run.

In the meantime tear the bread into rough chunks, about 2cm in size, and place in a bowl. Peel, quarter and deseed the cucumber, then cut into 5mm thick slices. Tip the tomatoes into a sieve over a bowl to catch the juices. Add 3 tablespoons of the olive oil and 2 tablespoons water to the juices, stir, and then sprinkle over the bread. Once the juice has been absorbed, add all the remaining ingredients, including the tomatoes. Toss to mix then transfer the salad to a serving bowl or dish. Taste for seasoning and drizzle with the remaining 4 tablespoons olive oil.

Tomato, Red Pepper and Anchovy Salad

This salad was born of a browse around an Italian deli where everything sold itself on the merit of being impossible to resist: a cache of large cherry tomatoes on the vine; green olives marinated with chilli and garlic; bushy leaves of rocket; fat pink anchovies and even fatter red peppers.

Serves 4
450 g cherry tomatoes (preferably on
   the vine)
   Extra virgin olive oil
   Sea salt, black pepper
3 red peppers
1 large avocado
100 g green olives, pitted
75 g salted anchovies
50 g rocket leaves
8 slices of French bread, 1cm thick
   and cut at an angle

Preheat the oven to 220°C, fan oven 200°C, gas 7. Place the cherry tomatoes in a small roasting dish, drizzle with a little olive oil and season with salt and pepper. Put the roasting dish in the oven and lay the peppers on the rack underneath. Roast for 20 minutes. Leave the tomatoes to cool for about an hour. Place the peppers in a bowl, cover with clingfilm and leave these to cool too.

Working over the bowl to catch any juices, remove the cores from the peppers, slip off their skins and remove the seeds. Tear the peppers into wide strips and return to the bowl. If the cherry tomatoes were on the vine, gently remove them from the stalk using a fork, leaving the tomatoes sitting in their juices in the dish. Quarter the avocado, discarding the stone, then peel off the skin and slice the flesh.

Gently toss the peppers, tomatoes and avocado with the olives, anchovies and rocket leaves in a large bowl or dish using your hands. Include any juices given out by the tomatoes and peppers. You shouldn't need to season the salad further.

Heat a ridged griddle and toast the bread on both sides. Place two pieces of toast on each of 4 plates and drizzle over a little olive oil. Pile the salad over half the toast. Trickle another tablespoon of olive oil over each plate and serve at once.

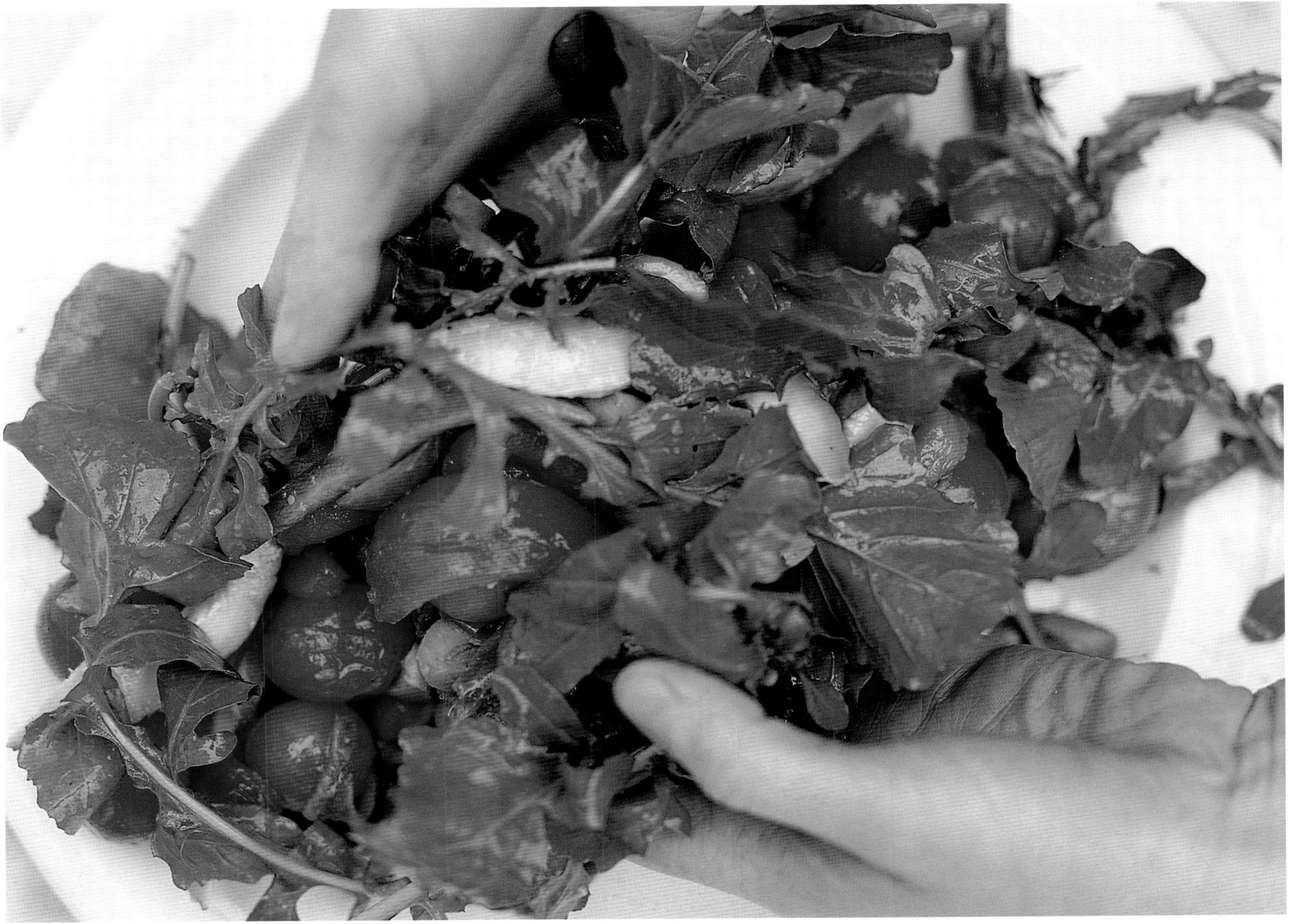

Oven-roasted Tomatoes

These candy-sweet tomato petals
are exquisite eaten with tart
cheeses and thick slices of toasted
French bread drizzled with olive oil.
More appealing than sun-dried
tomatoes, they are sublimely
sweet and intense, while being
tender and oily. A good fate for
tomatoes that are otherwise
lacking in flavour.

In particular, serve oven-
roasted tomatoes with a selection
of goat's cheeses, some wrapped
in chestnut leaves, others so runny
they flow out from the rind, and
small powerful cheeses marinated
to a dark ivory in brandy. Some
black olives, a large green salad and
you're there.

Serves 6
1.5 kg medium tomatoes
4 garlic cloves (unpeeled), smashed
5 thyme sprigs
Sea salt
Caster sugar
Extra virgin olive oil
Handful of basil leaves

Heat the oven to 130°C, fan
oven 120°C, gas ½. Bring a large
pan of water to the boil. Cut out a
small cone from the top of each
tomato to remove the core.
Plunge the tomatoes into the
boiling water for 20 seconds and
then into cold water. Remove
and slip off the skins, then halve
and deseed the tomatoes.

Lay the tomato petals out on
a non-stick baking tray. Scatter over
the garlic and thyme, and season
with salt and a sprinkling of sugar.
Drizzle with 4 tablespoons olive oil
and bake for 2 hours. Allow to cool.

Place the tomatoes in a bowl
or a jar interspersed with the basil
leaves, and cover with olive oil.
Either serve straightaway or cover
and chill for up to 3 days, bringing
back up to room temperature
before serving.

New Potato Salad with Sour Cream and Tarragon

This salad pays homage to the marriage of potatoes with mayonnaise. Sour cream is that much subtler in its coating, and that much more instant.

Serves 4
750 g small waxy potatoes, peeled
   or scrubbed
   Cayenne pepper, to dust

Dressing
150 ml sour cream
   Squeeze of lemon juice
½ teaspoon caster sugar
   Sea salt
1 tablespoon finely
   chopped shallot
2 teaspoons finely
   chopped tarragon

Place the potatoes in a steamer set over a 3cm depth of boiling water in the pan. Cover and cook for about 15 minutes until tender. Rinse the potatoes under the cold tap to wash off the starch on the surface. Alternatively cook the potatoes in a large pan of salted water until tender when tested with a skewer, then drain them into a colander. Leave the potatoes to cool while you make the dressing.

Whisk the sour cream in a large bowl with the lemon juice, sugar and some sea salt. Stir in the shallot and tarragon. You can prepare the salad to this point in advance and assemble it at the last minute.

Add the potatoes to the bowl with the dressing and gently toss to coat them. Transfer to a serving dish or bowl and dust with cayenne pepper. Serve as soon as possible.

Favourite Potato Salad

A lively salad that tastes even better if the flavours are allowed to mingle overnight.

Serves 4–6
750 g small waxy potatoes, peeled
   or scrubbed

Dressing
2 tablespoons white wine
9 tablespoons extra virgin olive oil
4 tablespoons chopped mixed
   herbs, such as parsley, chives,
   basil, chervil, tarragon
2 spring onions, trimmed and
   finely sliced
   Sea salt, black pepper

Place the potatoes in a steamer set over a 3cm depth of boiling water in the pan. Cover and cook for about 15 minutes until tender. Rinse the potatoes under the cold tap to wash off the starch on the surface. Alternatively cook the potatoes in a large pan of salted water until tender when tested with a skewer, then drain into a colander.

Thickly slice the hot potatoes, place in a bowl and pour over the wine and olive oil. Gently toss in the herbs, spring onions and some seasoning. Leave to cool to room temperature and check the seasoning. Serve straightaway, or cover and refrigerate, returning to room temperature 30 minutes before serving.

Tabbouleh

Tabbouleh is a test of strength for any Lebanese restaurant and has nothing to do with the stodgy, wheat-laden salad that has come to be sold in tubs. It is a salad of freshly chopped herbs and has no shelf life to speak of—a good restaurant will make it twice a day. The parsley should be young, and the wheat, a silent partner should be fine brown burghul, added as a smattering after the salad has been mixed. (Burghul has a variety of other names, including bulgar wheat and cracked wheat.)

Serves 4
1½ tablespoons fine bulgar wheat
120 g bunch of flat-leaf parsley, tough
   stalks removed
2 tomatoes, sliced and
   then chopped
1 handful of mint leaves, chopped
1 large spring onion, finely sliced
   and then chopped
1 teaspoon sea salt
½ teaspoon black pepper
3 tablespoons extra virgin olive oil
2 tablespoons lemon juice

Rinse the bulgar wheat in a fine-mesh sieve and set aside to absorb the residual moisture. Chop the parsley, holding the bunch and slicing from leaf to stalk. Combine the parsley, tomatoes, mint and spring onion in a bowl. Add the seasoning, the oil and lemon juice and toss to combine. Mix in the bulgar wheat to serve. If you do end up with leftovers then seal the surface with a lettuce leaf, cover with clingfilm and refrigerate.

Wild Mushrooms in Oil

Jars of things that tempt on the basis of looks are so often a disappointment—duck confit, quinces and cherries in syrup, preserved artichokes and wild mushrooms to name a few. Only one thing for it, and that's to buckle down to preparing your own. This salad is best displayed in a shallow white china dish, and it's good enough to sit around out of the fridge for some hours if you want to prepare it in advance. Serve it with lots of crusty bread, and some Parma ham for a treat.

Serves 4
Broth
12 black peppercorns
¼ teaspoon fennel seeds
¼ teaspoon coriander seeds
1 shallot, peeled and
    finely chopped
300 ml water
    Juice of ½ lemon
5 tablespoons extra virgin olive oil

Mushrooms
450 g mixed wild and cultivated
    mushrooms, scraped, trimmed
    and halved or quartered if large
    Sea salt, black pepper
2 tablespoons extra virgin olive oil
2 tablespoons coarsely chopped
    flat-leaf parsley
    Squeeze of lemon juice
120 g cherry tomatoes,
    sliced (optional)

To prepare the broth, tie the spices in a small square of muslin and place in a medium saucepan with all the remaining ingredients. Bring to the boil, then cover and simmer over a very low heat for 10 minutes.

Add the mushrooms and bring back to the boil. Cover the pan, turn the heat down low and simmer for 10 minutes, stirring once. Transfer the mushrooms to a bowl. Boil the broth to reduce to about 150ml, then season it. Discard the spices and pour the reduced liquor over the mushrooms. Leave to cool.

Once the mushrooms are cool, stir in the 2 tablespoons of olive oil and the chopped parsley. Sharpen with a squeeze of lemon juice, taste to check the seasoning and stir in the cherry tomatoes if using.

Char-grilled Courgettes with Pine Nuts

A hot griddle is sympathetic to courgettes that can otherwise lack character. Long, thin strips of courgette branded with the bars of a grill and marinated in olive oil make pleasant summer fare, indoors or out.

Serves 6
50 g pine nuts
4 medium courgettes, trimmed
    Extra virgin olive oil
    Sea salt, black pepper

Heat a dry frying pan over a medium heat and toast the pine nuts in it, stirring constantly until they are golden and fragrant. Remove to a bowl.

Slice the courgettes lengthways into 5mm thick strips. Heat a ridged griddle over a medium heat. Lay some of the courgette slices out on a board, brush the top surface with olive oil and season. Cook, oiled-side down, on the griddle until striped. Brush the upper surface with oil (but don't season); turn and cook this side too. Repeat with the remaining courgette slices, transferring them to a container as they are cooked. Splash over some olive oil, cover and leave in a cool place until ready to serve. Stir the pine nuts into the salad shortly before serving.

Celeriac Rémoulade

The French know only too well how cold ham and salami welcome Celeriac Rémoulade, and every butcher hawks a tub alongside prized homemade pâtés and sausages. It's a good-natured salad that will sit happily in the fridge for a couple of days.

Serves 6
1 celeriac bulb (about 800g)
1 teaspoon sea salt

Mayonnaise
1 large organic egg yolk
2 tablespoons Dijon mustard
250 ml groundnut oil
1 tablespoon lemon juice

Cut the peel off the celeriac and finely grate the flesh. This is easiest to do using the grating attachment on a food processor. Toss the celeriac with the sea salt in a bowl and leave to stand for 20 minutes.

For the mayonnaise, whisk the egg yolk and mustard together in a bowl, and then whisk in the oil, very slowly to begin with until it takes, then in slightly longer streams. Whisk in the lemon juice.

Place the celeriac in a clean teatowel and wring out as much liquid as possible. Return it to the bowl and tease the lump with your fingers to unravel the strands. Add the mayonnaise and mix with a wooden spoon. There shouldn't be any need for additional salt and pepper. Transfer the salad to a serving bowl. Either serve straightaway or cover and chill until required, bringing the salad back up to room temperature 30 minutes before serving.

Avocado Salad

A ripe avocado boasts such wantonly creamy flesh it seems a shame to detract from the experience with anything else, such as a lettuce leaf or prawn. Hass avocados, the ones with knobbly dark green skins, are a little harder to peel than the thin-skinned types but possess delectably dense flesh. They should be meltingly ripe and tender, though not remotely mushy or blackened.

Serves 4–6
4 ripe Hass avocados
1 tablespoon groundnut oil
1 tablespoon lemon or lime juice
Sea salt, black pepper
1 tablespoon finely chopped chives

Quarter the avocados, removing them from the stone, then carefully peel and cut the quarters in half lengthways.

Lay the avocados on a serving plate and drizzle over the groundnut oil and lemon or lime juice. Season and scatter over the chopped chives. Very carefully, using your hands, lift and turn the avocado just once. Serve immediately.

Fennel, Carrot and Radish Salad with Olives

One step beyond crudités, the vegetables in this salad are sliced wafer thin and soften up agreeably after a spell in olive oil.

Serves 6
1 fennel bulb, trimmed
6 radishes, trimmed and finely sliced
2 slim carrots, trimmed, peeled and finely sliced
½ red onion, peeled and finely sliced
100 g green and black olives, pitted and finely sliced
3 tablespoons extra virgin olive oil
1 teaspoon balsamic vinegar
Sea salt, black pepper

Cut off the outer sheath from the fennel, then halve the bulb and slice finely. Combine the fennel, radishes, carrots, onion and olives in a bowl. Toss with the olive oil and balsamic vinegar, cover and leave in a cool place until ready to eat.

Season the salad just before serving; if you do this in advance the salt will draw out juices from the vegetables and they'll lose their freshness. Transfer the salad to a clean bowl to serve.

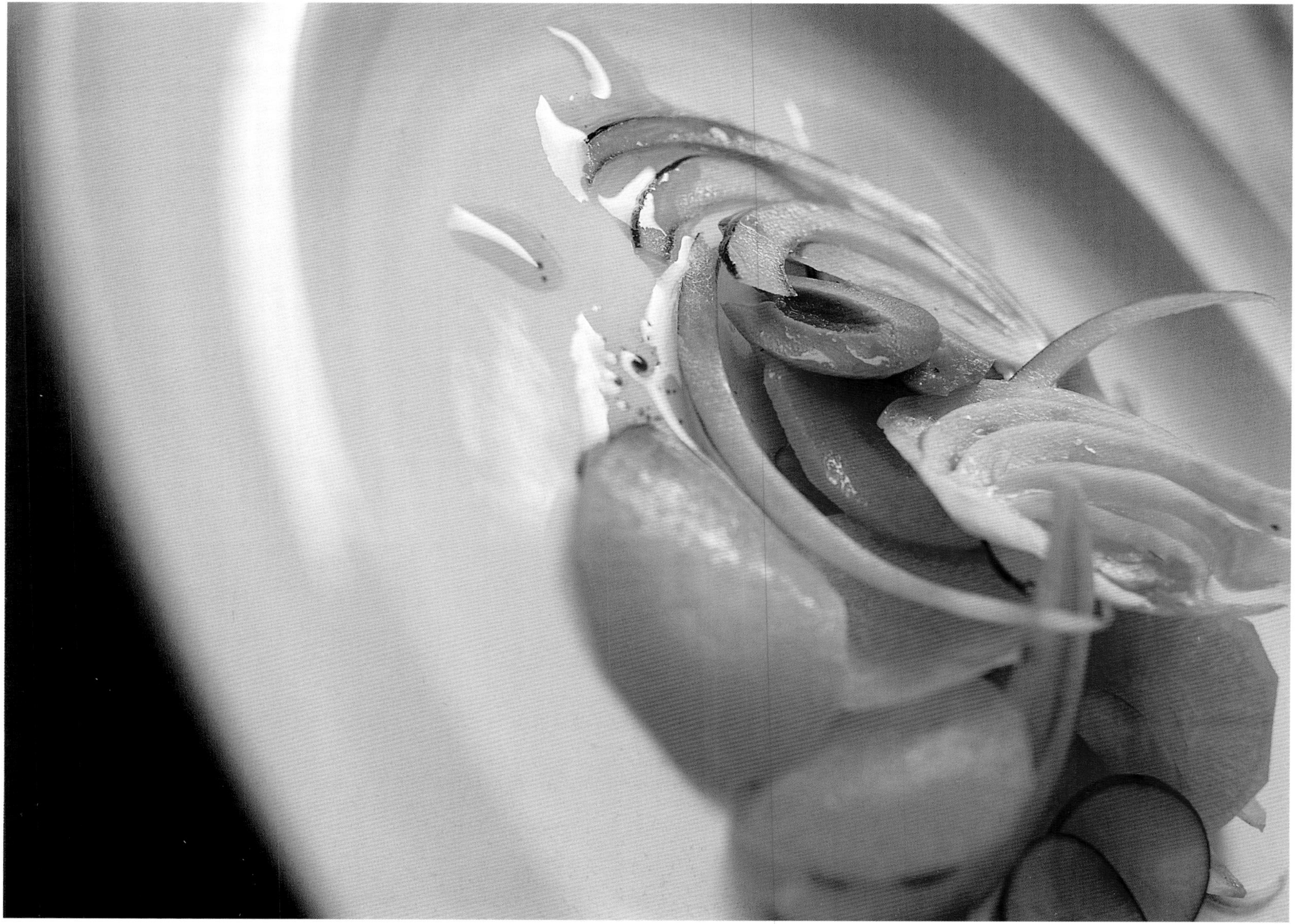

Carrot and Pine Nut Salad

This salad treads where coleslaw fears to go, succeeding in being delicious and good for you at the same time. The Lebanese claim their pine nuts are longer, thinner and more refined than Chinese ones. If you happen to be in the vicinity of a Middle Eastern haunt it's worth popping in.

Serves 4
50 g pine nuts
350 g organic carrots, peeled
2 tablespoons finely
chopped parsley

Dressing
½ garlic clove, peeled
Sea salt, black pepper
1 tablespoon lemon juice
2 tablespoons groundnut oil

Heat a dry frying pan over a low heat and toast the pine nuts in it, tossing constantly until they are well coloured. Transfer to a small plate and leave them to cool. Finely grate the carrots; you can use a food processor fitted with a fine grating disc to do this if you like. Combine the grated carrot and chopped parsley in a bowl.

For the dressing, either crush the garlic in a press, or chop it on a board and sprinkle with salt then crush to a paste, using the flat edge of a knife. Transfer to a small bowl, add the lemon juice and some seasoning, and whisk to combine, then whisk in the oil. You can prepare the salad to this point in advance.

Just before serving, toss the carrot and parsley with the dressing, then mix in the pine nuts.

Green Bean Salad

Fine French beans are a perennial treat, their thinness is all-important —fatter ones tend to mealiness. This makes a little more dressing than you need, but it keeps well in the fridge for a few days and can be applied to any green vegetable or potato salad.

Serves 4
350 g fine green beans, topped
and tailed
2 shallots, peeled and
finely chopped

Dressing
3 large organic eggs
1 rounded teaspoon English
mustard powder
1 rounded teaspoon caster sugar
2 teaspoons tarragon vinegar
5 tablespoons single cream
Sea salt, black pepper

For the dressing, bring a small pan of water to the boil, add the eggs and cook for 10 minutes. Pour off the water then run cold water into the pan until the eggs are cool. Break the eggs open and place the egg yolks in a blender together with the other dressing ingredients and blend until smooth.

Bring a large pan of salted water to the boil, add the beans and boil for 3 minutes or until just tender but retaining a slight bite. Using a slotted spoon, transfer them to a sink of cold water to refresh, then drain on kitchen paper or a teatowel and place them in a bowl.

Pour on enough dressing to coat them generously, add the shallots and toss to mix. Taste to check the seasoning, then transfer the salad to a serving bowl.

Variation
For a more instant dressing, the mustard dressing on page 181 will do nicely.

Salad of Frisée, Lardons and Croûtons

The croûtons absorb the flavour of the bacon and the dressing, emerging deliciously crisp at the edges and flavourful. The only possible downside is obtaining your frisée in the first place. The selection of salad leaves in most supermarkets is poor, with, for the most part, not a frisée or head of escarole in sight. Quite aside from the charms of such salad greens, they keep well for days in the salad drawer of the fridge. Frisée can vary in size greatly. If it's a huge blowsy affair, select enough leaves for four and keep the rest for another salad.

Serves 4

½ to 1 head of frisée

120 g green beans, topped, tailed and halved

6 large cherry tomatoes, cut into wedges

175 g lardons, or diced unsmoked streaky bacon

2 thick slices of Campagne or coarse-textured white bread, cut into 1.5cm dice

Dressing

1 tablespoon Dijon mustard

2 teaspoons red wine vinegar

Sea salt

3 tablespoons groundnut oil

The best way to prepare a frisée is to hold it by the stalk and give it a radical trim around the edges to remove the dark green leaves, which are tough and bitter. Now cut out the stalk and discard the periphery of outer leaves. Separate and tear up the remaining pale green fronds and wash them in a sink of cold water. Shake them dry and place in a large salad bowl.

Bring a small pan of salted water to the boil, add the green beans and simmer for 3–4 minutes leaving them firm to the bite. Drain and refresh in cold water, then toss them into the frisée leaves with the cherry tomatoes.

To make the dressing, whisk the mustard with the vinegar and some sea salt in a small bowl, then whisk in the groundnut oil.

Heat a dry frying pan over a medium-low heat and fry the lardons for about 4 minutes, stirring occasionally. Add the bread to the pan and continue to cook for another 4 minutes, tossing frequently until the bacon is frazzled and crisp and the croûtons are toasted at the edges. Toss the salad with the dressing. Scatter the contents of the pan over the salad, toss and serve at once, while the bacon and croûtons are still warm.

Warm Salad with Chicken Livers, Bacon and Grilled Potatoes

Puy Lentil, Roasted Pepper and Anchovy Salad

If you can, try to include some young dandelion leaves in this salad. Any that happen to be growing in your back garden will do, as long as you don't have pets.

Serves 4

8 medium new potatoes, peeled or scrubbed as necessary
Selection of salad leaves, such as rocket, red oakleaf lettuce, frisée, for 4
5 tablespoons extra virgin olive oil
Sea salt, black pepper
100 g pancetta or unsmoked streaky bacon, rind removed and diced
250 g chicken livers, trimmed
3 tablespoons white wine
1 teaspoon balsamic vinegar
1 teaspoon grainy mustard

Poached eggs

4 large organic eggs
Splash of white wine vinegar

Cook the potatoes in a pan of boiling salted water until tender, then drain. Poach the eggs in a large pan of water acidulated with the vinegar and reserve in cold water (see page 068).

Prepare the salad leaves and place in a large bowl.

About 10 minutes before serving heat a ridged griddle or a dry cast-iron frying pan. Halve the potatoes lengthways and toss them in a bowl with 2 tablespoons of the olive oil and some seasoning. Cook the potatoes on the griddle for several minutes on each side until streaked with brown. Bring a pan of water to the boil to reheat the poached eggs.

Heat a dry cast-iron frying pan, add the pancetta or bacon and cook until it is golden and crispy. Add the chicken livers, season and cook for 1 minute each side. Transfer the bacon and chicken livers to a plate. Pour the wine and balsamic vinegar into the pan and reduce to about 1 tablespoon, scraping up any sticky bits from the base of the pan. Take off the heat and stir in 3 tablespoons olive oil and the mustard.

Pop the poached eggs into the boiling water for 1½ minutes to heat through. Toss the leaves with the hot dressing and mix in the chicken livers and bacon. Pile this salad on to four plates and surround with the potatoes. Top each salad with a poached egg and serve.

This is another good-natured salad that can be made some hours in advance. Vegetarians can replace the anchovies with black olives.

Serves 6

6 red or orange peppers
8 to 10 thyme sprigs
2 bay leaves
4 garlic cloves, peeled and sliced
4 tablespoons extra virgin olive oil
Sea salt, black pepper
1 teaspoon balsamic vinegar
100 g Puy lentils
6 anchovy fillets, slit in half lengthways

Preheat the oven to 190°C, fan oven 180°C, gas 5. Core, deseed and quarter the peppers. Arrange them in a crowded single layer in a roasting pan, about 35 by 25cm. Tuck in the herbs and scatter over the garlic. Drizzle over the oil and season with salt and pepper. Roast for 50–55 minutes, stirring and basting at least twice to ensure the peppers emerge succulent and evenly singed at the edges.

As you remove the peppers from the oven, sprinkle with the vinegar and stir to mix into the juices. Leave to cool.

To finish the salad, bring a medium saucepan of water to the boil, add the lentils and simmer for 30 minutes until tender. Drain into a sieve and rinse under cold running water. Remove the herbs from the peppers, and add the cooked lentils and anchovies, gently mixing to coat them with the roasting juices. Transfer to a serving dish, cover and keep cool until ready to eat.

This salad is almost a full English breakfast. There shouldn't be any call for salt—pancetta does the trick and, ideally, this should be smoked. Failing that, lardons or even streaky bacon will do.

Serves 4
4 large organic eggs
125 g French beans, topped and tailed
650 g new potatoes, peeled
150 g pancetta, rind removed and cut into 1.5cm wide strips
2 tablespoons red wine vinegar
6 tablespoons extra virgin olive oil
Black pepper
1½ tablespoons snipped chives
25 g rocket leaves

Bring a pan of water to the boil, add the eggs and boil for 8 minutes; remove and cool in a sink of cold water. Add the French beans to the pan and cook for 4 minutes. Drain and refresh in cold water; drain well.

Cook the potatoes in a pan of boiling salted water until tender. In the meantime, shell and quarter the eggs. Drain the potatoes into a sieve and set aside to cool slightly while you finish the salad.

Heat a dry frying pan, add the pancetta and fry until crisp, then remove to a bowl and drain off fat. Off the heat, add the vinegar to the hot frying pan—it will splutter fiercely and reduce. Then add the oil and season with pepper.

Cut the potatoes into chunks depending on size. Toss in a salad bowl with the pancetta, French beans, chives and dressing. Mix in the rocket leaves, and then carefully tuck in the eggs. Serve at once.

Roast Shallots

Roast shallots come into their own when you have run out of fresh vegetables. Like any vegetable roasted or baked in its skin, all the flavours are captured and concentrated. A little butter, salt and pepper are all that are needed to enhance them. That said, they do need to be banana shallots—the tapered torpedoes—otherwise you would do better with red onions. Anything too small will shrivel up in the process of roasting.

Serves 4
1.3 kg banana shallots, or red onions (unpeeled)
Sea salt, black pepper
50 g unsalted butter

Preheat the oven to 170°C, fan oven 160°C, gas 3. Place the shallots or onions in a shallow roasting tin and bake them in their skins for 1¼ hours.

Slice off the base of each onion and carefully squeeze the inside out from its skin. Arrange the onions in a dish, slice open and season with salt and pepper. Dot with butter and serve as this begins to melt.

Roast Peppers

These are delectable served with grilled or roasted chicken and lamb, barbecued meats, or toasted goat's cheese. Alternatively, you can serve them as an hors d'oeuvre, alongside olives, slivers of Parmesan, salami, gherkins and caper berries. They are at their best served at room temperature, newly cooled. Avoid traffic light packs of red, amber and green peppers. The latter are merely unripe and lacking in sweetness. It's the fleshy red and yellow ones you want. The slender, thin-skinned peppers often sold as 'Mediterranean' are delicious, sweet and make good crudités, but are not for roasting.

Serves 6
6 red or orange peppers
8 to 10 thyme sprigs
2 bay leaves
5 garlic cloves, peeled and sliced
4 tablespoons extra virgin olive oil
  Sea salt, black pepper
1 teaspoon balsamic vinegar

Preheat the oven to 190°C, fan oven 180°C, gas 5. Core, quarter and deseed the peppers and arrange in a crowded single layer, in a baking dish or roasting pan. Tuck in the herbs, scatter over the garlic and drizzle over the oil. Season with salt and pepper.

Roast for 45–50 minutes, stirring and basting at least twice to ensure the peppers emerge succulent and evenly singed at the edges. When they come out of the oven, sprinkle with the vinegar and lightly stir to mix with the juices. Cool before serving.

Roast Aubergine

Here aubergine is roasted as thick slabs that blacken and caramelise on the outside, sealing the juices inside. Serve as an accompaniment to roast lamb or chicken.

Serves 6
700 g aubergines, stalks removed
  Extra virgin olive oil
  Sea salt, black pepper

Preheat the oven to 190°C, fan oven 180°C, gas 5. Cut the aubergines into slices, about 1.5cm thick. Brush with olive oil and place in a single layer on a baking sheet. Season with salt and pepper. Roast in the oven for 40 minutes until tender and caramelised.

Roast Beetroot, Carrot and Peppers

Beetroot and carrots with their leaves attached are more desirable than those denuded of their foliage. If you can find them by the bunch so much the better—the foliage is a healthy indicator of freshness.

Serves 4
450 g carrots
4 uncooked beetroot (the size of a small apple)
2 red peppers
Extra virgin olive oil
Sea salt, black pepper
4 tablespoons breadcrumbs
2 tablespoons chopped flat-leaf parsley
2 tablespoons chopped basil
Finely grated zest of 1 lemon
Squeeze of lemon juice
1 garlic clove, peeled and finely chopped
350 g ricotta cheese

Preheat the oven to 230°C, fan oven 220°C, gas 8. Scrub the carrots and beetroot, but don't peel them. Cut off the leaves if these are still attached. Slice the peppers in half through the core and remove the seeds. Place the vegetables in a roasting tray, drizzle over a little olive oil and season them. Roast for 30–40 minutes, tossing them halfway through. Remove and leave them to cool. Turn the oven down to 140°C, fan oven 130°C, gas 1.

Toss the breadcrumbs with a pinch of salt and a little oil, spread these out on a baking tray and toast for 30 minutes, tossing them around once or twice. By the end they should be golden and crisp. Allow them to cool.

Combine the chopped herbs, lemon zest and garlic in a small bowl with the lemon juice, 6 tablespoons of olive oil, and some seasoning. Slip the skin off the beetroots and halve them. Arrange the carrots, peppers and beetroot on plates and sprinkle with a little salt. Place a spoonful of ricotta cheese in the centre, drizzle over the herbed oil and scatter over some toasted crumbs.

Variations
Add a dollop of pesto instead of the herbed oil.

Serve the vegetables with grilled or roast chicken or fish, leaving out the ricotta.

Arrange the roasted vegetables with some rocket leaves and dress with a balsamic vinaigrette. Scatter over some black olives.

Serve the roasted vegetables with toasted goat's cheese instead of ricotta.

Roast Pumpkin with Garlic and Chilli

Given that pumpkin is such a watery old soul it is a wonder it roasts so well. True, it doesn't have the stamina of potatoes, parsnips or carrots, but that's a part of its charm. The outside, especially if it is tossed in flour, turns chewy and crisp at the edges while the inside melts in the mouth. Despite their radically diverse appearances the difference between varieties is not as great as you might imagine. This doesn't obscure a favourite however. Rouge vif d'Etampes is somehow just that little bit sweeter, firmer and more delectable than the rest. Butternut squash too is always a good bet.

Serves 4
1 kg pumpkin flesh, cut into crescents
Plain flour, for coating
6 garlic cloves (unpeeled)
3 red chillies
3 bay leaves
5 thyme sprigs
4 tablespoons extra virgin olive oil
Sea salt

Preheat the oven to 200°C, fan oven 190°C, gas 6. Toss the pumpkin pieces in a bowl with enough flour to coat them. Arrange them in a roasting dish and tuck in the garlic cloves, chillies and herbs. Drizzle over the oil, scatter over some sea salt and roast for 50–60 minutes, turning the pumpkin a couple of times during the process of cooking to ensure it colours evenly. The chillies can be eaten with the pumpkin; scrape the flesh off the skin and discard the seeds as you go. (Illustrated overleaf)

Creamed Spinach

It's not the baby spinach you want here but the big blowsy leaves that cook down to an exquisitely slippery mass. As the spinach cooks in just the water that clings to its leaves, it is important to use a saucepan with a thick base and tight-fitting lid. This will seem like a vast amount of spinach in its raw state—one of nature's little tricks as you will be lucky to have much more than a tablespoon per person by the end.

Serves 6
900 g spinach
150 ml crème fraîche
30 g unsalted butter
Sea salt, black pepper
Freshly grated nutmeg

Trim the spinach of coarse and frayed stalks and discard any wilted leaves. Wash the spinach thoroughly in a sink of cold water. Shake dry and place in a large saucepan, cramming it down to get it all in—if necessary use two saucepans. Cover tightly and cook over a medium heat for 10–15 minutes, pressing the spinach down halfway through. Drain into a sieve and press out as much liquid as possible. Be thorough about this, it is a constant source of amazement how much water this vegetable contains.

Put the crème fraîche, butter and some salt, pepper and nutmeg in the saucepan and return to a moderate heat. Once the butter has melted, simmer for several minutes until the cream thickens. Add the spinach and stir to coat it. Serve straightaway if possible. The spinach can be reheated but will lose its bright green sheen.

Buttered Spinach with Garlic

Spinach loves to be spoilt with copious amounts of butter—like scrambled eggs it seems to get better with every knob it absorbs. The garlic makes this a chicken or fish thing—grilled, roasted or laced with olive oil, lemon, herbs and spices. With the addition of a poached egg, it also makes a sublime supper.

Serves 6
900 g spinach
1 garlic clove, peeled
Sea salt, black pepper
90 g unsalted butter

Trim the spinach of coarse and frayed stalks and discard any wilted leaves. Wash the spinach leaves thoroughly in a sink of cold water. Shake dry and place in a large saucepan, cramming it down to get it all in—if necessary use two saucepans. Cover with a lid and cook over a low heat for 10–15 minutes, pressing it down halfway through. Drain into a sieve and press out as much liquid as possible. Spinach needs to be drained very thoroughly.

Either purée the garlic in a press, or chop it and sprinkle over a little sea salt, then crush to a paste on a chopping board using the flat of a knife. Heat the butter and garlic in the saucepan, with some pepper, and salt (if not used in crushing the garlic). Once the butter is seething, add the cooked spinach and stir to coat it. Heat through and serve. The spinach can be reheated but it will lose its lovely bright green sheen.

Creamed Corn

The canning giants pretty much have the gist of corn—it is quite naturally nibbed, or nibbed in a cream sauce. Canned sweetcorn has an appeal all of its own akin to frozen petit pois, which bear no relation to the real thing but are none the less delicious. However, canned corn is a far cry from cobs stripped down with your own fair hands. Properly creamed fresh sweetcorn makes a worthy companion for roast chicken.

Serves 6
4 corn-on-the-cobs
25 g unsalted butter
1 onion, peeled and finely chopped
Sea salt, black pepper
200 ml crème fraîche
Freshly grated nutmeg

Remove the husks and silk from the corn cobs, and slice off the kernels. The easiest way to do this—to avoid the kernels shooting all over the kitchen—is to hold the corn upright on the board, and starting halfway down the cob, slice downwards. Then upend it and repeat with the other half. Melt the butter in a medium saucepan, add the onion and cook with a pinch of salt for a few minutes until it is soft and translucent, stirring occasionally. Add the corn and continue to cook for 5–7 minutes until it is deep yellow and turning tender, again stirring occasionally.

Stir in the crème fraîche, cover and cook over a low heat for 10 minutes until the corn is coated in a thickened cream sauce. Season with pepper and nutmeg, and more salt if necessary.

Glazed Carrots

Having gone to the trouble of preserving the sweet succulence of whatever meat is starring at dinner, it seems a heresy to dish it up with vegetables on the raw side of being cooked. The trend for 'lightly steamed' vegetables is almost as bad as yesteryear's over-boiled ones. Carrots actually benefit from being well cooked; these ones are meltingly tender and buttery by design. For the best flavour use a homemade chicken stock, although water will still render tasty results.

Serves 6
800 g large carrots, preferably with foliage
125 ml chicken or vegetable stock, or water
40 g unsalted butter, diced
1 teaspoon sea salt
1 teaspoon caster sugar
2 tablespoons finely chopped parsley (optional)

Trim and peel the carrots and cut them into batons, about 5cm in length. Place them in a medium saucepan with the stock or water, butter, salt and sugar. Bring the liquid to a simmer, then cover and cook over a low heat for 8 minutes.

Give the carrots a stir, turn the heat up and cook uncovered until all the stock has evaporated and the carrots are glossy, about 8 minutes. Toss in the parsley if using and serve. If necessary the carrots can be reheated.

French Beans with Bacon

Crisp lardons of bacon nestling between the beans are welcome treasure. As you cook the French beans you could also throw in a few broad beans, skinned if they are beyond being tender, a few peas or fresh haricot 'coco' beans.

Serves 4
100 g unsmoked lardons, or diced
    streaky bacon
  2 shallots, peeled and
    finely chopped
  5 tablespoons white wine
 25 g unsalted butter
    Sea salt, black pepper
500 g fine French beans, topped
    and tailed

Bring a large pan of salted water to the boil. In the meantime, heat the bacon in a small frying pan over a medium heat until the fat renders, then continue to cook for 6–8 minutes until crisp and golden, stirring occasionally and adding the shallots a few minutes before the end. Add the wine and simmer until it has all but evaporated, then whisk in the butter and season.

Add the beans to the boiling water and cook for 3–4 minutes until just tender, then drain them into a sieve. Return the beans to the pan, add the contents of the frying pan and toss. Transfer to a bowl and serve.

Sautéed Mushrooms

The diversity of a mixed bag of mushrooms is to be relished. The exquisite scent of the more refined specimens brushes up against the old rogues of the bunch with considerable panache—the rough with the smooth.

Serves 4
  5 tablespoons olive oil
  3 shallots, peeled and
    finely chopped
  2 garlic cloves, peeled and
    finely chopped
900 g mixed wild and cultivated
    mushrooms, picked over and
    sliced as necessary
100 ml white wine
225 ml double cream
    Sea salt, black pepper
    Squeeze of lemon juice
  1 heaped tablespoon finely
    chopped flat-leaf parsley

Sauté the mushrooms in about three lots; it's important not to overcrowd the pan. Heat the oil in your largest frying pan over a medium heat, add the shallots and cook for a minute or two until they soften. Turn the heat up and add the garlic. Fry the mushrooms in the pan (in batches), tossing them constantly until they are soft and starting to colour. If any liquid is given out in the process, keep cooking until it evaporates. As they are are cooked, transfer the mushrooms to a bowl.

Return all the mushrooms to the pan, add the wine and cook until this evaporates. Add the cream, salt, pepper and lemon juice. Cook until the sauce thickens and then stir in the chopped parsley. Serve straightaway.

Serving suggestions
Serve the mushrooms on toasted brioche, with a poached egg on top.

Pile them to the side of scrambled eggs.

Use the mushrooms as a base for serving grilled quail or chicken.

Serve them piled on top of baked potatoes.

For a pasta sauce, leave out the parsley and add a spoonful or two of grated Parmesan in lieu.

Perfect Peas

Peas should be perfect, or at least perfectly cooked. Being so small, sweet and tenderly green, this would seem to be their divine right. Quite why we do not make more of the nascent shoots of the plant —that are so exquisite wilted in butter and tossed into cooked peas —is a mystery. In California punnets are quite the norm and hardy enough to withstand a Transatlantic flight home. In lieu, you could throw in some blanched mangetouts or broad beans, skinned if at all tough or mealy.

Serves 4
900 g peas in the pod
25 g unsalted butter
½ teaspoon sea salt
½ teaspoon caster sugar
50 ml water

Shell the peas. Place the butter, sea salt, caster sugar and water in a medium saucepan and bring to a simmer over a high heat. Add the peas and cook, tossing, for 2–3 minutes. They will turn a luscious green, remaining plump, and will literally burst as you eat them.

Peas with Pancetta

In addition to its place beside a roast, a bowl of peas with pancetta is to be savoured as a light supper on its own.

Serves 6
25 g unsalted butter
2 tablespoons olive oil
1 red onion, peeled and chopped
1 garlic clove, peeled and finely chopped
75 g pancetta or unsmoked streaky bacon, diced
400 g shelled peas
90 ml white wine
Sea salt, black pepper
2 tablespoons coarsely chopped flat-leaf parsley

Heat the butter and olive oil in a large saucepan over a medium heat. Add the red onion and sweat for about 5 minutes until it begins to colour. Add the garlic and pancetta, and fry, stirring occasionally, until this begins to crisp. Add the peas, wine and some seasoning. Cover and cook for 5 minutes, adding the chopped parsley just before the end. Serve at once.

White Wine and Butter Leeks

The velvet sleekness of a pile of buttery leeks softens any meat or fish they are served with. In this instance the wine and butter fuse into a sauce that coats them.

Serves 4
700 g leeks
50 g unsalted butter
150 ml white wine
Sea salt, black pepper

Trim the roots and cut off the dark green shoots from the leeks. Remove the outer layer of leaves and rinse them. Cut into 5mm thick slices and rinse well in a sieve under the cold tap.

Place the leeks in a saucepan with the butter, wine and seasoning. Bring the liquid to the boil, cover the pan and cook over a low heat for 25–30 minutes. Remove the lid. The leeks should be coated in a butter sauce, but if there is more liquid remaining, turn up the heat and continue to cook until it has all but evaporated.

Courgette stuffed with courgette is a very Alain Ducasse thing. Courgette flowers are a testament to their own freshness. The blooms do not allow any deception being delicate and fay, they will wilt at the slightest neglect and demand to be eaten straightaway. The flowers possess a sweet milky succulence. The prize morsel inside is the clutch of juicy yellow stamens, which to a courgette is what cheeks are to a cod.

Serves 4
600 g courgettes, ends removed
40 g unsalted butter
Sea salt, black pepper
8 courgette flowers, with courgette attached
2 tablespoons extra virgin olive oil
1 onion, peeled, halved and sliced
2 garlic cloves, peeled and thinly sliced
150 ml white wine

Coarsely grate the courgettes; you can use a food processor fitted with a coarse grating disc to do this. Melt the butter in a medium saucepan over a medium heat. Add the grated courgettes and season with salt and pepper. Sweat for 10–15 minutes, stirring occasionally, until you have a dry, textured purée. Set aside to cool.

Gently prise open the courgette flowers and stuff each one with a couple of teaspoons of the wilted courgette, twisting the tops of the flowers to secure them. Heat the olive oil in a large saucepan over a medium heat, add the onion and sweat for several minutes until it is soft and translucent, without colouring it.

Add the garlic and moments later, add half the courgette flowers, turning them in the oil. Pile them to one side of the pan and repeat with the remainder. Pour in the wine, season and bring to the boil. Cover and braise the courgettes over a low heat for 8–10 minutes until they are tender.

Serve the courgette flowers with their juices, carefully lifting them so as not to separate them from their baby courgette in the process. They are also delicious eaten cold.

This voluptuous golden emulsion is a profound expression of garlic, and much has been written of its desired quality. The rosy heads that come from Provence with their fat pearly cloves are perfect. You can use as few as two, or a whole head plus, but a happy medium of around six cloves is about right—still no shrinking violet.

Our dedication to good food stops short of making aioli with a pestle and mortar, however appealing that might be if someone else were cooking. There is a compromise—invest any physical energy in crushing the garlic cloves to a paste with a sprinkling of salt, and then whisk the mayonnaise by hand. It's that much easier than the pestle and mortar route and can still boast more authenticity than a whirring blade.

As for the oil, it is virtually impossible to produce a light mayonnaise that relies entirely on extra virgin olive oil. A powerful Tuscan oil would be a disaster. Provencal olive oil is altogether gentler and you can just about get away with using 100% of this oil if it is the right time of year—some months after the harvest when it will have mellowed. Sicilian oils too are gentle—Ravida oil will have mellowed sufficiently by the summer. But playing safe, half extra virgin and half groundnut oil is a better bet. Try to make the aioli a couple of hours ahead to allow time for the flavours to develop.

Serves 6–8
Sea salt
6 cloves garlic, peeled and chopped
2 large organic egg yolks
350 ml groundnut oil
225 ml extra virgin olive oil
2 teaspoons lemon juice
1 teaspoon pastis, such as Pernod

Sprinkle a little salt over the garlic, then crush and chop it to a paste using the flat edge of a knife. Alternatively use a garlic press, adding a little salt to the resulting pulp. Whisk the egg yolks and garlic together in a large bowl. Very gradually whisk in the groundnut oil, just a few drops at a time to begin with and then, once the mayonnaise has taken, in a more generous stream. Then whisk in some of the olive oil in a steady stream. As the mayonnaise becomes too thick to whisk, add some of the lemon juice followed by the Pastis, and then keep whisking in the oil. Taste it and add a little more lemon juice if necessary. Store it covered in the fridge and bring back to room temperature before eating.

Rescue remedy

If the aioli does the unmentionable and splits, whisk another egg yolk in a clean bowl and gradually whisk in the curdled mayonnaise. To reduce the risk, include a teaspoon of Dijon mustard in with the egg yolk at the beginning.

Mayonnaise

Homemade mayonnaise is strangely surrounded by mystique, akin to witchcraft. One Italian olive oil producer prided himself on his mayonnaise skills for decades, until as an old man he learnt to his astonishment that you don't have to whisk in the oil in a clockwise direction to avoid it splitting. Perhaps as a young man he had tried making it, succeeded and deemed this to be the reason for his success. Mayonnaise is a cinch to make, requiring no more than a few minutes gentle exertion of a whisk. There is just one trick of the trade and that is to include a spoonful of Dijon mustard in with the egg yolk at the very beginning. As well as stabilising the process it adds a welcome savour.

This is a classic mayonnaise for serving with cold crab, lobster, langoustines and poached fish such as salmon and turbot, as well as vegetables and potatoes. Its delicacy relies on the use of groundnut oil, which ensures a mayonnaise that is creamy and light in texture. Extra virgin olive oil is far too bold for a plain mayonnaise and best saved for aioli. Even then, it calls for a judicious hand.

Serves 6
1 medium organic egg yolk
  (at room temperature)
1 teaspoon Dijon mustard
  Pinch of fine sea salt
220 ml groundnut oil (approximately)
  Squeeze of lemon juice

Place the egg yolk in a bowl with the mustard and salt and whisk to blend. Now add just a dribble of oil and whisk it in, then another and another until the sauce thickens and you are confident the mayonnaise is taking.

You can now start to add the oil in bolder streams, whisking with each addition. By the end the mayonnaise should be so thick it clings to the whisk and sits in mounds in the bowl. Sharpen it with a squeeze of lemon juice. Cover and chill until required. It should keep well for several days. If by any misfortune it splits, employ the rescue remedy.

Rescue remedy
If the mayonnaise does split, whisk another egg yolk in a clean bowl and gradually whisk in the curdled mayonnaise.

Variation
Lower fat mayonnaise
Add an additional pinch of salt when you start making the mayonnaise, and an additional squeeze of lemon juice at the end. Finally fold 125g fromage frais into the prepared sauce.

Green Sauce

This classic Italian sauce is resonant with fresh herbs and anchovies. Very much a sauce for seafood, serve it over any grilled or poached fish, or with a big bowl of steamed clams or mussels.

Serves 4
3 heaped tablespoons coarsely chopped basil
2 heaped tablespoons coarsely chopped mint
6 heaped tablespoons coarsely chopped flat-leaf parsley
½ clove garlic
6 salted anchovies in oil
2 tablespoons capers, rinsed
¼ teaspoon chopped green chilli
1 tablespoon lemon juice
6 tablespoons extra virgin olive oil
1 teaspoon Dijon mustard
½ teaspoon sea salt

The easiest way to make this sauce is in a food processor. Alternatively, you could finely chop the ingredients by hand and then combine them. Place the herbs, garlic, anchovies, capers and chilli in a food processor and whizz until the mixture is finely chopped. Add the lemon juice and then the olive oil in a thin steady stream, and finally incorporate the mustard and salt.

Lebanese Garlic Cream

This is rough and ready—no pretence to suavity here. Whizz it up and serve with chicken or lamb kebabs in warm pitta bread or with a plain roast.

Serves 6
5 garlic cloves, peeled
1 large organic egg
150 ml groundnut oil
150 ml extra virgin olive oil
Juice of ½ lemon
Sea salt

Place the garlic cloves in a food processor and pulse to chop them finely. Add the egg and continue to whizz, and then slowly trickle in the oils, as though making a mayonnaise. Once the sauce starts to thicken, you can add the oils in a steadier stream. Finally add the lemon juice, season with salt and transfer to a bowl.

Tartare Sauce

Serve this with any milky white fish, its skin grilled or roasted to a crisp sheathe—it could be sea bass, halibut, haddock or grey mullet.

Serves 4
2 medium organic egg yolks
1 teaspoon grainy mustard
350 ml groundnut oil
Squeeze of lemon juice
1 heaped tablespoon finely chopped gherkins
1 heaped tablespoon finely chopped capers
1 heaped tablespoon finely chopped flat-leaf parsley

Whisk the egg yolks and mustard together in a bowl. Then gradually whisk in the oil to make a mayonnaise; by the end it should be too thick to whisk. Add a good squeeze of lemon juice, then the gherkins, capers and parsley.

Horseradish Sauce

Try to track down some fresh horseradish root, nothing quite beats its fiery nasal bite. If this isn't possible, jars of preserved grated fresh horseradish are quite acceptable. Start by adding 2 tablespoons of horseradish to the crème fraîche, adding more to taste if you like it hotter.

Serves 6
200 ml crème fraîche
2 to 3 tablespoons finely grated horseradish
Sea salt

Blend the crème fraîche and horseradish together in a bowl and season with salt to taste. Transfer the sauce to a clean bowl, cover and chill until required.

Cherry Tomato Sauce

An all-round tomato sauce with an exceptional flavour. It's a little more expensive than a standard tomato sauce, but well worth the extra.

Makes about 800ml
1.35 kg cherry tomatoes, halved
1 heaped teaspoon sea salt
1 teaspoon caster sugar
100 g unsalted butter
4 tablespoons extra virgin olive oil

Place the tomatoes in a medium saucepan, cover and cook over a low heat for 20–30 minutes until they collapse, stirring occasionally. Pass through a sieve or a mouli-legumes and return to the pan, rinsing it out if necessary. Add the remaining ingredients and simmer very gently, uncovered, for 1 hour until thickened but still of a thin pouring consistency.

Jerusalem Artichoke Purée

Serve this at room temperature with air-dried or honey-roast ham, in lieu of a sauce.

Serves 6
Juice of 1½ lemons
1.1 kg Jerusalem artichokes
3 tablespoons extra virgin olive oil
2 shallots, peeled and
finely chopped
Sea salt, black pepper
150 ml whipping cream, whipped

Acidulate a bowl of water with the juice of 1 lemon. Peel the artichokes and immerse them in the water. Heat the olive oil in a large saucepan, add the shallots and sweat for a minute or two. Drain the artichokes and add them to the pan, turn to coat in the oil and season them with salt and pepper. Add a little water to give a depth of 3–4mm. Put the lid on the pan and cook for 20 minutes until the artichokes are very soft. If any liquid remains, cook uncovered until it evaporates. Transfer the contents of the pan to a blender and process to a purée. Allow to cool—it will firm up considerably.

Combine the purée with the whipped cream and season with salt, pepper and a little of the remaining lemon juice. You can chill the purée but bring it back to room temperature before serving.

Leek Purée

A close relative of vichyssoise, this is halfway between a sauce and mash. Serve it with grilled chicken and fish, or with a poached egg on top and some toast.

Serves 4
225 g maincrop potatoes, peeled
and cubed
225 g sliced leeks
600 ml semi-skimmed milk
1 garlic clove, smashed in the skin
1 thyme sprig
1 bay leaf
Sea salt, black pepper
3 tablespoons double cream
15 g unsalted butter

Place the potato, leeks, milk, garlic, herbs and a little salt in a saucepan. Bring to the boil and simmer for 15–20 minutes. Drain the potato and leek mixture, discarding the herbs and garlic. (You can use the cooking liquor for soup or a béchamel).

Tip the leek and potato mixture into a food processor and reduce to a coarse purée, giving it a quick burst at high speed, try to do this quickly or it may turn gloopy. Return the mixture to the pan and add the cream and butter to make a sloppy purée. Season with salt and pepper and reheat to serve.

Prune and Walnut Stuffing

Exceptionally succulent and moist, this stuffing is perfect for guinea fowl, duckling or the neck of a turkey. Just scale it up according to the size of your bird. Don't attempt to cook the stuffing separately— the raison d'être of a stuffing is to soak up the juices of the bird as it cooks. Better to have just a small spoonful each than a tasteless desiccated lump.

4 servings
180 g ready-to-eat stoned prunes
6 tablespoons brandy or Calvados
50 g unsalted butter, softened
2 shallots, peeled and
finely chopped
3 celery heart sticks, finely sliced
40 g walnuts
3 tablespoons chopped parsley
⅓ teaspoon finely chopped tarragon
3 tablespoons breadcrumbs
Sea salt, black pepper
Squeeze of lemon juice

Put the prunes and brandy in a small saucepan over a medium-low heat until all the liquor is absorbed.

Heat half the butter in a small frying pan. Add the shallots and celery and sweat over a gentle heat for about 8 minutes until soft and translucent, without allowing them to colour.

Finely grind the walnuts in a clean coffee grinder and blend with the remaining butter in a bowl, using a wooden spoon. Work in the herbs and the breadcrumbs, then add the sweated vegetables. Coarsely chop the prunes and incorporate these, then season with salt and pepper and add a squeeze of lemon juice. Use to stuff your bird in the usual way.

Commercially produced chutneys are invariably over-vinegared, pasty and bland, whereas homemade ones are lusciously sticky and taste of the vegetables, fruit and spices that have gone into them. For the novice, rest assured it is virtually impossible to go wrong, and, having made one batch, you will almost certainly be hooked. A jar of home-made tomato chutney and a big hunk of farmhouse Cheddar in the fridge are great standbys.

The vinegar and sugar
Chutneys are by definition sweet and sour. The balance and quality of the vinegar and sugar are all-important—malt vinegar is no kinder in chutney than it is to fish and chips. By the same equation, use an unrefined soft brown sugar rather than a refined white one for a richer flavour.

The pan and jars
Either use a large stainless steel preserving pan, a maslin pan (as shown) or simply a large saucepan. Avoid aluminium, as vinegar will cause the metal to pit, tainting the preserve. Clip-top kilner jars are available from ironmongers in 500ml and 1 litre sizes. Before filling the jars, heat them in a medium hot oven (about 180°C, fan oven 170°C, gas 4) for 5 minutes.

Storing the chutney
Partly through impatience we break with the tradition of maturing chutney for at least 3 months before eating it, and dive in as soon as it's cool. This said, chutney does mellow with age, and it will be as good if not better after several months.

Available from major supermarkets, Aspall Organic Cyder Vinegar gives this chutney a wonderfully mellow, fruity finish.

Makes 1.5 litres
1.3 kg beefsteak tomatoes
500 g eating apples, cored
700 g red onions, peeled
    and chopped
500 ml cider vinegar
  4 garlic cloves, peeled and
    finely chopped
  1 tablespoon finely chopped
    root ginger
400 g raisins
450 g soft brown sugar
  ½ teaspoon cayenne pepper
  7 cm cinnamon stick
  1 tablespoon sea salt

Cut out a cone from of the top of each tomato to remove the core. Immerse the tomatoes in a pan of boiling water for 20 seconds, then plunge into cold water. Skin and chop the tomatoes. Without peeling, cut the apples into 5mm dice.

Put the tomatoes, apples and onions in a large saucepan. Add the remaining ingredients, stir and bring to a simmer. Cook over a low heat for 3–3½ hours, stirring occasionally, but more frequently towards the end to prevent the chutney from sticking.

There should still be a small amount of sticky syrup floating on the surface, bearing in mind the chutney will firm up on cooling. To test, draw a trough in the chutney using a spoon: it shouldn't collect more than a small amount of syrupy liquor; if it fills up with vinegary juices it needs further

cooking. You can also spoon a little chutney on to a cold plate, leave it to cool for a few minutes, then judge whether it is the right consistency. Once cooked, discard the cinnamon. Fill three hot 500ml kilner jars (see left) with the hot chutney, then close them and leave to cool.

In its finest form, gravy is essentially the flavour of the meat or bird given back to it, the starting point being the sticky caramelised juices left clinging to the pan when the roast is removed. These are eked out by deglazing the pan with a drop of wine, Madeira or port, and then stretched a little further with water or stock, and any juices given out when the roast is carved. A couple of tablespoons of this richly flavoured sauce are all that is needed to enhance the succulence of the meat.

Such gravy does however demand a judicious choice of vegetables on the side. The days when it was fashionable to drown your roast in thickened gravy coincided with the tradition of serving two over-boiled vegetables that needed all the help they could get. We had more in mind a rich gratin, creamy vegetable purée or just one other vegetable. The gravy is there to take care of the meat.

Three steps to perfect gravy
Skimming the juices
First skim off any excess fat from the roasting tray leaving just one or two tablespoons. The sticky bits left clinging to the bottom of the pan form the foundation of your gravy, and the more there are the better. Though even when there appears to be next to nothing, it's surprising how far their flavour will stretch with the help of a little wine and stock.

Deglazing the pan
There are no golden rules about whether you add red or white wine to the roasting tray. When roasting beef or lamb you may like to add Madeira or port instead. Place the roasting pan on a fairly low heat, add the wine and simmer for several minutes, scraping up the sticky residue on the bottom. If you taste the sauce at this point it should be quite strong and probably adequately seasoned from the initial seasoning you gave the meat.

Thinning the gravy
If you are using water or vegetable cooking water (which in truth has very little flavour), you should add a relatively small quantity. If you are using stock however you can afford to add more without diluting the flavour. Use chicken stock for chicken, and either lamb or beef stock for red meats. Simmer the gravy long and hard enough for the juices to amalgamate into a smooth sauce, then add any juices given out on carving the roast.

Roast chicken
On removing your roast bird to a carving plate to rest, tip any juices from inside the chicken back into the roasting pan. Proceed as usual deglazing the pan with 90ml dry white wine. Now add 90ml water or 180ml chicken stock and continue to simmer for several minutes.

Roast lamb
Make gravy in the usual way, deglazing the pan with 90ml red wine or Madeira. Once the wine has cooked off, add a teaspoon or two of redcurrant jelly and stir until it melts, then thin the gravy with 180ml beef or lamb stock and continue to simmer until it amalgamates. Roast lamb gives out lots of pink juices when it is carved that can be added back.

Roast beef
Deglaze the pan using 90ml red wine or port if you like it slightly sweet. Stir in ½ teaspoon Dijon mustard then thin it with 180ml beef stock and proceed as usual.

Tips for success
The quality of your gravy will depend on the quality of your meat or poultry. The more flavour it has, the more flavourful the gravy.

For gravy-making you need a sturdy roasting dish that is suitable for the hob, anything flimsy with an uneven base will burn the juices. See page 273 for recommendations.

Remember that making gravy is an imprecise art—the amount of wine or stock you add should be determined by the size of the roast and the amount of juices in the pan. Be guided by intuition and taste as you go. What are euphemistically known as cook's nips are off the agenda. The ends of glasses and bottles that are combined and kept beside the stove for such occasions will be little better than vinegar. Any wine you use should be decent enough to drink.

Try to use fresh stock, rather than stock cubes. And don't bother to sieve the finished gravy—while common practice in restaurants, one of the joys is all the bits from the roast that come in it.

Pour the gravy into a jug at the very last minute once everyone is seated to ensure it comes to the table piping hot.

Tricks of the trade

Old-fashioned mushroom ketchup was the answer of many a Victorian cook to pepping up their steak and kidney pudding. It's still around today, a useful little bottle for keeping beside the Lea and Perrins. Just a few drops will add a sparkle to a slightly flat gravy.

A smidgeon of Dijon or grainy mustard can be added to boost the flavour, as can a few drops of Lea and Perrins.

Scent the gravy with thyme by adding a few sprigs to the pan when deglazing it and removing them at the end.

Add a few green peppercorns to a chicken or beef gravy.

Add some chopped herbs and skinned and diced tomato to a gravy for chicken or lamb.

Add some chopped black olives to lamb gravy and enrich with a knob of butter. This is delicious served with ratatouille.

In France the giblets from your guinea fowl or chicken automatically come wrapped in a little sachet of foil. If you do happen to be fortunate enough to acquire the giblets with the bird and you're not in the mood to use them, pop them into the freezer. They'll come in handy at Christmas when you need all the gravy you can muster.

Stock
Giblets (heart, liver, neck and gizzard), chopped
90 ml red wine
Bouquet garni (1 thyme sprig, 1 bay leaf, 2 parsley stalks)
1 carrot, peeled and chopped
1 leek, trimmed and chopped
1 onion, peeled and chopped

To finish
180 g mixture of leek, carrot and celery, chopped
90 ml red wine

For the stock, preheat the oven to 220°C, fan oven 200°C, gas 7 and roast the giblets in a little fat for 20 minutes until slightly coloured. Transfer them to a saucepan, add plenty of water to cover and bring to a gentle boil. Simmer for about 1 hour, skimming until all fat and froth is removed, and topping up with water if necessary. Add the wine, bouquet garni and chopped vegetables, cover and simmer for 1 hour. Strain the stock and reserve.

To finish the gravy, drain off the surface fat from the roasting tray. Add the mixed vegetables to the remaining pan juices and cook until syrupy and golden. Add the wine and reduce by half. Add the stock and simmer for 15 minutes. Season and strain the gravy into a jug.

The Cheese Course

Full cheeseboards, while magnificent to behold, rarely slot with any grace into dinner. Invariably they are too much, too late, and at their most enjoyable after a bowl of soup or in the company of a salad. When cheese does appear as the second or third course, it is more apt to serve just one variety that transcends the ordinary.

The French custom of serving the cheese course in advance of pudding has a rationale. It saves confusing your palate by taking it from savoury to sweet and back again. Sugar has a tendency to blanket our tastebuds, so anything that comes after is not only slightly warped by the experience but dulled too. Serving cheese the French way demands only that dry white wine be replaced by a glass of red, which will also see you through the pudding if there is no sweet wine to come.

Of accompaniments, a small green salad is always a pleasant aside. The recipe on page 181 has a slightly more pungent dressing than usual, though the salad needn't be dressed. We often resort to some plain leaves of Belgian or red chicory, which provide a sweet succulent bite in contrast. If you're set on crackers, then Carr's water biscuits are the most elegant and achieve the best balance of being hard and fine at the same time. Other than that, the following combinations are most agreeable.

Stilton and quince cheese

The russet hue of quince cheese is true to the perfumed pulp of this exquisite fruit. As sweet as jam but grainy in texture, the smallest sliver delights a morsel of Stilton, a cheese that has been described as an iron fist in a velvet glove.

Stilton should be rich, creamy yellow and spreadable like butter when it is ripe, with a restrained marbling of veins displaying the colour of lichen. Stilton from the Colston Bassett Dairy is justly famous.

Roquefort and walnuts

Cracking walnuts and extracting the kernels is almost as pleasurable as eating them. The mellow charm of these nuts is an apt match for the salivating power of Roquefort. This most complex of all blue cheeses is intensely salty and almost wet around the mould ripened centre. The blue veining has the moist air currents that flow through the chalky caves in Roquefort where the cheese is matured to thank.

Lancashire and chutney

A good homemade chutney is ever a good accompaniment to Cheddar, and it's worth making a few kilner jars of Tomato Chutney (page 217) to see you through the year for this purpose alone. The sharply intense crumb of tasty Lancashire, one of the finest farmhouse cheeses around, is particularly well offset—especially that of Mrs Kirkham whose reputation as a cheesemaker precedes her.

Cheddar and cob nuts

Cob nuts are quaintly British, appearing in the shops in September, blushing a verdant pale green that like the leaves on the trees, colours to brown as the season progresses. And though they still make good eating later in autumn they are at their best early on, with that slight wetness possessed of new nuts. Serve them with a mellow Cheddar like Montgomery's, Chewton or Keen's.

Parmigiano-reggiano and pear

The dry crumbly nature of fresh Parmesan marries beautifully with the dripping succulence of a ripe pear, and with its aroma. Shave the finest slivers off a roughly hewn chunk—a little Parmesan goes a long way. Although rich in character this cheese is surprisingly gentle served this way.

Salers and apple

Catch this combination on a good day and the only thing that can render it any more sublime is a 'café Calva' to follow. When you taste a truly great apple you realise just how inferior much of the fruit on the market is. The potential of a majestic apple lies in its acidity offset by a sweetness that results in an extraordinary intensity of flavour. As to salers, even the best Cheddar pales beside this AOC cheese. It has an extraordinary scent that can be attributed to the mountain pastures where gentian, bilberry and liquorice grow. The milk comes from Salers cows, huge russet beasts that have defied modern methods of milking and farming.

Goat's cheese and dates

Part of the charm of small goat's cheeses is that no two are ever the same, as they differ from one maker and region to another. Nothing too mature here, a young goat's cheese with soft curdy insides and a rim of runny cheese within the rind will make tasty eating with some Medjool dates.

Vacherin mont d'or and watercress

Vacherin mont d'or from the Joux valley in the Jura, is scented by the resin in the hoop of spruce bark used to enclose the cheese, making it a moodily seasonal offering around Christmas. The form is to lift off the reddish crust and remove the creamy insides using a teaspoon, an experience to be savoured with, at most, a sprig or two of watercress.

Perail and chicory

The inside of this small round sheep's milk cheese with its delicate scent of meadow flowers has the same milky liquid charm as vacherin mont d'or, but it's not as grand. Perail is a cheese to enjoy with chicory when the company numbers just two or three, or you can serve it as a light lunch with some radishes and French bread.

Rhubarb Jelly

Roasted rhubarb sitting in a flimsy
jelly of its own juices has the same
Edwardian appeal as aspic and
damson gin, only to be bettered
with a dollop of cream scented
with orange flower water.

Serves 6
900 g rhubarb (trimmed weight),
    cut into 2cm lengths
225 g caster sugar
1½ by 11g sachets of
    powdered gelatine
1 tablespoon lemon juice

Preheat the oven to 180°C,
fan oven 170°C, gas 4. Arrange the
rhubarb in a shallow gratin or
baking dish, sprinkling it with the
sugar as you layer it. Cover with foil
and bake for 45 minutes. Carefully
tip the rhubarb and juices into a
sieve set over a bowl. Once all the
liquor has drained from the fruit,
transfer it to an 18–20cm dessert
bowl. Pour the rhubarb juice into a
measuring jug.

Put 4 tablespoons of just-boiled
water into a small bowl. Sprinkle on
the gelatine and leave for several
minutes to dissolve, then stir. If it
hasn't fully dissolved, place the
bowl within a second bowl of just-
boiled water and leave it for a few
minutes longer, then stir again.

Stir a couple of tablespoons of
the rhubarb liquor into the gelatine
solution, then mix this back into the
rest of the rhubarb juice. Add the
lemon juice and make up to 600ml
with boiling water. Carefully pour
this over the rhubarb, and level the
surface with a spoon. Leave to cool,
then còver with clingfilm and chill
for 6 hours or overnight until set.

Whisked Wine Jelly

Wine jellies possess hidden powers to intoxicate, especially if you absentmindedly dip into the bowl on a midsummer morning. There is no need here to polish up your moulding skills, as you're going to slush the jelly with a whisk once it's set, appearance doesn't really come into it. Serve this spooned over whatever summer fruits take your fancy—cherries, peaches, raspberries, loganberries or strawberries.

Serves 4–6
1 bottle Sauternes or other dessert wine
40 g caster sugar, or to taste
11 g sachet powdered gelatine

Bring the wine to the boil in a saucepan and then immediately remove from the heat. Add sugar to taste (the amount will depend on the sweetness of the wine). To counter the acidity of the fruit, your jelly should be sweeter than you might want to drink the wine. Transfer 3–4 tablespoons of the hot wine to a small bowl and sprinkle over the gelatine. Leave it to stand for a few minutes and then stir to dissolve. If the gelatine hasn't completely dissolved, stand the bowl in a saucepan of just-boiled water until it does.

Combine the dissolved gelatine with the remainder of the wine. Pour into a bowl and leave to cool, then cover and chill in the fridge for several hours until it has set, preferably overnight.

To serve, run a whisk through the jelly to break it up into a soft jewelled mass and spoon it over whatever fruit you choose to serve.

Strawberry Fool with White Chocolate

A quivering set that melts in the mouth. Only the ripest most perfumed strawberries will do— ones with the same intensity of flavour as wild strawberries, which can in fact be used to decorate the fool should you come across any.

Serves 6
1 lemon
600 ml double cream
1 vanilla pod, slit
⅓ by 11g sachet powdered gelatine
125 g caster sugar
350 g strawberries, hulled
225 g raspberries

To serve
225 to 250g medium strawberries, hulled and halved
2 tablespoons finely grated white chocolate

Finely pare the zest from the lemon in strips, using a potato peeler. Place the cream, lemon zest and vanilla pod in a medium non-stick saucepan. Bring to a simmer and reduce by a third, stirring from time to time. Take off the heat and set aside to infuse for 15 minutes. Towards the end of this time, put 3 tablespoons of just-boiled water into a small bowl. Sprinkle on the gelatine and leave for several minutes to dissolve, then stir. If it hasn't fully dissolved, stand the bowl in a saucepan of just-boiled water until it does.

Add the gelatine to the cream and stir to blend. Add the sugar and stir until this has dissolved. Purée the fruit with a squeeze of lemon juice in a blender and then stir into the cream base. Pass the mixture through a fine sieve into a 20cm serving bowl.

Cover with clingfilm and leave the fool to set in the fridge for at least 4 hours or overnight.

To serve, arrange the strawberry halves on top of the fool and scatter the grated chocolate over the top.

Chocolate and Vanilla Cream Pots

These creamy little pots of custard derive from La Bastide de Moustiers, Alain Ducasse's Provençal auberge where they also serve a third petit pot scented with coffee. If you have small dishes or pots in which to make them that's fine, otherwise set them in a larger bowl and serve a spoon of each, accompanied with dessert biscuits.

Serves 6
500 ml full-cream milk
500 ml double cream
 10 medium organic egg yolks
225 g caster sugar
 90 g dark chocolate, cut up small
  1 vanilla pod, cut up
    Dessert biscuits, to serve

Preheat the oven to 150°C, fan oven 140°C, gas 2. Bring the milk and cream to the boil in a saucepan. Whisk the egg yolks and sugar together in a large bowl, and then whisk in the boiled milk. Pour half of the mixture into another bowl.

Add the chocolate to one bowl and leave until melted, then stir until smooth. Add the vanilla to the other bowl and leave to infuse for 10 minutes. Whisk and strain the different mixtures into clean ovenproof bowls. Stand them in a bain marie or roasting tin containing enough boiling water to come two thirds of the way up the sides of each one. Cook in the oven for 1 hour 15 minutes. Allow to cool, then cover and chill.

Place a spoonful each of the vanilla and chocolate custards on each plate. Accompany with crisp dessert biscuits.

Pear and Raspberry Mascarpone Trifle

All the essentials of a good trifle are present and correct—almond-scented macaroons and sponge cake, sticky raspberry jam, thick creamy custard, poached fruits and the heady hit of brandy.

Serves 6–8
Pears
300 ml water
175 g caster sugar
  1 vanilla pod, slit, or 1 teaspoon vanilla extract
  2 Comice pears
  3 tablespoons Poire William eau-de-vie or brandy

Trifle
100 g amaretti or macaroons
500 g mascarpone
  3 medium organic eggs, separated
 50 g caster sugar
125 g Madeira sponge cake, cut into 5mm thick slices
150 g seedless raspberry jam
  1 tablespoon lemon juice
 15 g toasted flaked almonds

To poach the pears, place the water, sugar and vanilla pod or extract in a small saucepan and slowly bring to the boil so the sugar dissolves. Peel and halve the pears. Add them to the syrup so that as far as possible they are submerged. Cover with a circle of baking parchment and poach until the pears are tender when pierced with a skewer; this can take anywhere between 4 and 15 minutes depending on their ripeness. Allow to cool in the syrup, then remove and drain thoroughly. Quarter, core and finely slice the pears. Mix 5 tablespoons of the syrup with the eau-de-vie or brandy. Break the macaroons into a shallow bowl and pour on half of the flavoured syrup.

To prepare the custard, beat the mascarpone with 2 egg yolks in a large bowl (the third yolk isn't required for the trifle). In another bowl, whisk the egg whites until they hold their shape, then gradually sprinkle over the sugar and whisk well with each addition, until you have a glossy meringue. Fold this into the mascarpone.

To assemble the trifle, smear a spoonful of the custard over the base of a deep 20cm bowl. Lay the cake on the base and sprinkle over the remaining brandied syrup. Spread with two thirds of the raspberry jam, then smooth over half the custard. Scatter over the macaroons leaving behind any syrup they haven't absorbed. Layer the pears over and spread with the remaining custard. Cover and chill for at least 2 hours.

To serve, blend the remaining jam with the lemon juice in a bowl. Drizzle this over the surface of the trifle and scatter over the toasted flaked almonds.

Ice-cream

You can spend hours toiling over your home-baked bread, peel a mound of quail's eggs and stuff a jar of olives, but a spoonful of freshly made vanilla ice cream—melting over a warm apple tart—will make the most cynical succumb.

The best ice-cream consists roughly of half whipped cream and half custard with the scales tipped in favour of the former. As ever it's about consistency. Ice-cream that is freshly churned is as delicate as the teasing shower of snow that promises to settle but melts before your eyes. Ideally it should be eaten within hours of being made before it has a chance to freeze solid, and certainly within a couple of days.

Tips
Always chill your mixture thoroughly before freezing it.

Alcohol such as rum, whisky and brandy or fruit eau-de-vies can be added, but as they inhibit freezing only add a couple of tablespoonfuls.

Use the following recipes as a base for improvising your own flavours. But remember when tasting the mixture that it needs to be sweeter than you would normally have custard.

Ice-cream is at its best served straight from the machine, thick and sticky rather than scoopable. If you want it a tad firmer, transfer it to the freezer for an hour or two. If the ice-cream has been frozen for longer than this, give it 30 minutes out of the freezer to allow it to soften before serving.

Vanilla Ice-cream

Purists don't look beyond the perfect vanilla ice, the palest ivory in colour and flecked with the black of vanilla seeds.

Serves 6
300 ml full-cream milk
  6 medium organic egg yolks
150 g caster sugar
  1 vanilla pod
350 ml double cream

Pour the milk into a small saucepan and bring to the boil. Whisk the egg yolks and sugar in a bowl, then whisk in the hot milk. Return this to the pan and heat gently, stirring constantly, until you have a thin pouring custard that coats the back of the spoon, taking care not to overheat it. Pour it straightaway into a bowl. Slit the vanilla pod lengthways, cut it up and add it to the custard. Cover the surface with clingfilm (to prevent a skin forming) and leave to cool.

Liquidise and pass the custard through a sieve into a clean bowl; cover the surface with clingfilm and chill. Whip the cream, whisk it into the custard and freeze according to the manufacturer's instructions for your ice-cream maker.

Variations
Strawberry
Omit the vanilla pod. In a blender, purée the custard base with 225g strawberries and 25g caster sugar until smooth. Pass through a sieve to remove the seeds and then freeze as above.

Cinnamon
Make as for vanilla ice-cream, replacing the vanilla pod with a 7cm cinnamon stick, broken into pieces.

Chocolate Ice-cream

The ultimate rich chocolate ice.

Serves 6
350 ml full-cream milk
  1 tablespoon cocoa powder, sifted
125 g good quality dark chocolate
    (such as Lindt), broken up
  6 medium organic egg yolks
125 g caster sugar
300 ml double cream
  1 teaspoon vanilla extract

Heat the milk with the cocoa powder in a small pan and simmer for 5 minutes. At the same time, melt the chocolate in a small heatproof bowl set over a pan of simmering water. Whisk the egg yolks and sugar in another bowl and then whisk in the hot cocoa milk.

Return the custard to the pan and heat briefly, stirring, to thicken. Transfer to a blender, add the melted chocolate and whizz until smooth. Pass through a sieve into a clean bowl. Stir in the cream and vanilla extract. Cover the surface with clingfilm and chill in the fridge. Freeze according to the instructions for your ice-cream maker.

Variations
Double chocolate chip
Stir in 40g finely chopped dark chocolate a few minutes before the end of churning.

Chocolate nut
Add 50g chopped walnuts or toasted flaked almonds a couple of minutes before the end of churning.

Mocha
Add a heaped teaspoon of instant coffee to the hot cocoa milk and stir to dissolve.

Maple Syrup and Stem Ginger Ice-cream

The mellow sweetness of maple syrup makes an elegant foil for the warming bite of preserved ginger.

Serves 6
150 ml maple syrup
6 medium organic egg yolks
300 ml full-cream milk
350 ml double cream, whipped
50 g preserved stem ginger in syrup, drained and chopped

Whisk the maple syrup and egg yolks together in a bowl. Bring the milk to the boil in a small saucepan. Whisk it into the egg yolk and syrup mixture and then return to the pan. Heat this very gently, stirring until it coats the back of a wooden spoon. Be careful not to let it boil otherwise it will curdle. Strain the custard into a clean bowl, cover the surface with clingfilm and allow to cool, then chill in the fridge.

Combine the cream with the custard and freeze according to the manufacturer's instructions for your ice-cream maker. Add the ginger a few minutes before the end of churning.

Variations
Honey hazelnut
Substitute honey for the maple syrup, and roasted and chopped hazelnuts for the ginger.

Maple, ginger and whisky
Add 2 tablespoons whisky to the ice-cream mixture and freeze according to the ice-cream maker's instructions. This is a delicious supper party ice-cream, served with brandy snaps.

Butterscotch Ice-cream

The strangeness of this ice-cream is also its strength, a hefty dose of sea salt that sets the caramel alive. It is the fudge-maker's big secret, the finest toffee and fudge achieves a crafty balance of sweet and salty.

Serves 6
Butterscotch
225 g unsalted butter
170 g golden caster sugar
1 teaspoon sea salt
50 ml water
150 ml double cream

Custard
225 ml double cream
475 ml milk
9 large organic egg yolks
50 g golden caster sugar

To make the butterscotch, place the butter, sugar, salt and water in a medium saucepan and simmer for about 8 minutes, stirring occasionally, until the mixture darkens and appears condensed. Remove from the heat and stir in the cream, which will splutter. Leave the butterscotch to cool.

To make the custard, bring the cream and milk to the boil in a small saucepan. Whisk the egg yolks and sugar together in a bowl, then whisk in the hot creamy milk. The mixture should thicken instantly into a custard. Pass it through a sieve on to the butterscotch. Stir to combine, then cover the surface with clingfilm and leave to cool.

Freeze according to your ice-cream maker's instructions, then turn into a suitable container and place in the freezer. If frozen for longer than 4 hours allow to soften for 20–30 minutes before serving.

Affogato al Caffe

A connoisseur's ice-cream float
where a scoop of vanilla ice-cream
is attended by a shot of freshly
brewed espresso coffee. It's a
tale of two ingredients made to
complement each other, the hot
bitterness of one and the cooling
sweetness of the other. The form
in eating it is to first scrape off the
outside where the espresso clings,
and then when you are about
halfway through and the ice-cream
has softened, work it into the
coffee until you have a creamy
whipped coffee ice-cream.

Serves 4
4 scoops vanilla ice-cream,
  frozen solid
4 shots of freshly brewed
  espresso coffee

Whereas normally you would
soften an ice-cream straight
from the freezer in the fridge
before serving it, here it should
be frozen hard. If you are using
homemade ice-cream, churn and
freeze it overnight.

Place four scoops of ice-cream
in four small bowls. Trickle a shot of
freshly brewed espresso over each
one and serve at once.

Roast Fruits

Caramelising fruits in a hot pan on the stove renders their flesh meltingly succulent, the skins sticky and golden at the edges. And there is scarcely any need to interrupt the intrinsic beauty of their natural shapes. Simply remove the stone from peaches and plums; halve pears and nick out the core of seeds; leave figs roundly intact, save for cutting a cross in the top to allow them to swell and open.

Roasting is perhaps contravening the Trades Description Act, they are first sautéed in clarified butter, then glazed under the grill with a sprinkling of sugar, and finally splashed with a little fruit liqueur or eau-de-vie. The call is for nothing more elaborate than a cooling slick of ice-cream or cream, and the crumble of a buttery shortbread biscuit. Each of the following serves 4.

Clarifying butter

Gently melt the butter in a small pan, skim off the surface foam, decant the yellow clarified butter and discard the milky residue in the base. You can clarify butter well in advance, and keep it chilled in the fridge for the same period as the butter's shelf life.

Apples

Peel, quarter and core 3 eating apples. Heat 40g clarified unsalted butter in a large frying pan over a medium heat and cook the apples for 4–5 minutes each side until golden on the surface. Sprinkle over a tablespoon of caster or vanilla sugar and grill until the sugar is melted and bubbling. Drizzle with a tablespoon of Calvados.

Pears

Peel 3 ripe pears, halve them and cut out the core, leaving the stalk attached. Heat 40g clarified unsalted butter in a large frying pan over a medium-low heat. Add the pears, cut-side down, and cook for 3–4 minutes until lightly golden, then turn and repeat with the other side. Sprinkle over a tablespoon of caster or vanilla sugar and place under the grill until the sugar is melted and bubbling. Drizzle with a tablespoon of Poire William liqueur or Calvados.

Bananas

Peel 4 fairly small ripe bananas and cut in half lengthways. Heat 40g clarified unsalted butter in a large frying pan over a medium heat. Add the bananas, cut-side down, and cook for 2–3 minutes then turn and repeat with the curved side. Sprinkle over a scant tablespoon of light muscovado sugar, dispersing any lumps with your fingers. Place under a grill until the sugar is melted and caramelised. Drizzle with a tablespoon of Tia Maria, Kahlua, Amaretto or dark rum.

Plums and peaches

Halve 6 plums or 3 peaches and prise out their stones. Heat 40g clarified unsalted butter in a large frying pan over a medium heat. Add the fruit, cut-side down, and cook for 3 minutes until lightly golden. Turn the fruit and cook the other side for 2 minutes. Sprinkle over a tablespoon of caster or vanilla sugar and place under the grill until melted and bubbling. Drizzle with a tablespoon of Amaretto, or Courvoisier or other brandy.

Pineapple

Cut the skin off a large pineapple and cut it into about eight 1cm thick slices. Carefully cut out the central core. Heat 40g clarified unsalted butter in a large frying pan over a medium heat. Sauté the pineapple slices, two at a time, for 3 minutes each side. Arrange them in overlapping slices in a gratin dish. Liberally dust with icing sugar and glaze under the grill. Drizzle with a tablespoon of Calvados or dark rum.

Figs

These are more successfully roasted whole in the oven. Preheat the oven to 220°C, fan oven 200°C, gas 7. Cut the stalks off 8 figs and slice a cross about 2cm deep in the top of each one. Stand the figs in a small baking dish spacing them slightly apart. Scatter over 25g demerara sugar and pour on 125ml port. Roast the figs for 25 minutes basting halfway through.

Serving roast fruits

Ice-cream and warm fruit is ever a winning combination, whatever takes your fancy—praline, vanilla, strawberry or spiced. Otherwise a fruit sorbet—raspberry and blackcurrant are favourites. Alternatively serve roast fruits with a dollop of mascarpone, crème fraîche or whipped cream. Depending on the sharpness of the fruit this can be sweetened with a little sifted icing sugar. It can also be flavoured with vanilla extract, ground cinnamon or orange flower water. More mundanely, when you don't want to pile on the calories, fromage frais, Greek yogurt or a plain organic one will do nicely.

A thick buttery chunk of shortbread perfectly offsets the soft, sweet and sour flesh of roast fruits. Walkers, established in 1898 and still family run, produce excellent shortbread that is stubbornly true to form—made using butter, flour and sugar, nothing else. Look out for their 'homebake' range—these biscuits are especially soft and crumbly. The only other make we would care to recommend is Duchy Originals.

Roast Plums and Raspberry Sorbet

Pink on pink.

Serves 6
12 large juicy red plums, stalks removed
50 g demerara sugar
4 tablespoons water
3 tablespoons Grand Marnier or Cointreau (or water)
Squeeze of lemon juice
10 g unsalted butter, diced
500 ml tub raspberry sorbet

Preheat the oven to 190°C, fan oven 180°C, gas 5. Place the whole plums in a shallow baking dish that will hold them snugly in a single layer. Scatter over the sugar and drizzle over the water and liqueur. Roast for 25–30 minutes, basting halfway through.

Transfer the plums to a bowl. Sharpen the syrup with a generous squeeze of lemon juice and whisk in the butter. Pour the sauce over the fruit and serve warm with a dollop of raspberry sorbet. The plums are also delicious served at room temperature; in which case omit the butter from the sauce.

Pan-poached Nectarines in a Spiced White Wine Syrup

Here the scent of lemon grass cleverly mingles with rosemary and cinnamon. You can take the frying pan straight to the table, leaving the spices in the syrup. Dressing up is minimal—a scoop of ice-cream or crème fraîche and a biscuit.

Serves 6
6 nectarines

Syrup
1 bottle dry white wine
175 g caster sugar
2 rosemary sprigs
½ lemon grass stalk,
   split lengthways
3 green cardamom pods, cracked
7 cm cinnamon stick
2 thin slices fresh root ginger
6 black peppercorns

Combine the ingredients for the syrup in a large cast-iron frying pan. Bring to the boil and let it seethe for 30–35 minutes until the syrup is thick and well reduced.

Cut the nectarines in half along the groove and twist the halves to separate them. Carefully loosen the stone starting at the stalk end and remove it. Add the nectarines to the syrup, curved-side down, bring it back to a simmer and poach them for 3–4 minutes. Turn them over and cook for another 3 minutes. Remove from the heat and leave for 15 minutes before serving.

You can also serve the nectarines at room temperature, in which case cover and chill them once they are cool leaving in the aromatics, and bring them back up to room temperature before eating.

Hot Buttered Cherries with Vanilla Ice-cream

These cherries are sautéed with stalks and stones in place—a part of their attraction, it also does away with the task of pitting them.

Serves 6
110 g unsalted butter
110 g golden caster sugar
  2 tablespoons kirsch or other
     fruit eau-de-vie
750 g red or black cherries
500 ml tub vanilla ice-cream
     Fine dessert biscuits, to serve

Melt the butter and sugar together in a large frying pan. Once it is seething add the kirsch and simmer for 1 minute until the sauce is smooth. Add the cherries and cook for 5 minutes stirring them occasionally, then leave them to cool for a few minutes.

Serve the warm cherries in their syrup with a scoop of vanilla ice-cream on top and a couple of dessert biscuits to the side.

Summer Pudding

Dark, sultry and eccentrically British, summer pudding consists of a shell of white bread soaked in crimson juices encasing a compote. For a connoisseur's pudding it's surprising how rarely you come across a really good one. With the short list of ingredients, it should be the most straightforward dish in the world to create. And while it's not difficult to get right, it's easy to get it wrong.

The fruit

The essential starting point is red and blackcurrants, which are responsible for the rich purplish juice that soaks into the bread. We like to make up the rest of the melange with a high proportion of raspberries, and a few blackberries and loganberries if we can lay our hands on them. The fruit must be ripe, tender and juicy. Blackberries in particular can be dry and tough, especially those grown in hot arid countries. The varieties cultivated here during the summer are usually excellent, and often a huge advance on anything you might find in the wild.

The bread

It may be the easiest thing in the world to grab a packet of sliced white bread at the supermarket, but at your peril. Sliced white will only turn slimy once it has been soaked. You need the body and open weave of good bread that can hold its own. It should be sliced by hand from a loaf of day-old white bread, not necessarily stale, but past its best. When lining the pudding basin the pieces of bread should be fitted together as seamlessly as possible, any cracks will allow the juice to seep out once the pudding has been inverted.

Soaking the pudding

Invariably summer pudding will turn out perfectly, but there will be times when the berries won't have been as juicy as normal and there will be patches of white. With this in mind, take a few precautions. Firstly, set aside a small cup of juice and berries before filling the pudding in order to patch up any white bits. Secondly, leave the pudding to stand for 30–60 minutes once you've turned it out, to allow the juices to soak into the base; any that trickle out can be spooned back over the pudding.

Serves 6
225 g redcurrants
225 g blackcurrants
170 g caster sugar
700 g raspberries, blackberries or loganberries
¾ loaf of day-old (un-cut) white bread (approximately)
Clotted cream, to serve

Using a fork, remove the currants from their stalks and place in a small saucepan. Add the sugar and heat gently for 4–5 minutes until the fruit is soft but still retains its shape, and is sitting in a pool of syrup. Place half of the currants in a sieve over a bowl and press to extract the juice.

Return the juice to the pan, discarding the residue. Fold in the other berries, stir well and heat very gently for a minute or two, not to cook them but to encourage them to release their juices. Leave the fruit to cool, then check the sweetness and add a little more sugar if necessary. Set aside about two thirds of a teacup of the fruit and juice; cover and refrigerate.

Cut the loaf into 8–10 slices, about 7–8mm thick and remove the crusts. Use the bread to line a 1.8 litre pudding basin. Place a square of bread on the base of the basin with four pieces around the sides, and fill in the triangular gaps as neatly as possible. Tip the fruit into the basin and press it down well using a wooden spoon. Make a lid with more bread, and trim the edges in line. Place a small plate on top—one that's slightly smaller than the diameter of the pudding bowl. Weight this down (cans are ideal for this). Leave the pudding in the fridge overnight.

To serve, run a knife carefully round the edge of the pudding to loosen it, and then invert on to a plate. Leave the pudding to stand for 30–60 minutes, which will bring it back up to room temperature as well as allowing the juices to soak into the base. Spoon the reserved fruit and juices over, soaking any bits of bread that haven't turned red. Serve with clotted cream.

A perfect meringue is soft and mousse-like beyond its composed exterior and collapses into a heap as you eat it. For all their simplicity, meringues can be difficult to get right, but when they do live up to their potential they are a fine confection, that needs little in attendance—chantilly cream scented with coffee, chocolate or vanilla, or some roast fruits whose tartness will offset all that sugar.

The egg whites

These should be at room temperature. If you keep your eggs in the fridge, take them out an hour beforehand. In addition the eggs should either be organic or free range. Inferior quality eggs will have watery whites that may fail to rise.

The sugar

Meringues conform to a basic ratio of 1 large egg white to 60g of sugar. We advocate a refined caster sugar for meringues, not least to encourage that snowy white hue. Either use caster sugar, or half-caster and half-icing sugar.

Enemies

Meringues have two arch-enemies. The first is water: even a drop in the bowl or on the whisk will prevent the whites from rising. The other is grease: your bowl and whisk must be scrupulously clean.

Utensils

Use a large bowl, but not one with a base so wide that the white is too shallow to whip effectively. As to the whisk, electric whisks and mixers do not create as much volume as a balloon whisk, or hand-turned rotary whisk (that is solidly built with bars some 5mm wide).

Basic meringues

Just a handful of large blowsy meringues placed centrally on the table for people to break up and help themselves makes for informal eating. Alternatively if they are to be sandwiched together for tea you can make them smaller, in which case reduce the cooking time accordingly.

Makes 6
3 large organic egg whites
180 g caster sugar

Preheat the oven to 130°C, fan oven 120°C, gas ½. Place the egg whites in a large bowl and whisk them until they rise into a froth the consistency of shaving foam. From here sprinkle over a heaped tablespoon of sugar at a time, whisking well with each addition until you have a smooth, glossy meringue. You can increase the sugar to 2 tablespoons towards the end. In theory the meringue should be stiff enough for you to hold the bowl upside-down above your head, though we don't recommend you risk this.

Line one or two baking trays with baking parchment. Drop heaped tablespoonfuls of the mixture on to the paper leaving plenty of space between each meringue. If you like you can make them bigger or smaller than this.

Place the meringues in the oven and turn it down to 110°C, fan oven 100°C, gas ¼. Cook for 2 hours; if you are using two trays then switch them around halfway through. The meringues by the end should be crisp on the outside, and if you tap the base it should sound

hollow within. Remove and leave them to cool. They can be stored in an airtight container for 2 weeks.

Variations

Chocolate

Stir 1 heaped tablespoon of sifted cocoa powder into the finished meringue mixture. Dust over some more cocoa when serving them. Delicious served with butterscotch ice-cream.

Almond

Scatter some flaked almonds over the meringues before baking them. Dust with icing sugar when you come to serve them. Good with vanilla custard and poached fruits such as rhubarb and plums.

Hazelnut

Scatter a few chopped hazelnuts over the meringues before baking them. Good for serving with caramelised apples and pears, and whipped cream.

Pistachio

A few chopped pistachios sprinkled over before baking creates an unusual meringue that is surprisingly adaptable. You can serve these with raspberries and blackberries, as well as with pears in red wine, chocolate and coffee creams, or with lemon and orange sorbet.

Brown sugar

Replace the white sugar with a light muscovado sugar and bake the meringues for 2 hours at 130°C, fan oven 120°C, gas ½.

More restrained than the schoolboy's pudding of fame, if not a lot—its messiness is part of its charm. Beyond the constraints of a school dining room, indulge your choice of fruits, leaning towards raspberries and wild strawberries.

Serves 4–6
3 medium organic egg whites
170 g caster sugar
800 g red berries, hulled
40 g icing sugar
2 tablespoons raspberry eau-de-vie (optional)
Squeeze of lemon juice
450 ml whipping cream, whipped

Preheat the oven to 150°C, fan oven 140°C, gas 2. Whisk the egg whites in a bowl until softly peaking. Sprinkle over the sugar, a spoonful at a time, whisking well with each addition until the meringue is smooth and glossy. Line a baking sheet with baking parchment and using a palette knife, spread the meringue to a 1cm thickness, roughly 30cm square. Bake for 45 minutes; the outside should be crisp, the inside soft. Allow to cool.

Meanwhile, purée a third of the berries in a blender with the icing sugar, eau-de-vie if using, and lemon juice. Pass through a sieve into a bowl; taste for sweetness and add more sugar or lemon juice as necessary. Add the remaining fruit to this sauce and toss to mix.

Break the meringue into large pieces. Arrange half in a deep 20cm bowl or individual bowls. Cover with half the fruit, then half the cream. Repeat the layers. Serve as soon as possible; the meringue softens after a while, but is still good to eat.

Baked Couscous Pudding with Raisins

This is one of the better uses of couscous we can think of. If you are a rice pudding aficionado it should have you just as captive. It would be missing a trick not to scent the pudding, either by sticking a vanilla pod or cinnamon stick into its midst while it bakes. Alternatively you could add a sliver of orange peel or a drop of rosewater.

Serves 6
70 g couscous
100 g caster sugar
600 ml full-cream milk
300 ml double cream
50 g raisins
Pinch of salt (optional)
Freshly grated nutmeg

Preheat the oven to 170°C, fan oven 160°C, gas 3. Place the couscous, sugar and milk in a saucepan and bring to the boil. Add the cream and raisins, and a pinch of salt if you like. Bring back to the boil and then transfer to a 1.5 litre shallow gratin or ovenproof dish.

Grate plenty of nutmeg over the surface. Bake for 35 minutes until the pudding is thick and creamy underneath its golden skin. It is at its best about 15 minutes out of the oven, and still good cold though it firms up as it cools.

Prune Clafoutis

It's no great surprise that the French don't go in for proper puddings when superlative pâtisserie flaunts itself in the window of the most modest village shop. Clafoutis Limousin is one of the few French puddings that can match any British creation. Juicy black cherries, or in this case prunes simmered in rum, are baked in a surround of sweetened batter. It is at its most delicious eaten hot, or lukewarm about 30 minutes out of the oven. There's no need for additional cream, but no rules against it.

Serves 4–6
Prunes
150 ml dark rum, plus 1 tablespoon
150 ml water
50 g caster or vanilla sugar
200 g prunes, ready-soaked and stoned

Batter
75 g plain flour, sifted
50 g caster or vanilla sugar (see note), plus extra for dusting the dish
3 medium organic eggs
425 ml milk
25 g unsalted butter, plus extra for greasing the dish
Icing sugar, for dusting

To make the batter, whizz the flour, sugar, eggs and milk in a blender until smooth and leave to rest for 30 minutes.

For the prunes, place the 150ml rum, the water and sugar in a small saucepan and bring to the boil. Add the prunes and simmer for 15–25 minutes until all the liquid has been absorbed and they are coated in a sticky syrup.

Preheat the oven to 220°C, fan oven 200°C, gas 7. Butter a 35cm oval gratin dish (or other shallow ovenproof dish of equivalent dimensions). Dust with caster or vanilla sugar, tipping out the excess. Re-whisk the batter if necessary and then pour it in to the dish. Scatter the prunes and syrup evenly over the surface. Dot with the butter and bake for 25–30 minutes. When it comes out of the oven it will be impressively puffed and golden, sinking after a few minutes. Sprinkle over the remaining tablespoon of rum. Dust with icing sugar to serve.

Note
To make vanilla sugar, cut up a vanilla pod and whizz with 225g caster sugar in a food processor, then pass through a sieve. Store in a jar until required.

Poppy Seed Cheesecake

Soft and creamy with the thinnest crust, everything that slice of cheesecake in the Polish deli promised to be and wasn't. A glass of chilled vodka won't go amiss.

Serves 6–8
Base
25 g unsalted butter, softened
25 g fresh white breadcrumbs
 1 teaspoon caster sugar

Filling
 50 g sultanas
  4 tablespoons lemon or other flavoured vodka
700 g cream cheese
225 g caster sugar
  2 medium organic eggs
350 ml whipping cream
 40 g plain flour, sifted
1½ teaspoons vanilla extract
  1 to 2 tablespoons poppy seeds

Place the sultanas in a bowl, pour over the vodka and leave to soak overnight.

Preheat the oven to 190°C, fan oven 180°C, gas 5. To prepare the base, grease a 20cm springform cake tin, using all of the butter. Mix the breadcrumbs with the sugar and press it on to the sides and base of the tin.

To make the filling, blend the cream cheese and sugar in a food processor or mixer. Beat in the eggs and cream, and then carefully fold in the flour and vanilla extract. Mix in the sultanas and any residual soaking liquor. Carefully spoon the mixture into the tin. Dust the surface with poppy seeds so it is lightly covered with a thin layer. Bake in the oven for 45 minutes until just set and puffy around the edges, it should wobble if moved from side to side. Turn the oven off and leave the cheesecake inside with the door ajar (or propped open with a wooden spoon) for 1 hour.

Remove the cheesecake from the oven and cool completely. It is at its best a day later, served at room temperature. If you chill it, return to room temperature 30 minutes before serving.

Cherry, Almond and Pine Nut Streusel

A streusel sports crumble on top, shortbread underneath and, in this case, black cherries in between. It's a good balmy summer's day pudding for when they're in season.

Serves 6
200 g plain flour
110 g ground almonds
110 g caster sugar, plus 1 tablespoon
225 g unsalted butter, chilled and diced
 40 g flaked almonds
 40 g pine nuts
550 g black cherries, pitted
     Icing sugar, for dusting
     Whipped or clotted cream, to serve

Preheat the oven to 180°C, fan oven 170°C, gas 4. Place the flour, ground almonds and 110g caster sugar in a food processor. Add the butter and process the mixture to crumbs (it's essential that the butter is cold otherwise it will cream into a dough). As it starts to resemble a crumble, transfer half of the mixture to a bowl and toss in the flaked almonds and pine nuts.

Continue to process the remaining mixture until it forms a smooth pastry dough. Press this into the base of a 20cm cake tin with a removable base. Scatter the cherries on top and dust with the remaining tablespoon of caster sugar. Scatter the crumble and nut mixture over the top of the cherries and bake for 45 minutes until the top is golden and crisp and the cherry juices have begun to bubble. Remove and allow the tart to cool, then dust with icing sugar and serve with whipped cream.

French Puff Pastry Apple Tart

The simplest of all apple tarts and arguably the most delicious. Serve it with vanilla ice-cream, the real kind, flecked with specks of black vanilla seeds, and soft to the point of melting.

Serves 4

350 g puff pastry
  4 Granny Smith or other tart eating apples, peeled, quartered and cored
 50 g unsalted butter
  4 teaspoons caster sugar
  2 tablespoons apricot jam

Preheat the oven to 220°C, fan oven 200°C, gas 7. Roll out the puff pastry thinly on a lightly floured surface and cut out four circles, 15cm in diameter, you can use a plate or a bowl as a guide. Lay the pastry rounds out on a baking tray.

Slice the apple quarters lengthways as thinly as possible—this is important, otherwise they won't lie neatly. Lay the apple slices on the pastry rounds in a circle so they radiate out from the centre, then place a couple of slices in the very middle. Dot the butter over the tarts and sprinkle over the sugar. Bake for 15–20 minutes until the pastry is golden and risen at the edges and the apples have started to colour.

Warm the apricot jam in a small saucepan and press it through a sieve. Brush the apricot glaze over the tarts and serve straightaway or whilst still warm, with ice-cream.

Treacle Tart

With a hint of apple and lemon that cuts through the gooey sweetness, this delights where so many other treacle tarts fail. A recipe from Peter Gordon.

Serves 6
Sweet lemon pastry
230 g plain flour
130 g unsalted butter, chilled and diced
    Finely grated zest of 1 lemon
 70 g icing sugar, sifted
  1 small organic egg yolk
  1 drop of milk

Filling
  2 medium organic eggs
    Finely grated zest and juice of 1 lemon
350 ml golden syrup
300 ml double cream
100 g brioche crumbs (or bread or croissant crumbs)
  1 eating apple, peeled and grated
    Icing sugar, for dusting
    Crème fraîche, to serve

Place the flour and butter in a food processor. Give it a quick burst at high speed to reduce to a crumb-like consistency, then add the lemon zest and icing sugar and give it another quick burst. Mix in the egg yolk and enough milk to bring the dough together. Wrap it in clingfilm and chill in the fridge for 1 hour or overnight.

Preheat the oven to 180°C, fan oven 170°C, gas 4. Roll out the pastry thinly on a lightly floured work surface and use to line the base and sides of a 23cm tart tin, 4cm deep, with a removable base. The easiest way to do this is to slip the base of the tin under the rolled out pastry and then into the tin—

you will probably end up partly pressing the pastry into the tart tin. Run a rolling pin across the top to trim the edges. Line the case with baking parchment and baking beans (any dried pulse will do) and cook for 15 minutes. Take out the paper and beans and cook for a further 5–10 minutes until the case is evenly golden. Remove from the oven.

Turn the oven down to 160°C, fan oven 150°C, gas 2½. For the filling, whisk the eggs, lemon zest and juice together, then add the golden syrup and cream and whisk until the mixture emulsifies. Add the brioche crumbs and grated apple and mix well. Immediately pour the mixture into the pre-cooked tart case, place it on a baking tray and bake for 50–55 minutes. The filling should be golden and slightly puffy, if you move the tart around it should wobble without being at all liquid.

Either serve the tart warm about 30 minutes out of the oven, or at room temperature. Dust it with icing sugar immediately beforehand and accompany with crème fraîche.

Orange and Almond Cake with Cardamom Syrup

Made with ground almonds and drenched in a citrus syrup, this is far more luxurious than any sponge could ever aspire to be. Very much destination dessert rather than tea.

Serves 6

Cake

100 g ground almonds
20 g flaked almonds
200 g caster sugar
40 g white breadcrumbs
1½ teaspoons baking powder, sifted
4 large organic eggs
200 ml sunflower oil
Finely grated zest of 1 orange
Finely grated zest of 1 lemon
80 g cranberries (optional)

Syrup

Juice of 2 oranges
Juice of 1 lemon
170 g caster sugar
5 green cardamom pods, cracked

Preheat the oven to 200°C, fan oven 190°C, gas 6. Mix the dry ingredients for the cake together in a large bowl. Beat in the eggs and the oil, then stir in the citrus zests, and cranberries if using. Pour the mixture into a greased 20cm cake tin with a removable base. Bake for 40 minutes until the cake is golden and a skewer inserted into the centre comes out clean.

Meanwhile, make the syrup. Place all the ingredients in a small pan, bring to the boil and simmer for 3 minutes. Once cooked, leave the cake in the tin for a few minutes then remove the collar and slip it on to a deepish plate. Pierce holes in the top and spoon over half the syrup, discarding the cardamom pods. Leave to cool. Serve with the remaining syrup spooned over.

Apple Cake with Calvados Cream

More in the way of cake to serve as pudding, here wafer-thin apple slices are set into a moist almond sponge—crème fraîche flavoured with a dash of Calvados as a complement.

Serves 6

2 Granny Smith's apples
2 squeezes of lemon juice
175 g golden caster sugar
175 g unsalted butter, diced
3 medium organic eggs, separated
175 g ground almonds
1 teaspoon baking powder, sifted
2 tablespoons Calvados (optional)
Icing sugar, for dusting

Calvados cream

300 g crème fraîche
25 g icing sugar, sifted
1 tablespoon Calvados

Peel, quarter and core the apples. Cut two of the quarters into wafer-thin slices, toss with a squeeze of lemon juice in a bowl and set aside. Slice the remaining apple quarters more thickly. Toss with a squeeze of lemon in another bowl, then sprinkle with a tablespoon of the sugar and toss to coat. Set aside for 10 minutes while you prepare the cake mixture.

Preheat the oven to 150°C, fan oven 140°C, gas 2 and butter a 20cm springform cake tin, with a removable base. Cream the butter and remaining caster sugar together until light and fluffy; you can do this in a food processor or electric mixer. Beat in the egg yolks, and then incorporate the ground almonds and baking powder, working the mixture as little as possible to keep it light. Transfer the mixture to a large bowl.

Stiffly whisk the egg whites in another bowl. Fold half into the cake mixture and then fold in the remainder. Add the Calvados if using, and any juice given out by the thickly sliced apples. Drain these thoroughly on kitchen paper and gently fold them into the mixture. Transfer it to the prepared cake tin and smooth the surface.

Drain the reserved finely sliced apple and arrange on top of the cake, sticking some of the slices in at an angle. Bake in the oven for 1 hour 15 minutes or until golden, and a skewer inserted into the centre comes out clean.

Run a knife around the edge of the cake and leave it to cool for several hours, then remove from the tin. Being such a moist cake it keeps well in a covered container, and can be reheated if you want to serve it warm.

For the Calvados cream, blend all the ingredients together in a bowl, cover and chill until required.

Dust the cake with icing sugar and serve in slices accompanied by the Calvados cream, or crème fraîche if preferred.

Chocolate Gâteau with
Crème Chantilly

Something like a chocolate brownie but more sophisticated.

Serves 6–8

Chocolate gâteau

150 g dark chocolate, broken up
75 g golden caster sugar
150 g unsalted butter, diced
1 tablespoon runny honey
4 large organic eggs, separated
200 g ground almonds
75 ml milk
Cocoa powder, for dusting

Crème Chantilly

300 ml whipping cream
40 g icing sugar, sifted
2 tablespoons strong black coffee

Preheat the oven to 180°C, fan oven 170°C, gas 4. Butter a 20cm springform cake tin, with a removable base. Put the chocolate, caster sugar, butter and honey in a heatproof bowl over a pan of simmering water. Melt the ingredients together gently, stirring frequently, until amalgamated and smooth.

Transfer the mixture to a large bowl and beat in the egg yolks and ground almonds, then stir in the milk.

Whisk the egg whites in a large bowl until they are stiff and then fold them into the cake mixture, a third at a time. Transfer it to the prepared cake tin and give the tin several sharp taps on the work surface to get rid of any air bubbles. Bake in the oven for 35–40 minutes until the cake is risen and a skewer inserted into the centre comes out clean. Run a knife around the collar of the cake to loosen it and leave it to cool.

To make the crème Chantilly, whisk the ingredients together in a large bowl until the cream forms soft peaks. Unless you are serving the cake straightaway, transfer the cream to a smaller bowl, cover and chill until required. If prepared more than 30 minutes ahead however, you will need to re-whisk the Chantilly just before serving.

Serve the cake in slices with the crème Chantilly spooned on top, dusted with cocoa powder.

This has the social aspirations of being like the River Cafe's chocolate nemesis, soft as silk in the centre, with the thinnest cakey crust around the outside.

Serves 6

450 g good quality dark chocolate (ideally Meunier), broken into pieces
120 g unsalted butter
2 heaped tablespoons caster sugar
4 medium organic eggs
1 tablespoon plain flour, sifted
Cocoa powder, for dusting
225 g wild strawberries or raspberries, to serve (optional)

Preheat the oven to 220°C, fan oven 200°C, gas 7. Butter a 20cm springform cake tin with a removable base. Put the chocolate, butter and half the sugar in a heatproof bowl over a pan of simmering water and gently melt, stirring occasionally, until smooth.

Put the eggs and remaining sugar in a food processor and whizz for 10 minutes until the mixture has increased in volume several times and is very thick and pale, almost white. Transfer to a large bowl and carefully fold in the flour, then gently fold in the melted chocolate mixture. Occasionally, if you are using a chocolate with a high percentage of cocoa, the mixture can split, in which case whisk in 2–3 tablespoons of water to emulsify it. At this point the mixture will still be quite runny it sets partially as it cooks and further as it cools.

Pour the mixture into the cake tin and cook for 6 minutes. The rim should have just set while the centre will still appear to be liquid. Leave the cake to cool, then cover and leave in a cool place, but not the fridge, overnight.

To serve, run a knife around the edge of the collar and remove it. Dust the surface of the cake with cocoa, and serve in slices, scattered with berries if wished.

Date and Honey Madeleines

These cakes are buttery, meltingly tender and especially moist if you make them with Medjool dates. The traditional scallop-shaped cakes fluted on the underside are the stuff of specialised baking (unless of course you happen to have a madeleine tray). We make do with fairy cake moulds. Serve them as a sweet treat with coffee or tea— elevenses, teatime or after dinner. Equally, madeleines sit elegantly alongside poached or roast fruits.

Makes 15–20
110 g pitted dates, chopped
90 ml water
½ teaspoon bicarbonate of soda
2 large organic eggs
25 g vanilla or caster sugar
Finely grated zest of 1 lemon
2 tablespoons clear honey
50 g self-raising flour
Pinch of salt
½ teaspoon baking powder
50 g ground almonds
110 g unsalted butter (plus 15g for greasing), melted and cooled
Icing sugar, for dusting

Put the dates in a small saucepan with the water and bring to the boil. Simmer for 4 minutes until they turn quite mushy, then stir in the bicarbonate of soda and leave to cool. Whisk the eggs and sugar together in a bowl until they are almost white, then add the lemon zest and honey. Sift the flour, salt and baking powder together and lightly whisk into the egg mixture. Incorporate the ground almonds, taking care not to overwork. Gently fold in the melted butter, and the dates and their water. Chill the mixture for 30 minutes. In the meantime, preheat the oven to 200°C, fan oven 190°C, gas 6.

Brush the insides of the cake tins with a little melted butter. Spoon the mixture into the prepared moulds, two-thirds filling them. Bake for 8–10 minutes until golden, then run a knife round the edge of the tins and turn the madeleines out on to a wire rack. Dust with icing sugar and eat warm or barely cooled, though they will still be delicious cold.

Stuffed Dates

Very good with syrupy black coffee.

Makes about 18
270 g dates
170 g mascarpone
3 tablespoons maple syrup
1 tablespoon finely chopped pistachios

Slit the dates open to remove the stone. Blend the mascarpone with 2 tablespoons of maple syrup in a bowl. Fill the dates generously with this mixture. Scatter over some pistachios and drizzle over the remaining syrup to serve.

Vin Santo and Cantuccini

Dipping cantuccini into a glass of syrupy vin santo wine is pudding in itself, when you want something lighter or simply to continue drinking. The experience is something like a deconstructed trifle without the fruit and cream. Cantucci di Prato (near Florence) are long flat biscuits, by design as hard as rock. Slices of sweet bread, flavoured with aniseed, that are re-baked. Very much a dunking biscuit, cantuccini soften and absorb the wine without collapsing.

As to vin santo, a tonic wine, it is heady, amber and highly aromatic, common in Tuscany and Trentino. Its richness is achieved by drying the grapes, sometimes for months, before they are pressed. The wine is then matured for several years in barrels and several more in the bottle.

The Occasion

It was a desire to bridge the gap between how we eat on a daily basis and how we receive our friends that largely inspired this book. Partly because we want to eat beautiful food day in and day out, and partly because we hate the idea of having to put on a show when we entertain. The whole idea of dinner parties and the food that goes with them seems outdated. We are all aware of the decline that has taken place in the social table, a decline not experienced by our continental neighbours.

A recent dinner in France followed a gracious, time-honoured path and in its simplicity was exquisite. We sat down at the table and were offered an aperitif and some pastries. Next a large platter of oysters from the local beach that we ate with pain de Campagne, some unsalted butter and red wine vinegar to season them. After that came a plate of thickly sliced roast lamb or 'gigot,' a thin onion 'jus' and a bowl of haricots. Next a very lightly dressed salad of mâche, picked from the garden, which some of the company ate with cheese and others with the remains of the gravy. Finally a Tarte Tatin was presented, and the cognac and coffee. It didn't matter that our host and hostess weren't renowned gourmets, they were practised in the foods they served and the menu followed a course. First comes the fish, and then the meat either with a vegetable or potatoes but never both. If the main course had been fish, then the first course might have been ham or a pâté, either way the sequence was set.

For some such strictures might seem narrow, but they act as a guiding hand in the pursuit of

quality. This is especially true when the menu is determined by what is produced within a 30 kilometre radius—in itself a guarantee of seasonal produce. Having access to every ingredient and dish from around the world is a fine thing in principle, but the reality is less than satisfactory when there is no cultural setting or context, tradition or proper understanding of where the food comes from or how it has been produced.

Far better to learn how to roast a chicken properly and therefore in seven different ways, to appreciate when the dark meat has a depth of flavour and the breast a succulence without being watery, to identify the characteristics of particular breeds and to ascertain from the appearance of a bird something of its likely eating. So too, better to master the art of making and embellishing a green salad, to become acquainted with the individual flavours and textures of different leaves. Equally advantageous, to learn how to make perfect meringues and then vary them. All this rather than learn many different dishes, all disparate. Repetition is essential to quality— we repeat, we learn.

As a starting point we sat down and pondered how we approach the task of feeding our families. Straightaway we came face to face with the weekly supermarket shop. Although we derive great pleasure from farmers' markets and small retail outlets, such shopping tends to be confined to the luxury of the weekend. Neither can we pretend that browsing the supermarket shelves is sufficient inspiration to construct the week's menus on the spot and fill the trolley accordingly. It's a

lovely thought that we should plan our lives according to the experience of shopping in a continental market, but the reality isn't quite like that. Most of us have a comparatively narrow set of categories into which supper will fall during any one week—roast chicken one night, spaghetti another, soup the day after and a salad somewhere down the line. It seemed altogether calmer to base the book on the way we are, instead of perpetuating the myth that you should be able to dip into Thailand on Monday, Italy on Tuesday, Morocco on Wednesday, and a spot of French provincial cooking at the weekend.

Whatever the occasion and setting, we have steered away from food that tries to impress and be different. The media attention afforded to all things gustatory comes with an inevitable drive for novelty. That's all very well, except that much of what is readily achievable and indeed most delicious is now considered too dull for mention. Whatever happened to plain cooking, the kind that allows ingredients to speak for themselves? At a time when there is a significant drop-off in the amount we cook, the food presented to us is becoming ever more complex and unattainable. Perhaps we need to take a step back in order to go forwards.

The menu
Supper midweek rarely stretches beyond a single course, a token gesture of an appetiser beforehand or a slice of cheese and a few nuts after is as elaborate as it need be. But if it is midweek in the company of friends, then the evening needs to be spread out, in which case it can take in three or even four

courses. If the menus seem at all scant, weave into the picture a fine loaf of crusty white bread that lingers on the table until the main course is over, in line with French habits. Frequently we prefer to eat our fish or meat on their own without potatoes, a hunk of bread to mop up the sticky juices. Lucky are they that live within a short walk of a good bakery. Sadly, most of us must resort to buying a long-keeping loaf such as pain de Campagne or sourdough bread, and to pop a loaf or two in the freezer.

For simplicity the menus that follow are divided into weekday family suppers and those in the company of friends. Then Saturday lunch which tends to be a fairly rushed affair, followed by Saturday dinner when you may have more time to cook and more people to cook for. Sunday lunch is the longest laziest meal of the week regardless of whether there are two or six people. Sunday dinner is ever short, sweet and to the point, often coming after a weekend of indulging—a time for eating lightly and retiring to bed.

We have moved away from the traditional pear-shaped meal. Also from the kind of starter or first course that demands you sit at the table. It is so much easier and for that matter more enjoyable when the role of the appetiser is extended to take in the first course. As guests lounge around enjoying a drink, they can dip slivers of raw vegetables into anchoiade and a paste of crushed goat's cheese, graze on slices of Parma ham with a small salad of parsnips and raisins, or toy with brittle shards of Melba toast, fresh taramasalata and olives.

We have trimmed any fish or meat main course to include at most some mash, a vegetable purée or one uncomplicated vegetable—certainly nothing resembling 'the trimmings'. After that might come a salad and then a slice of cheese, but again nothing as formal as a cheeseboard with crackers, just one perfectly matured offering with a few nuts to crack in its company or leaves of chicory.

Few of us have time to make puddings as a matter of course. Few of us either can eat them every day without putting on weight. We would rather save them for a treat at weekends or when someone's coming to dinner. Fill their place midweek with whatever fruit is in season— sweet juicy pears in the autumn, meltingly tender raspberries in the summer, succulent figs and mirabelles following on.

The setting is all-important to the enjoyment of the occasion. When the weather permits, it is much more enjoyable to settle down to a table in the shade on a sunny day, or to enjoy the cool of the evening after a blazing afternoon. A summertime breakfast especially is to be savoured in the cool freshness of the morning, the first cup of coffee or piece of fruit of the day that always tastes so much more vibrant than anything that follows.

There is no real need for special outside lights, plates and cutlery, or for that matter, different food. Nor is there any need for a picnic to be a performance in fine dining in the middle of a field. A wicker hamper decked with china, cutlery and glasses and the type of food that goes with it, is more likely to deter than encourage. Keep it rustic. Little whets the appetite like the smell of smoke out of doors, beaches can be combed for driftwood to build a fire, and inland a portable field grill set up. Marinated lamb and chicken kebabs make for enticing grilling, with flat breads warmed on the grid to wrap around them. And afterwards the dying embers should see you through a pot of espresso coffee.

Menus are of limited use and serve here as examples of how we like to eat more than recommendations to be adhered to. We still hope you will find ideas for every occasion, be it lunch on your own, supper for two when you haven't shopped, or an uncannily balmy evening in May when you can't bear to drag yourself out of the garden in the first preprandial bliss of summer.

Weekday Supper

083 Spaghetti Puttanesca
180 Salad of Cresses

071 Soft Scrambled Eggs
204 Buttered Spinach with Garlic
     Figs

120 Plaice à la Meunière
222 Salers with a Green Salad

195 Puy Lentil, Roasted Pepper and
     Anchovy Salad
230 Affogato al Caffe

048 Dressed Mozzarella
064 Mussel Soup with Tomato
     and Chilli

046 Quails' Eggs, Savoury Salt
     and Grissini
097 Venetian Peas and Rice

142 Chicken Breasts Escoffier
222 Goat's Cheese and Dates

     Smoked Salmon
063 Courgette and Lemon Soup

146 T-bone for Two
206 Sautéed Mushrooms
     Pears

Weekday Supper with Friends

042 Roasted Garlic, Toasted Goat's
     Cheese and Parma Ham
134 Chicken and White Wine Stew
     with Gremolata
172 Mashed Potato
     Green Salad
226 Strawberry Fool with
     White Chocolate

036 Radishes with Butter and
     Sea Salt
111 Normandy Fish Pie
233 Roast Plums and
     Raspberry Sorbet

189 Wild Mushrooms in Oil
097 Risotto with Fontina
     Green Salad
252 Vin Santo and Cantuccini

108 Grilled Squid with Lemon
     and Chilli
078 Wild Mushroom Torte
     Green Salad
247 Chocolate Gâteau with
     Crème Chantilly

     Parma Ham
190 Celeriac Rémoulade
119 Monkfish à l'Americaine
172 Saffron Mash
245 French Puff Pastry Apple Tart

181 Rocket and Parmesan Salad
095 Risotto with Roast Chicken
     and Gravy
235 Hot Buttered Cherries with
     Vanilla Ice-cream

201 Roast Beetroot, Carrot
     and Peppers
102 Mussels with Tomato
     and Chorizo
246 Orange and Almond Cake with
     Cardamom Syrup

     Olives, salami, roast
     garlic, gherkins
120 Charmoula-grilled Halibut
170 Spiced Sweet Potatoes
240 Baked Couscous Pudding
     with Raisins

048 Naked Mozzarella
119 Gigot of Monkfish
193 Green Bean Salad
235 Pan-poached Nectarines in a
     Spiced White Wine Syrup

Saturday Lunch

078 Croque Monsieur
182 Classic Tomato Salad

194 Salad of Frisée, Lardons
    and Croûtons
222 Cheddar and Cob Nuts

    Parma Ham
190 Celeriac Rémoulade

038 King Prawns with Garlic
193 Green Bean Salad

072 Tomato Frittata
180 Salad of Cresses

    Goats' Cheeses
186 Oven-roasted Tomatoes
181 Rocket and Parmesan Salad

139 Grilled Marinated Quail
167 Savoury Lentils

054 Bruschetta
181 Rocket and Parmesan Salad

041 Taramasalata
    Olives, Crudités and Flat Bread

Saturday Dinner with Friends

044 Parma Ham with Parsnip Salad
101 Squid Ink Risotto with Scallops
226 Whisked Wine Jelly

061 Gingered Carrot Soup
131 Roast Guinea Fowl with
    Pistachio and Lemon Crumbs
222 Parmigiano-Reggiano and Pear
252 Vin Santo and Cantuccini

056 Salted Almonds
115 Sea Bass baked in Salt
172 Mashed Potato
204 Buttered Spinach with Garlic
229 Butterscotch Ice-cream

046 Guacamole and Corn Chips
163 Meatballs with Marjoram and
    Pine Nuts in Tomato Sauce
243 Poppy Seed Cheesecake

048 Mozzarella with Warm
    Tomato Dressing
155 Pot-roasted Leg of Lamb with
    Black Olives
    New Potatoes
245 Treacle Tart

063 Cream of Cauliflower Soup
125 Olive Oil Roast Chicken
210 Aioli
180 Salad of Cresses
230 Affogato al Caffe

108 Warm Salad of New Potatoes
    and Oysters
136 'Guinea' Coq au vin
    Green Salad
239 Eton Mess

083 Spaghetti with Bottarga
076 Spinach, Garlic and Goat's
    Cheese Soufflé
246 Orange and Almond Cake with
    Cardamom Syrup

038 King Prawns with Garlic
094 Saffron Risotto
201 Roast Pumpkin with Garlic
    and Chilli
229 Maple Syrup and Stem Ginger
    Ice-cream

Sunday Lunch

128 All-in-one Chicken Roast
206 French Beans with Bacon
249 Chocolate Mousse Cake

066 Gazpacho
125 Butter-roasted Herbed Chicken
208 Perfect Peas
224 Rhubarb Jelly

158 Roast Rib of Beef with
    Yorkshire Pudding
214 Horseradish Sauce
175 Champ
205 Glazed Carrots
227 Pear and Raspberry
    Mascarpone Trifle

063 Cream of Cauliflower Soup
157 Roast Lamb with Flageolet Bean
    Gratin and Vine Tomatoes
220 Stilton and Quince Cheese

125 Olive Oil Roast Chicken
210 Aioli
169 Jacket-roasted New Potatoes
    Green Salad
236 Summer Pudding

119 Gigot of Monkfish
200 Roast Peppers
227 Pear and Raspberry
    Mascarpone Trifle

197 Warm Potato and
    Pancetta Salad
113 Poached Salmon with
    Sauce Verte
236 Summer Pudding

056 Salted Almonds
144 Moroccan Chicken Salad with
    Preserved Lemon
187 Tabbouleh
222 Goat's Cheese and Dates

058 White Onion Soup
093 Tomato and Basil Lasagne
    Wild Strawberries

Sunday Dinner

109 Jansson's Temptation
250 Stuffed Dates

082 Midnight Spaghetti
222 Roquefort and Walnuts

073 Souffléed Omelette
    with Gruyère
232 Roast Figs

150 Steak 'au poivre'
176 Sautéed Potatoes

051 Quiche Lorraine
180 Salad of Cresses

044 Chicken Liver Parfait
064 Garlic Soup with a Poached Egg

137 Lemon Chicken in Paper with
    Straw Potatoes
180 Salad of Cresses

206 Sautéed Mushrooms
175 Baked Potatoes

061 Leek and Potato Soup
222 Lancashire Cheese and Chutney

Equipment

Although kitchen equipment can run to a cast of thousands, virtually all recipes revolve around a core—pots and pans, knives and a chopping board. The quality of these objects is one of the keys to success in cooking. In what follows we have sought to define the optimum collection—not necessarily the most skeletal but one that will ensure the seamless progression of whatever you are cooking from start to finish.

Pots and Pans

Saucepan technology has never been the most alluring topic of conversation, but an understanding of how different pots and pans suit particular cooking methods enables you to make an informed decision.

Pots and pans need to be made from materials which conduct heat and don't taint food. At one time unlined lead was in general use for pans, but fell from favour for obvious reasons. Copper succeeded lead, but always lined with another material, since copper oxide is injurious to health. Tin was the traditional choice for this, but while it contained copper, it also wore off with heavy use within about six months and was comparatively soft and so liable to melt at high temperatures. You can still buy copper pans and the linings are becoming increasingly durable. Some even come with a pot of polish, but you still need to find time to buff them to a lustrous sheen. To put the efficiency of metals in perspective, copper is twenty times more conductive than stainless steel, nearly ten times as conductive as cast iron, with aluminium about halfway in between.

Aluminium

The discovery of aluminium or a means of extracting the metal from its ore, only began to have an impact at the end of the nineteenth century. Over the next fifty years the cost of extracting it fell, and soon into the twentieth century it was popularised as being light, rust-free and durable. It continued to be the most popular choice for saucepans throughout the middle years of the twentieth century. However, as anyone who has cooked in an aluminium pot knows, over time it becomes pitted as the metal oxidises—acidic foods in particular eat into the surface. Nor is it as hard as could be. It is also relatively difficult to clean and keep looking spick and span. In terms of efficiency, the high conductivity of the metal, while rendering the base of the pan responsive to heat changes, means the sides readily give up their heat to the surroundings. By the 1960s cooks were ready to consider other metals as possibilities.

These are probably the main reasons why it no longer exists as the household favourite, but it didn't help when it became linked to the degenerative brain disorder Alzheimer's disease during the last decades of the twentieth century. No substantiated link between the the use of aluminium pans and the likelihood of developing Alzheimer's has been proven, but if you want to delve into the subject further, read 'The Curious Cook' by Harold McGee. If aluminium pans are your preferred choice, you should avoid using them to cook long-simmered or acidic foods. It is also inadvisable to store foods in the saucepan in the fridge—this applies to all saucepans. It's always best to transfer food to a glass, ceramic or stainless steel bowl, or plasticware before chilling it.

Anodized aluminium

In the US in particular the answer to the problems posed by the pitting and denting of aluminium has been to anodize it. This involves treating the surface to create a layer of aluminium oxide, which is far harder than aluminium itself and acts as a barrier between the metal and the food. The upside is good-looking matt black pans with good conductivity. The downside is that the layering is only skin deep and, in due course, wears off to re-expose the aluminium. And as ever it is comparatively soft and with time the base tends to warp, which may not present a major problem for gas hobs, but may cause difficulties on ceramic or halogen ones where a totally flat base is essential.

Perhaps the worse drawback is that the pans must be washed by hand—a dishwasher can wreck the finish in a single cycle. If the pan has a non-stick interior, then washing it up by hand is easy, but in time, not only does the anodised layer wear off, so too does the non-stick coating. Smart as these pans may look in the shop, they are not a good long-term investment.

Non-stick pans

Non-stick pans represent the largest sector of household pot and pan purchases. Whatever else we want as consumers, we certainly don't want our food to stick. We would also like our pans to be rendered clean after a quick swill under the hot tap. As anyone who has ever come face to face with the remnants of scrambled eggs will vouch, a non-stick pan is worth almost any sacrifice.

There are occasions when a non-stick frying pan is virtually indispensable. Fish, when it is very fresh—within 2 hours of being caught—cooks like a dream. However, 48 hours thereafter (which is when most of us obtain it), the flesh and skin will have exuded an oily film that causes it to stick to the pan and tear. On this account it's worth frying fish in a non-stick pan as a matter of course. This will ensure beautifully intact fillets and skin that is golden and crisp. Equally, a non-stick pan is worth its weight in gold when frying aubergines, which greedily drink up oil and will stick and burn all too readily. Chicken breasts and bacon too, can be fried until crisp without any additional fat.

Non-stick pans do not provide a universal solution. A non-stick surface is basically a plastic, hence the slip-slide effect. Colouring pieces of meat for a casserole is a disaster, as they skid around like a dancer on ice when the point is for the sugars and juices in the meat to catch on the metal and caramelise.

The technology relating to non-stick pans is still far from perfect. True, there are some manufacturers offering lifetime guarantees on their coatings, but what they are really saying is that they are quite happy to replace or re-coat the few pans that will still be in use in thirty years time. At present the greatest advance has been to flame-spray stainless steel at a very high temperature with a fine coating of steel particles. This technique creates a roughened surface of minute hills and valleys harder than the layer of stainless steel below it. When this is subsequently coated with a non-stick material, metal utensils—which normally cause the damage —only come into contact with the hills, rendering the coating that much more durable. The drawback is that it doesn't and cannot perform as effectively as a normal non-stick coating. At present the best and most technologically assured manufacturers are settling for a compromise between durability and performance.

Cooking with cast iron

Cast iron has the comfort that comes with experience. It's been used for generations and is unique in providing a slow, nurturing, succulent heat, gently drawing out the best in braises and pot-roasts. Cast iron is not the quickest metal to heat up but, once hot, retains the heat—steadily and for that much longer than copper or aluminium.

The downside of cast iron is its weight, not so problematic in a casserole, which is only lifted in and out of the oven once or twice during the process of cooking. It can, however, seriously hamper the function of a large frying pan which one wants to be able to lift with one hand. Small cast iron frying pans and medium-size ones are fine—in fact some of the best to be found on the market. Cast iron saucepans, like large frying pans, are to be avoided, as they'll not only be unnecessarily heavy, but slow to respond to changes in heat.

The term cast iron actually refers to an alloy of iron with a percentage of carbon that hardens it. The one thing we don't recommend is untreated cast iron. Unless you care for your pans assiduously, they will be prone to rusting which, if left, will eat deeper and deeper into the vessel.

The usual way of containing the rust is to oil and heat a pan to create a barrier between the metal and the air. This barrier is never wholly effective and always at the mercy of scouring pads and detergents. The long-term solution is to coat cast-iron pans with vitreous enamel, a thin layer made by fusing powdered glass on to the surface of the metal. Even though the enamel is non-conductive, the layer is so thin it does not affect the ability of the iron below it to conduct heat efficiently. Enamel is usually coloured, but it also comes in a discreet matt black finish that resembles untreated cast iron and is our preferred finish. For a list of enamelled cast ironware manufacturers, see page 294.

State of the art saucepans

Most professional quality saucepans—including French Bourgeat 'Traditional Plus' pans and Demeyere's 'Apollo' range—conform to a type. The basic shell is made from stainless steel. As this is a poor thermal conductor, it advantageously ensures that heat is well retained within the pan. To improve the conductivity of the base and avoid hot spots, a disc of varying construction—containing one or several metals—is welded to the bottom, about 1cm in from the edge. Such pans are excellent quality and we would recommend both manufacturers. One drawback is their design. The pans are comparatively rough around the edges and look better in a professional kitchen than the home.

The Belgian manufacturer Demeyere offers a new range called Atlantis with a flush base that affords 25–33% more heat-conductive area than the usual type of pan where the welded base stops short of the edge. These saucepans perform that much more efficiently.

The minimum number of pans any household needs is three, though four is usually more appropriate, ranging in size from 16–24cm. In addition, one very large maslin pan that can be used for cooking food in quantity, as well as for stocks and preserves, will prove invaluable.

Frying pans

We would recommend two sizes of frying pan. A small one is useful for cooking small amounts of food, dry-frying spices and making omelettes. Le Creuset's 23cm cast iron skillet in their Granite range is ideal. For general frying and cooking larger amounts of food, you need one or two large frying pans. Although non-stick frying pans are rarely design icons, they are beneficial for certain foods and every kitchen's arsenal should include one. The Duraglide frying pans in Demeyere's Apollo range perform extremely well.

It's important to use the right size of pan for the task. If it is too large in relation to the food, residues that spread out from the item you are frying will burn. Equally, if the pan is overcrowded, the food on top will steam rather than fry because it won't be in contact with the hot surface—one reason why recipes sometimes suggest that you use two frying pans at once.

Cast iron frying pans take a relatively long time to heat up, but achieve a consistent heat devoid of hot spots and probably offer the best performance. Our preference is Hackman's Dahlstrom 26cm pan.

Stainless steel frying pans generally have a highly conductive base containing aluminium, but poorly conductive stainless steel sides. The drawback here is that any flames that hit the sides will create hot spots and cause the food to burn. We are therefore quite wary of these pans, with the exception of Demeyere's stainless steel frying pans. These consist of a 7-ply material going right the way up the sides that achieves an even distribution of heat and enlarges the potential cooking surface.

Casseroles

Every household needs a minimum of one cast iron casserole for pot-roasting and for stews. If cared for, this should last a lifetime.

Staub, one of the market leaders, produces a stunning range of matt black casseroles with brass handles and an induction-proof, dark blue enamel base that doesn't rust. A special feature is a set of spikes under the lid that encourages steam to condense and drip back on to the food, so basting it throughout the cooking process. The 31cm oval cocotte will accommodate a chicken or a leg of lamb.

Roasting pans

Cast iron roasting pans cannot be recommended highly enough. The material nurtures the roast, protecting it from the ravages of heat. Juices tend to caramelise rather than burn in the way that can happen in aluminium and stainless steel pans. They are perfect for making gravy on top of the stove.

Most households benefit from two sizes of cast iron roasting pan. Chasseur's 32 by 21cm and 40 by 24cm roasting dishes, produced by Invicta, are a good foundation. In addition, it is useful to have a couple of small dishes for tasks such as roasting nuts. Those produced by Staub are ideal.

The only alternative we would recommend is unseasoned black iron roasters (not iron at all but steel). They do require more in the way of maintenance, but still produce excellent results and have an undesigned quality.

Steamers

Unless you do a great deal of steaming, a petal steamer is more than adequate for vegetables. This opens out like a flower and fits inside any size of saucepan, with the advantage of being small enough to pop into a drawer. The lid of the pan must be tight fitting in order to retain the steam.

Griddles

The best griddles are made from cast iron—one that has a ridged side for grilling chicken and fish and a flat side for traditional griddling is particularly useful. Ideally a griddle should cover two rings to cope with larger quantities of food, and sport ridges of sufficient depth, to grill rather than fry. Le Creuset's Giant Grill fills all these criteria.

Maintenance of pans

Non-stick pans are damaged by metal utensils, so stick to wooden or plastic ones. If your pan came with a lengthy guarantee and shows more than its fair share of wear and tear, send it back.

Enamelled pans are vulnerable to damage and can scratch and chip. Clean with a mild detergent and, if necessary, leave to soak overnight rather than scrub with a scourer.

Stainless steel pans are relatively easy to maintain. The '18/10 grade' of stainless steel used in saucepan manufacture, comprising 72% iron, 18% chrome and 9–10% nickel, is hard and doesn't rust. It is the chrome that is responsible for the resistant shine, the chrome oxide on the surface acting as a protective barrier.

Stainless steel finishes are either high gloss or matt. Pretty as mirrored steel looks in the shop, it is every bit as difficult as copper to keep looking pristine, because it scratches and shows rainbow streaks. These are mineral deposits that can be removed using vinegar or lemon juice, but again this requires effort.

We prefer a matt finish, though this is still susceptible to fingerprints created by a chemical reaction between the acids in sweat and the metal. The range of pans we recommend gets around the problem with a patented electrochemical process called Silvinox that effectively removes the impurities from the surface of the metal. The resulting finish is yellower than normal, but the pans wash up like a dream. If you put them through a dishwasher they emerge looking as good as new, year after year.

Cast iron pans should not rust provided they are enamelled, but bearing in mind that enamel is delicate, metal utensils should be avoided if possible. As mentioned above, a gentle soak overnight is better than a scrub with wire wool, and they should always be left to cool before being immersed in water. These pans should also be heated over a low to medium heat rather than a high one.

Kitchen knives

It wasn't long ago that the average domestic kitchen sported a bread knife and one plastic handled serrated knife. We have the interest in how chefs cook to thank for the availability of good knives, but while the advent of quality is to be lauded, we are still some way off understanding how best to exploit such knives within a domestic context. The size of a knife should not only correspond to the task and the size of the hand using it, but the amount of food it will be working. In the home kitchen there is no real need for huge 25cm chopping knives.

The outline of the traditional riveted handle has not to date been improved. It feels comfortable in the hand and light. The handles of our recommended Wusthof knives are made from plastic that is virtually indestructible and are dishwasher proof.

Wusthof Trident, a family owned and run company, is recognised as being the finest manufacturer of knives in the world. It continues to use the traditional hot-drop forging method. Competitors have largely replaced this by welding together three separate pieces of steel, which fails to offer the same balance and cannot afford the same degree of strength as a single piece of metal. The hardness of Wusthof knives is set at 56 Rockwell, which is the optimum for holding the edge and making it easy to resharpen. The following knives are all contained with Wusthof's Classic range and, as a set, make a superb foundation.

Paring knife (10cm)

This is the knife you will take to a clove of garlic, to cut out the cone from the top of a tomato, to core an apple or halve a plum.

Utility knife (12cm)

This is possibly the most useful knife of the range. It's an unusual length and shape, beautifully proportioned, like an elongated paring knife. It will cope with all the tasks of the paring knife, but can also be used to cut a sliver of cheese, to slice bottarga or cut open a lemon.

Sausage knife (14cm)

The serrated edge of this knife glides through salamis, tomatoes and stubborn fruit like passion fruit.

Cook's knife (16cm)

Any smaller than this and the knife won't perform its function, much larger and it becomes unwieldy. A perfect knife for chopping and slicing.

Narrow slicer (20cm)

This flexible knife is the perfect all-purpose carver, whether for a roast chicken, beef or a gigot of monkfish.

Bread knife (26cm)

A serrated bread knife will receive an outing in most households several times a day. It needs to be long enough to facilitate the sawing action demanded by a large loaf.

Straight meat fork (16cm)

This will pierce a roast and hold it in place while you perform the honours with the carving knife.

Kitchen shears

Apart from the efficacy of these scissors, their traditional silhouette is particularly appealing.

Palette knife (20cm)

All you need to assist in turning fried foods and fillets, or loosening the edges of an omelette, and considerably more efficient than the wide spatulas normally sold for such tasks.

Staying sharp

An elliptical fine finish diamond steel is extremely efficient at realigning the edge on a neglected blade. Its surface is coated in industrial diamonds, which gives a finish like sandpaper.

To sharpen a knife the easy way, place the tip of your sharpener on the work surface and hold the heel of the blade against it at a 20° angle. Run the length of the blade down the sharpener twice, quite hard. Repeat with the underside and then again with the topside. Test to see whether it is sharp by trying to cut through a piece of paper. If necessary, give the topside another couple of swipes and try again. If you have the angle of the knife correct, this method is foolproof.

If your knives have become seriously blunt, you may want to have them professionally ground. Find a specialist rather than resort to the local keycutter, or send them instead to the Italian Maturi family in Leeds who have specialised in grinding knives for over a hundred years now (see page 294).

Storing knives

Magnetic steels are less obtrusive than knife blocks, which dominate the view and take up space on the worktop. Such steels can be fitted into a drawer. A canvas knife holder is a useful means of carrying your favourite knives from one place to another.

Opinel—the classic penknife

This is one knife you shouldn't be without. In France every self-respecting chef keeps one to hand for purposes as diverse as shaving a few slivers of black Perigord truffle, or removing the core of an apple. Opinel knives are a fine example of everyday design that is so good and so simple that you take it for granted. Its most brilliant facet is the safety ring, which holds the blade folded into the handle, making the knife safe to carry. When you want to use the knife, the ring is twisted to lock the blade into the open position.

Opinel knives range in size from a dinky 4cm blade, through to 12cm. It is the larger sizes 6–12 that come with the locking ring. The beauty of the design was recognised by the Victoria and Albert Museum in London in 1985 when they chose to include it in a good design guide as 'one of the 100 most beautiful products in the world'. It is also exhibited in New York's Museum of Modern Art.

Chopping boards

The vast array of shapes, sizes and materials would imply you need lots of chopping boards to cook well. The ideal is just one large wooden board that can sit permanently on the work surface. This board is as central to the process of cooking as the hob or sink.

Large boards make for simplicity. In most restaurant kitchens every chef, while limited in space, will have a large board in front of them on which to prepare whatever he or she is cooking. From start to finish this space is at the heart of the dish. A large board allows you to contain everything within one area.

The presence of wood in a kitchen becomes ever more calming as steel and other modern manmade materials gain in use. Apart from the aesthetics of a large slab, there is the pleasure of using it, the sound a knife makes and the way it feels—that familiar gentle thud so different from the clack of a steel blade on plastic. Thankfully, the demonisation of wooden boards as being unhygenic has been disproven—wood contains natural substances that are inhospitable to bacteria and, provided it is well-maintained, is as safe as polypropylene.

Which wood?

Good chopping boards will be made from hardwood, which might be cherry, maple, beech or olive, all of which have warm subtle colours. These are slow-growing trees, so the wood has a tight grain and isn't as porous as that of trees that mature quickly. Hardwood boards won't absorb odours as readily either, nor are they as prone to warping or cracking. Beyond this, it is largely a question of taste. Choose a grain that appeals to you, bearing in mind that the paler the wood, the more likely it is to stain.

Large boards are either cut as a single piece along the grain—which needs to have a thickness of at least 3cm to ensure it won't warp—or they are 'end-grain' boards which are even thicker. Comprising a chequerboard of small squares of wood cut across the grain and glued together, 'end-grain' boards are favoured by butchers for their durability, though this is less of a consideration for the average household. They can be anything between 8–15cm thick and therefore more unwieldy.

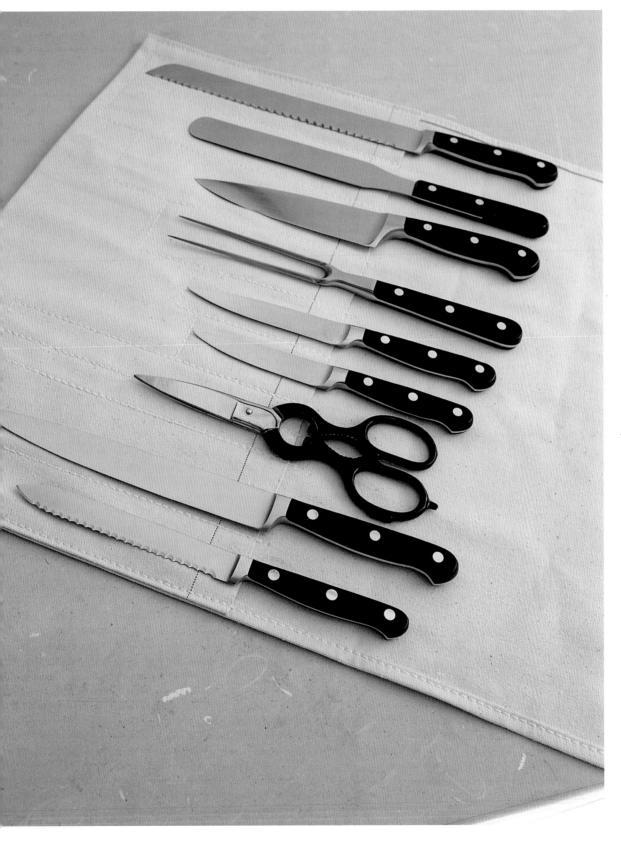

Different boards, different functions

The fastidious cook may like to keep a separate board for fruit and other sweet food that can be tainted by savoury odours—especially those of garlic, onion and chillies. Our answer is simply to flip the board over. Handles, grooves, lips and legs are unnecessary. If anything they complicate matters by reducing the function of the board to a specific task, such as carving meat or cutting bread, and they aren't as straightforward to clean.

Care of wooden boards

Every time you use your board, you will need to wipe it down thoroughly. You should avoid leaving a board sitting in a pool of water, as this causes warping. Now and again give it a really good clean by scrubbing with a paste made from baking powder and water, which should deodorise it in the process. Alternatively, sprinkle with salt and give it a good scrub with a hard bristle or wire brush then dry off thoroughly. If you stand the board upright, it will allow the air to circulate, otherwise it's best to clean and dry off one side at a time.

A new board will benefit from being oiled regularly—once a week for the first month and then every few weeks until it is about a year old and has the appearance of being well seasoned. Thereafter the occasional oiling will afford some protection from changes in temperature and humidity. Olive oil is to be avoided because it turns rancid after a while. Instead, use a tasteless vegetable oil like soya or sunflower, gently rubbing it in using a soft clean cloth.

A good, well-nurtured board will last a lifetime. If the surface is damaged, simply sand it down with an electric sander in the direction of the wood grain or glue lines (or take it to a timber merchant and ask him to do it for you). Brush off the dust with a soft brush and oil the board as described above.

Home-Making

Whether a drink before dinner is a glass of Champagne, wine or water, a Paris goblet is our choice. The cup itself has been endlessly copied in crystal and given a slender stem in the name of elegance, but it is the short stubby dimension of the original that is so appealing.

A tray is almost essential in offering the flexibility to move the occasion to wherever people have naturally gravitated. If it's a cold evening, most will be drawn to the fire, while in the summer we have to steel ourselves to move from the garden. The ideal tray is cleanly geometric and made of wood, with generous carrying space, adequate sides and comfortable handles. A classic Butler's tray is ideal.

Very occasionally there may be call for a decanter, and in this case the crystal Baccarat offers a stunning silhouette that captures everything that is beautiful about the shape of a wine bottle.

However informal the occasion, there is always cause for something small on the side. They have this down to a fine art in Spain, where it may be no more complicated than a sliver of Manchego cheese or Serrano ham. The French, too, would never dream of serving drinks before dinner without some small offering of food. Crisp salted almonds are delectable, and on from this, lightly poached quails' eggs or a slice of buffalo mozzarella. This is probably the best occasion, too, for savouring the luscious texture of smoked salmon, with just a grinding of black pepper and a few drops of lemon juice.

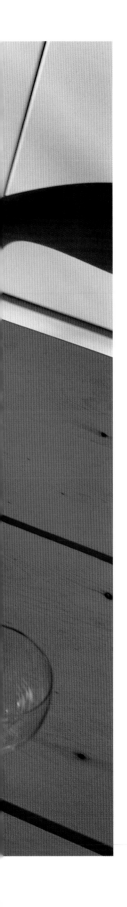

Beyond the simplicity of a bowl of nuts, there is much to be said for replacing the first course with something that lies halfway between the two. The chapter 'To begin' is about small tasters that can be eaten plate and fork in hand while standing around chatting and drinking. Whether or not you have a house full of friends or it's down to one or two, it makes for a fluid and relaxing start to lunch or dinner.

Laying a table

An elaborately laid table comes across as a statement of grandeur —all those glasses and silver. The less the better. Ideally the table should be virtually empty at the start of a meal, just the candlesticks if it's an evening, and white linen napkins—antique ones worn to a velvety softness loosely folded, with a knife and fork placed on top.

Cutlery

Part of the elaborate laying of a table has to do with the out-dated social convention of needing a different set of cutlery for every course. It's perfectly feasible to carry over a knife and fork used for an appetiser, as is often the habit in France and Italy, simply adding a knife or spoon as needed. The Victorians are largely to blame for elaborate dinner settings by creating a fork, spoon and knife for every conceivable function, as well as lifters, slicers and servers.

Fish knives and forks are the epitome of superfluous cutlery. Many of us fortunate enough to escape a set as a wedding present subsequently inherit them from a grandmother or aunt. The earliest recorded set dates back to 1847, before which fish was eaten with two forks. The functional purpose of a fish knife is its point with which to tease the flesh from the bone, but this is just as easily achieved with an ordinary knife. In fact, so obscure is the function behind the original design, some establishments today use them for kipper pâté and smoked salmon. Fish implements are no more necessary than other additional small knives and forks, or soup spoons when dessert ones are adequate to the task.

The most beautiful of all cutlery is fashioned from silver, with its lustrous grey-white sheen. Silver is sturdy enough to have survived the centuries while delicate enough to tell us a story. A spoon might have been wrought by hand with hammer and anvil, the edges of the bowl deliberately thickened for strength. The tines of a fork may be worn with use, or spikily intact after a life spent in a darkened box in the attic.

The Georgian period saw the appearance of the ultimately restrained fork. The three-pronged fork in general use at the end of the seventeenth century, had a comparatively short life. By the end of the eighteenth century, forks had four prongs and continued to do so throughout the Victorian era and the twentieth century. Perhaps the introduction of a fourth tine was to make it easier to eat peas—it had been customary for peas, as well as sloppy sauces and gravy, to be eaten with a knife.

Crockery

The ideal is just one size of plate. A 25cm dinner plate is large enough to cater for the main course without being too big for a pile of green leaves, a slice of Parmesan and a pear, or some toast for breakfast. Better too much space

on a plate than too little. Side plates are limited in function and it is in any case so much nicer to eat bread straight from the table and suffer the mess of a few crumbs. An all-purpose bowl, shaped as a straight-sided cup without a handle, graciously receives drinks like tea and coffee, as well as creamed soups, nuts, olives and cereal. A larger version can be used for anything from a green salad to fruit.

Wedgwood makes the most restrained off-white china. Called Queensware, it is one of the factory's oldest designs. It received its Royal Assent in 1765 when Josiah Wedgwood rose to the lofty height of 'Potter to her Majesty', then Queen Charlotte wife of George III. The plates have a curved base without a foot-rim, and a perfectly judged concave rim which prevents food from spilling over the side without taking up the whole of the inside of the plate, as so many modern designs are inclined to do.

Salt and pepper

If food is perfectly seasoned then, arguably, you don't need salt and pepper on the table, but this is to assume we all have the same taste. Salt grinders have a habit of clogging up if the salt is any good— French sea salt is literally wet. English Maldon salt—which is the finest on offer—is readily crushed between the fingers, in which case a small bowl such as the Wedgwood Queensware sugar bowl makes the ideal receptacle.

As to pepper mills, the only consideration in favour of large ones is the quantity they hold. The ideal is one that is comfortable to grasp—12cm is a sensible height that won't dominate the work surface or the table. An adjustable grinding mechanism can be useful —when flavouring delicate soups and purées, pepper is best added as a fine powder, but at other times it is more enjoyable coarsely ground. Occasionally there is a call for pepper that is even coarser— the answer is a pestle and mortar. This cannot be challenged for the way it releases the fragrance of herbs and spices which should be ground at the last minute. The matt finish of a vitrified ceramic pestle isn't affected by acidic foods which attack marble mortars, nor is it subject to the inevitable tainting of wooden ones.

Candlesticks

Rather as vases of flowers in the house can fall into the category of beautiful effects which can be debased through overuse, so too candles in excess can undermine rather than enhance atmosphere. They are best used with restraint, but their appeal endures— especially that of untapered ivory church candles, made with a high proportion of beeswax. A 23cm candle will outlast the most expansive dinner.

If money were no object then Georgian silver candlesticks possess a timeless elegance. A surprising choice, perhaps, given that their curves could undoubtedly be simplified, although not improved by subtraction. Victorian candlesticks can be a good alternative. A candle placed within a bowl is another possibility, although it lacks the appeal of a candle flame reflected in silver. It is one of the pleasures of the evening to select and light fresh candles.

Flowers

Flowers and plants really belong outside. Nonetheless, having flowers in the house, as well as affording temporary sensory pleasure, is an aspect of bringing the outside inside. Our preference is for a bunch of wild flowers or something cut from the garden. Failing that, a generous, tight bunch of a single variety looks good.

The quiet palette of John's interiors suits a strong bolt of colour—tulips that are almost black, or vermilion gerberas, a bunch of crimson roses or peonies, a vase of sunflowers, or poppies. Mistletoe also looks good when used in quantity.

The vases we prefer are clear, crystal volumes. Clarissa Berning's heavy lead crystal cubes look as though they have been cut from blocks of ice. Each piece is cast individually in a plaster mould and polished by hand. For bunches of longer-stemmed flowers, the organic forms of the Alvar Aalto range are perfect.

Flowers on tables distract from both food and people. Vases are best set on benches or shelves, positioned so that the light falls from behind, catching in the crystal and reflecting on surfaces. They are also more alluring in living areas than in bedrooms, where they suck out the air at night and pervade with scent.

Serving of food

If equipment is sufficiently handsome, it will double as cooking vessel and server. Our own choice of saucepans, casseroles and frying pans takes into account their look on the table, a consideration often cited of earthenware that should

extend to all cookware. An obvious advantage is that transferring the food is less effort, and there is less washing up. By the same token, everyday china can also be used for serving appetisers and salads, which saves having to keep special platters for the job.

Fruit bowls

Because fruit and vegetables need to be cared for in their raw state, they are better not treated as decorative objects and kept instead in proper, ventilated storage at the correct temperature and humidity. But there are still times when you want to offer up whatever seasonal fruit you may have procured— black cherries, figs, white peaches, mirabelles or wild strawberries— at the table. The solution is some beautiful flat artefact such as Clarissa Berning's lens-shaped crystal platter that is as alluring standing empty as it is piled high with just one type of fruit. The other possibility is to heap fruit into a bowl, such as the Wedgwood Queensware salad bowl.

The ritual of tea and coffee

The kettle resting on the hob has long been symbolic of home life. The old-fashioned kettle that stood on the range is at the heart of this in a way that an electric kettle will never be. Ironically modern designs of electric kettle now concentrate on trying to mimic the shape of the original as closely as possible.

Similar satisfaction is to be had from the purr of coffee brewing in a stove-top espresso pot. Despite attempts to modernise the original Bialetti design, nothing to date has improved on their classic Moka Express that has been in production since the 1950s—some 90% of Italian families own one.

The inspiration for Alfonso Bialetti's prototype was an early washing machine made from a boiler with a tub for the collection of hot water. The Express heats water to boiling point in the lower section, when it is forced under pressure upwards through the coffee grounds, the resulting coffee collecting in the upper chamber. The body wears to an attractive dull haze with time. It is indispensable on picnics—there are few greater luxuries than a freshly brewed espresso when you are in the middle of nowhere. As to cups and saucers, rather saucer-less, handle-less cups and the drinking technique they foster, the one small requirement being that you don't overfill them otherwise the rim gets too hot to hold.

Picnic

Eating outside should be as close in kind to eating inside, so there is no need for a change in plates or cutlery. The problem remains that if you have chosen to live with just one set of cutlery and plates and indulged that decision with the purchase of silver and china, you may not consider it suitable for use in a field. On the comfort of a lambswool rug, wine can be drunk out of Duralex tumblers and everything else enjoyed in hand, with the assistance of a set of Opinel knives to cut cheeses and salami if necessary.

Bulthaup
Kitchens
00 44 (0)20 7317 6000
www.bulthaup.com

Gaggenau
Ovens
BSH Home Appliances Limited
00 44 (0)1908 328 360
www.gaggenau.com

Miele
Dishwashers
00 44 (0)1235 554 455
www.miele.co.uk

Obumex
John Pawson kitchen system,
including hob
00 32 51 70 50 71
www.obumex.be

Equipment

Bourgeat
Pans
00 44 (0)1904 670 328
www.bourgeat.fr

Demeyere
Pans
00 44 (0)1282 613 644
www.demeyere.be

Hackman and Chasseur
Pans
00 44 (0)1730 811 811

Le Creuset
Pans
00 44 (0)800 373 792
www.lecreuset.co.uk

Peter Maturi
Knife-sharpener
00 44 (0)1132 453 887

Opinel
Knives
00 44 (0)1539 721 032
www.opinel.com

Staub
Pans
00 44 (0)1782 207 755
www.staub.fr

Wusthof Trident
Knives
00 44 (0)1782 207 755
www.dreizack.de

Home-Making

Alvar Aalto
Vases
Dexam International Limited
00 44 (0)1730 811 888

Baccarat
Decanters
00 44 (0)20 7409 7767
www.baccarat.fr

B&B Italia
Furniture
00 44 (0)20 7551 8155
www.bebitalia.it

Clarissa Berning
Cube vase and crystal platter
Dominic Berning
00 44 (0)20 7739 4222

Bialetti
Moka Express
Household Articles
00 44 (0)20 8651 6321
www.bialetti.it

Bruford and Heming Limited
Candlesticks and cutlery—pistol handled knives, Hanoverian three-pronged forks
00 44 (0)20 7629 4289

Calphalon
Classic water kettle
00 31 30 23 31 89 39
www.calphalon.com
www.potpan.com

Cucina Direct
Oak butler's tray
00 44 (0)870 2727 4300
www.cucinadirect.co.uk

Driade
Furniture
0 44 (0)20 7278 8456
www.driade.co.jp

Duralex
Glasses
00 44 (0)20 8992 4627
www.bormiolirocco.com

Luminarc
Paris goblets
00 44 (0)20 7316 0014
www.arc-international.com

Peugeot
Pepper mill
Richard Gilbert
00 44 (0)20 8731 3700
www.gilberts-foodequipment.com

Price's Patent Candle Co. Limited
Untapered 25cm beeswax candle
00 44 (0)1234 264 500

Wedgwood
Crockery
00 44 (0)800 317 412
www.wedgwood.com

When Objects Work
John Pawson tray and vase
00 32 58 29 81 86
www.whenobjectswork.com

Index

GR 4/05

First published in hardback in 2001
This paperback edition first
published in 2004
1 3 5 7 9 10 8 6 4 2

First published in the United
Kingdom in 2001 by
Ebury Press
Random House
20 Vauxhall Bridge Road
London SW1V 2SA
www.randomhouse.co.uk

Random House Australia (Pty)
Limited, 20 Alfred Street, Milsons
Point, Sydney, New South Wales
2061, Australia. Random House
New Zealand Limited, 18 Poland
Road, Glenfield, Auckland 10, New
Zealand. Random House South
Africa (Pty) Limited, Endulini, 5a
Jubilee Road, Parktown 2193,
South Africa. Random House UK
Limited Reg. No. 954009.

A CIP catalogue record for this book
is available from the British Library.

ISBN 0 09 189448 4
Printed and bound in China by
C&C Offset.

Photography
Christoph Kicherer

Design
John Pawson and William Hall

John Pawson's office
Alison Morris
Nicholas Barba

Editor
Janet Illsley

Food Stylists
Louise Pickford
Susie Theodorou

The authors wish to thank
Catherine Pawson, Jonathan Bell,
Rosemary Sandberg,
Angela Mason, Carol Corniguel,
Fiona MacIntyre, Denise Bates,
Helen Everson and Ciara Lunn.